Flying Mouth Of Hell

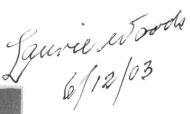

Laurie Woods
6/12/03

Author: LAURIE WOODS,
  Distinguished Flying Cross
     (Immediate Award)

First published in Australia – 2003
By **AUSTRALIAN MILITARY HISTORY PUBLICATIONS**.
13 Veronica Place, Loftus 2232 Australia.
Phone: 02-9542-6771 Fax: 02-9642-6787

Written by Laurie Woods.

Copyright remains the property of the author and apart from any fair dealing for the purpose of private study, research, criticism or review, as permitted under the Copyright Act, no part may be reproduced by any process without written permission. All enquiries should be made to the publishers.

Printed in Australia by
Watson Ferguson & Co. Moorooka, Qld 4105

National Library of Australia Cataloguing-in-Publication data:
Woods, Laurie, 1922-
Flying into the mouth of hell.

ISBN 0 646 33267 8.

1. Woods, Laurie, 1922- . 2. Australia. Royal Australian Air Force. Squadron, 460. 3 World War, 1939-1945 - Aerial operations, Australian. 4. World War, 1939-1945 - Personal narratives, Australian. I. Title.

940.544994

FLYING INTO THE MOUTH OF HELL
By LAURIE WOODS

The story of my Royal Australian Air Force service culminating in a tour of operations against the enemy, whilst an aircrew member on the Australian Lancaster 460 squadron immediately following the invasion of Europe by the allied forces where in the first three months following the invasion the aircrew casualties of Bomber Command exceeded those of the invading ground forces.

My story is based on Lancaster "K2" Killer – ND615
And the crews who flew in *"our plane"*

Dedicated to the aircrew of Bomber Command, and to all those mates who did not return, who served in the forefront of the war against the enemy for six long years, in which the squadrons were never withdrawn from operations.

Killed in Action…………………..	51%
Killed in Crashes………………..	9%
Seriously injured in crashes..	3%
Prisoners of War………………..	12%
Evaders……………………………	1%
Survivors unharmed………….	24%

We owe an immense debt of gratitude to the ground crews who through thick and thin in all kinds of weather strove to keep our aircraft operational. They shared with the aircrews all the dangers of fire, explosions, enemy incursions, and the dangers associated with a Bomber Command squadron.

CONTENTS

page

DEDICATION iii
FORWARD vii
AUTHOR'S NOTE ix
ACKNOWLEDGEMENT xi
PREFACE - THE BOMBER OFFENSIVE xiii
             - 460 SQUADRON (R.A.A.F) xv
HIGH QUALITY MEN OF COURAGE
             CREWS OF BOMBER COMMAND xvii

CHAPTER 1

        The Formative Years 21

CHAPTER 2

R. A. A. F. Training School (Aircrew) SOMERS Vic. 33
No 2 Air Observers School, Mt. Gambier 43
Bombing and Gunnery School at West Sale 45
No.2 Astro Navigation School, Nhill, ... 48

CHAPTER 3

Heading overseas 51
Crossing America 55
Camp Myles Standish 57
At Sea - "*Queen Elizabeth*" 65

CHAPTER 4

England at War – 1943 69

CHAPTER 5

Service in the RAF
No 4 (O) A FU West Freugh, Scotland 83
No 27 OTU Lichfield, Staffs. 86
Heavy Conversion Unit, Blyton ....
Lancaster Finishing School, Helmswell 97

CHAPTER 6

460 Squadron, (Australian) Binbrook 101
On Operations 117

Accidents and Indecisions 135
Over the Normandy Beachhead 145
A Hell of a Fright 147
Bull's Eye – No Recognition 167

CHAPTER 7

Experiments and Problems 169
Of This and That 175
Not So Lucky over Stettin 179
Without a regular Navigator 187

ILLUSTRATIONS.. 217

CHAPTER 8

Stolen Happy Moments 235

CHAPTER 9

Back on Flying Operations 241

CHAPTER 10

The Lucky Last Trip 245
Honours and Awards 253
Grounded no Flying 261
Heading Home 267
Australia 271
Reminiscing in the post-war era 275
Letter from Flight Sergeant Geoff Tallents 279
Anatomy of a Bombing Operation on 460 Squadron
By Sgt. John Watson 285
The RAAF and Bomber Command –
A Retrospective - Dr Alan Stephens 295
Churchill's speech "The Few"
House of Commons, August 20, 1940 301
Commander in Chief-Sir Arthur Harris 303
Epilogue – The exalted Few 319

FOREWORD

People who did not have the privilege of service in an active squadron overseas cannot appreciate the bond that existed between aircrew, who flew together "into the mouth of hell".

In fact that same bond existed to a smaller measure between all ranks, Officers, N.C.Os and airmen and was caused by the fact that everybody was giving and nobody was taking. We worked all hours, day and night without complaint and personal ambitions were not an issue in our pursuit of victory. The only aim was to prevent the takeover of our homeland by aggressors who had shown themselves to be ruthless with no respect for the rights and privileges of ordinary people.

Why so many young men, the elite of this country, volunteered to join the Air Force the most dangerous service of all was not, I am sure, for the above reasons. Rather it was because they were proud to be Australians with a history of volunteering for overseas service, had a lifestyle that gave them the confidence that they were any man's equal and a natural instinct to join in a fight.

We certainly did not join to "give our lives for our country", no, there was the excitement of going overseas and underneath it all a belief in loyalty. That we had to pay such a high price to gain victory was and always will be the tragedy of war.

I was, and still am, proud of my fellow Australians who not only carried on the traditions of our forefathers but enhanced them to greater heights of achievement.

There are some who question why we went to war saying it was futile, without reason, and was a wasted effort.

That is not so, because by our victory we passed on to our children a country free from foreign domination where they can live in peace and do what they want in their own way.

This book tells of one Tasmanian boy who achieved much to become an aircrew bomb aimer and complete a full tour of operations among the heroic crews of Bomber Command. It tells in detail, the high price paid by aircrew to achieve victory, the loss of comrades and the extreme hazards faced day after day which called for great courage and effort that in the end stole their youth.

On his last mission Laurie reached such great heights of valour in order to save his crew members from almost certain tragedy that I had no hesitation in strongly recommending him for the immediate award of the Distinguished Flying Cross which he so deservedly received.

Keith Parsons

9th November, 2002
Air Commodore K.R.Parsons, C.B.E., D.S.O., D.F.C., A.F.C.

INTRODUCTION - AUTHOR'S NOTE

It was only after visiting a couple of squadron mates and realising that they were getting very old that I made a decision to put down for my family, and for future generations, the story of my experiences on an average tour of operations in Bomber Command in 1944.

Having seen many hundreds of log books in his 40 plus years of research, Mike Garbett, author of the book "Lancaster" considers my log book one of the neatest and most complete logs he has had the pleasure of viewing. On recorded times of take off, routes to and from the target, and the bomb load and description. It has been an invaluable help in recording details in this book

My recollections were complete when I referred to a secret diary I had kept, against the rules and regulations, recording from day to day, names, places, details of raids etc. and of the experiences during my service in the Royal Australian Air Force.

In 1985 at the RAF Museum at Hendon, in company with our engineer, Sgt. Peter Odell, ex RAF, a fellow crew member on 460 Squadron, I stood in front of the Lancaster bomber spellbound. My thoughts were of Lancaster K2 "Killer" of "C" flight, 460 Squadron, bringing us safely through our tour of operations.

In 1999 at the Australian War Memorial in Canberra Australia, members of 460 Squadron gathered for the dedication of a plaque to those members of 460 Squadron who did not return.

We were invited to the hall where our famous "460" Lancaster, "G" for George was standing just prior to removal for refurbishment.

The members who wished, could climb aboard "G" for George. Without any exceptions everyone queued. What an enormous thrill, to climb into the familiar aircraft.

Surely it wasn't so cramped aboard, so little gangway, all the familiar smells, or was it just a flight of imagination. I'm sure had there been petrol on board, the engines would have been turning the propellers again.

Sitting in the pilot's seat brought back a flood of memories to me. After the short time aboard, no one seemed to want to move away from the plane, lingering and reminiscing, a thrill for the rest of our lives. Words cannot express the feeling, nor the love and admiration, and comradeship, we share with this mighty aircraft.

The Lancaster was a legend, a magnificent machine, where heroism was ever present, and a friend who enabled us to carry out raids over enemy territory, sharing with us the many frightening moments. Death constantly rode with us; we matured from young men, into fighting warriors, aged far beyond our years.

Feeling so much part of the Lancaster, for a long time we stood together, as the memories came flooding back. There was no need for words, the magic of the reunion with a "Lanc" was only destroyed when our wives asked "how much longer?".

ACKNOWLEDGMENTS

My thanks to Mrs Patricia Stafford – Clark, widow of Dr David Stafford – Clark, for her kind permission and encouragement to include the article
"Morale and Flying Experience", published in 1949 in the "Journal of Mental Sciences".
Squadron Leader Dr. David Stafford – Clark passed away on 9 September 1999. His untimely death could have been hastened by his voluntary exposure to various types of gas inhalation, in his unceasing efforts to help lessen the harmful effects of these weapons of war.
Those with whom he had come in contact sadly miss him. He will be remembered as the man who had the term LMF (Lack of Moral Fibre) banned from the Air Force records as a disgraceful brand.

My good friend Arthur Hoyle, DFC., noted author has been a wonderful help in knocking my story into shape. His experience and knowledge have been invaluable. Arthur, after two tours on 460 squadron, flew with our skipper Ted Owen in Transport Command after Ted had recovered from the severe wound in the face.

Arthur confirmed our opinion that Ted Owen was a very good pilot but quite mad when it came to flying. He was very keen if he had a chance on low flying always thinking he was an ace fighter pilot. It seemed that many pilots shared the same dreams. Arthur thought it quite amusing when Ted went off to sleep he always slept with his left eye open. The ack-ack splinter as big as a man's little finger had penetrated end on under the eye and left Ted with damaged nerves controlling the eyelids preventing him from closing his left eyelid. Unfortunately the nerves controlling the eye lid had been damaged and only many years later could he partly close the eye lid.

To the late Peter Firkins whose book "Strike and Return" rekindled a desire in me to make known to Australians some of the war experience of those who flew in the air war over enemy occupied territories of Europe and in particular Germany.

To my course mate Geoff Tallents, and his "letter Home",
To fellow 460 Squadron airman John Watkins, for his
"The anatomy of a bombing operation by 460 Squadron".

Specific data on damage to targets are from the "Bomber Command War Diaries".
by Martin Middlebrook and Chris Everitt.

Preface

THE BOMBER OFFENSIVE

The British night bomber offensive against Germany had been directed since early 1942 by Air Chief Marshal Sir Arthur Harris, who said, "A lot of people say that bombing can never win the war". His answer to that was "Well, it has never been tried yet and we shall see". And later he stated, "I would not regard any cities of Germany as worth the bones of one of our airmen".

The Royal Air Force Bomber Command, following the Battle of Britain, was the means to carry the war to Germany. The aircrews knew the odds weighed heavily against their own survival when carrying out air attacks on the industries of Germany. Flying a bomber, over Germany, with flak and fighters, and risk of collision, was one of the most demanding, and deadly experiences in World War Two.

A tour of operations was 30 trips, the life expectancy of a crew was 6 trips, and of the Lancaster 10 trips. The chance of completing the 30 trips was only 44%. Because of the heavy casualties on 460 squadron, there was not any one plane, which flew 100 operations.

Royal visits and heroic accolades were heaped upon the men of Bomber Command which lost 56,000 men killed in WWII.

In the first few weeks after D-Day the RAF was losing more men than the British 2nd Army in Normandy, and aircrew were amongst the most highly skilled manpower.

By early 1945 the cities of Germany were battered on an unprecedented scale. Dr. Goebbels wrote: "The situation grows daily more intolerable, we have no means of defending ourselves against the catastrophe".

Reports tell of so much sorrow and misery one hardly dares to think about them in detail. 600,000 Germans died. It is difficult to decide which is the more terrifying experience; to bomb or to be bombed.

If any airman, due to a breakdown in nerves, sickness, fright, or any other reason, was unable to, or refused to fly, he was branded LMF (lack of moral fibre). Aircrew were not very happy about this label. Someone could fly twenty trips and due to nerves, stretched beyond the limit of endurance, then be branded LMF. Unlike the brand of cowardice, which carried the death penalty in the First World War, LMF meant stripping of wings, (a qualification badge) stripping of rank, and a dishonourable discharge.

Once they flew over enemy occupied territory, waiting for the airmen was a Nazi defence force of 900,000 members. Some 900 night fighters 6,880 searchlights, and slightly in excess 20,600 anti aircraft (ack-ack) guns.

In the first three months of 1944, Bomber Command lost 80% of the aircraft and crews that had been on active squadrons at the end of 1943.

Approximately 9,000 members of the RAAF served in Bomber Command. They were about 1% of all Australian enlistments for all services. Yet they accounted for 21% of all Australian combat deaths during the war. Royal Australian Air Force lost aircrew, as follows:

European theatre (Germany and Italy)	6,666.
Bomber command	3,486
(1018 on 460 Squadron).	
Coastal command,	408.
Fighter command	171.
Middle East	1,135.
Training exercises	724.
India/Burma	242
South-West Pacific	3,342.
Other Areas	163
In the Korean fighting	41.
And in the Vietnam fighting	74.

460 Squadron - Preface

"Moving to Binbrook in May 1943, 460 Squadron, the senior Australian Lancaster squadron in a two year stay at Binbrook, established all kinds of records within Bomber Command.

It flew the most sorties in No 1 Group and in the whole of Bomber Command. (no mean achievement in a Group which strived for maximum effort at all times)

It suffered the heaviest Lancaster losses in 1 Group, (equivalent to being wiped out five times) the second heaviest in Bomber Command. It is also believed to have dropped the greatest tonnage of bombs—-24,000 tons--- of any squadron and set a monthly record of 1,867 tons in August 1944".

Extract from "Maximum Effort" by Patrick Otter.
Printed by Grimsby Evening Telegraph.

Commemorative Stone and Plaque in the
"Airmen's Garden of Remembrance" RAAF Station
Amberley, Queensland, Australia.

HIGH QUALITY MEN OF COURAGE
CREWS OF BOMBER COMMAND
By Squadron Leader, Dr. David Stafford – Clark,

"Bombing operations were like nothing else in the world. The aircrew flew in darkness relieved only by the dim orange glow of a lamp over the navigator's table and the faintly green luminosity of the pilot's instruments.

Three or four miles high, through bitter cold over hundreds of miles of sea and hostile land, with the thundering roar of engines shutting out all other sounds except when the crackling metallic voice of one member of the crew echoed in the others' earphones.

Aware of Danger
"For each man there was a constant awareness of danger; danger from the enemy, from sudden blinding convergence of searchlights, accompanied by heavy, accurate and torrential flak, from packs of night fighters seeking to find and penetrate the bomber stream.
Of danger from collision, from ice in the cloud, from becoming lost or isolated, from a chance hit in the petrol tank leading to loss of fuel, and a forced descent into the sea on the way back, if nothing worse, or worse still the plane being set on fire.

There was no single moment of security from take-off to touchdown, but often the sight of other aircraft hit by flak and exploding in the air, or plummeting down blazing to strike the ground, an incandescent wreck.
The chances of any particular individual surviving his thirty trips alive, unwounded and without being taken prisoner or having been forced down over enemy territory were generally accepted by the aircrew themselves as being one in five.

Everyone looked forward to the completion of his tour. So strong was the team spirit that it was not uncommon for a man to volunteer for as many as ten extra trips so that he and his crew could finish together, if he had joined them with more to his credit than they had done.

There was, however, a definite nervous toll on the man. His first three or four sorties were so full of novelty and amazement, that unless he was fundamentally unsuited to operational flying he would not suffer from actual fear to a great extent. But by the time he had completed five to eight sorties he discovered the magnitude of the task he had undertaken.

The extreme novelty of the operations had gone, succeeded by a growing recognition of the cost. By the 12th or 15th sortie he had the full realisation of the danger and the unpleasantness of the job and the long stretch of sorties before him. As his tour continued, morale rose until by the twenty fifth trip the cumulative stress and fatigue began to tell, and morale fell during the last sorties.

Their attitude to losses and death of friends was particularly striking. It was one of supreme realism, of matter of fact acceptance of what everyone knew perfectly well was inevitable.
They did not plunge into outspoken expression of their feelings, nor did they display any compromise with conventional reticence about the fact of violent death.
They said: "Too bad ………sorry about old so-and-so……….rotten luck." Their regret was deep and sincere, but not much displayed, nor long endured.

They were apt and able to talk of dead and missing friends, before mentioning their fate, just as they talked of anyone else or themselves. It took the loss of particular friends or leaders, flight commanders or squadron commanders to produce a marked reaction among a squadron. Then they might feel collectively distressed, have a few drinks, go on to a party and feel better.

But they made no effort to escape the reality of the situation, nor was there any of the drinking to forget, referred to in accounts of flying in the first war. They were young; they were resilient; they lived until they died.

They were never completely unconcerned about their fate, and some were quite matter of fact about the possibility that they might not "Last" until the end of the war.

A mushroom growth of superstition was noted, and personal mascots, ranging from hares' feet to a girl's stockings were taken very seriously.
One Captain of a 460 squadron aircraft forbade his crew to take out a very lovely red headed W.A.A.F. who had lost two men, one fiancee, one husband, in quick succession. He said, there was no point in tempting fate.

Temperament

A different attitude was observed between non-commissioned flying crews and that of their officers. They more frankly expected privileged treatment and special consideration, and except in the air, were more inclined to resist discipline than officers.

A small but definite proportion of aircrew sergeants differed completely from the rest of their colleagues. Their motive for joining was simply glamour and promotion, their attitude to flying and its risks unconsidered. Most of the minority were air gunners or flight engineers. Their mental attitude was often surprisingly adolescent and immature; off duty they pictured themselves as cinematograph heroes rather than as the men they were.

The cumulative stress of continued operational flying often produced in some men a reversal of their usual habits. The noisy exuberant extroverted type of fellow became silent, morose, and solitary. The naturally shy, or secretive individual, assumed a false jocularity, often accompanied by an unwonted alcoholic indulgence.

At any stage of the preliminaries to an operation – the operational meal, the main briefing, driving out to or standing by the aircraft – an order for alteration, cancellation, or delay might come through.

"No one who saw the mask of age which mantled the faces of these young men after a period of continued standing by, punctuated by inevitably false alarms, is likely to forget it.

Their pallor, the hollows in their cheeks, and beneath their eyes, and the utter fatigue with which they lolled listlessly in chairs about their mess, were eloquent of the exhaustion and frustration which they felt. In ten hours they seemed to have aged as many years.

Perhaps because the public was assumed "to want their heroes simplified" propaganda about the RAF tended to misunderstand and underrate the quality or the courage of aircrews.

The core of this quality, now more widely recognised, its most terrible and unforgettable characteristic was the subordination of the instinct of self-preservation. In an endeavour to fulfil a very high standard of war service; a determination to see the job through, despite the greater love for wife or child, or for life itself".

Author's note: "there were 110,000 aircrew who flew on operations in Bomber Command and 51% (55,564) were killed, many of them with no known graves.

The US 8th Air Force lost 26,000 killed"

CHAPTER ONE

K2 "KILLER"

The formative years

Deloraine, at the foot of the Great Western Tiers, is set in the midst of rich farmland and named by Scott the surveyor for the Tasmanian Government in 1840. Scott when surveying the Northern part of Tasmania camped on the bank of the Meander River, naming the place Deloraine. First settled by convicts and ticket of leave men it gradually developed into the centre of a rich farming district.

In Barrack Street the late Commodore Sir John Collins was born in the house next to my grandfather. As Capt Collins he became famous as the commander of H.M.A.S. Sydney in World War 11. A few doors further up the street I first saw the light of day on Boxing Day, 26th December, 1922.

My father was descended from a family of builders who specialised in building stone churches and other public buildings. John Julian Grigg, his wife Mary Ann and daughter, Elizabeth, aged 3 yrs, accompanied by brother, Jacob Julian and sister Elizabeth Grigg, migrated from Cornwall, arriving in Australia on the ship "City of Edinburgh" on the 31 August, 1837. In 1839 John's wife Mary Ann died in Sydney. He moved to Melbourne where he met and married in the old cathedral, on 21 March, 1840, Elizabeth Ann Ricketts, who had arrived from London accompanied by her brothers David and Thomas Ricketts. John Grigg and brother Julian worked on the construction of the new Cathedral in Melbourne, until the building construction was completed 2 October, 1842. By 1845 John and Elizabeth Grigg had moved to Ross in Tasmania where there were more opportunities for work on public buildings, churches and schools.

My great grandfather, named John after his father, was born at Ross on the 18 February, 1845. The family moved to Archers Estate via Longford, then to Westbury, where there was a convict station and a lot of construction works in stone being carried out. The family settled in Deloraine in 1856, where over the years they were joined by other members of the family migrating from Cornwall. John Grigg's daughter, Ada, married George Edward Ernest Woods, grandson of William Wood, convict, in 1898. Unfortunately when my father, Ariel John Woods was three weeks old, his mother died. He was reared by his grandfather John Grigg

My mother was descended from Benjamin Sherriff, convict, Leicester, Leicestershire, and Caroline Dine, convict, Lewes, Sussex. My mother remembered her great grandmother Caroline Dine as a lovely little old lady who walked everywhere. When visiting her daughter the old lady wrapped a few goodies in a large cloth which she knotted in such a manner that she could pass her stick through and then sling the bundle over her shoulder. This made it much easier for her to carry. My mother was not aware of her convict ancestry until my family research in 1995. She remembered her grandmother, when any male even her own sons came to visit her she would always meet them inside the house.

The prisoners, sometimes on the smallest pretext, were convicted and sent to places like Van Diemens Land, later Tasmania, as the British wished to set up a centre of population before the Dutch or the French were able to colonise the place. The convicts, once they had served their term, had the opportunity to make a better life in a new land, many of them prospering far beyond what they would have achieved had they not been transported.

My father, who was an itinerant worker at the time of my birth, was out daily digging potatoes in season in return for ½ a bag of potatoes per day to help feed his family of a daughter, 3¼ years, son 2¼ years, and of course the baby, myself, later to be joined by a sister and another brother. He was spending time in between jobs hunting for rabbits or in season picking blackberries, as he used to say "to keep the pot boiling". My father and mother tended their own vegetable garden to feed the family.

My schooling started at the age of six years and we walked just on one mile to school, home for lunch, and immediately after school home to help with the garden or in planting and cultivating potatoes in a paddock which Dad had rented in return for a couple of bags of potatoes. In the blackberry season we left home at 4.30am with our buckets to pick the rather plentiful blackberries around the area especially down along the river bank.

The return from the blackberries was used to buy our clothing and as in many families of that period it was a hand me down of clothing, patches and all, from the oldest to the youngest. My State schooling finished on the eve of my fourteenth birthday, and I had passed the merit certificate exam. My parents by this time thought that, perhaps, if I wished they might be able to afford to send me on to high school. School was part of growing up, I didn't hate it, nor was in love with it. My wish was to get a job in order to help the family financially.

From an early age after I learned to ride my Great Uncle Willies bicycle. I wanted a bike. From my older brother Ben I inherited all his hand me downs clothes and when he bought himself a racing bike I inherited his old bike. It wasn't long before I had a job delivering the early morning "Mercury" paper at 5/- a week and the Saturday Evening Express at 2/- each night. I was lucky to get a job delivering meat on Saturday mornings from the butcher for 2/- and two pound of sausages. After learning how to make sausages I had to make my two pounds of sausages plus more for the butcher's stock.

From this I saved enough money to buy my first pair of brand new pants at age twelve years. Then I saved enough to buy a racing bike frame and then gradually by buying the seat, and the handle bars that suited me best, the proper racing wheels, I built up my own pride and joy, my own racing bike.

Deloraine with a population of 1200 people and the Meander River running through the centre had nothing for teen age amusement. It was therefore a matter of choice in creating your own type of recreation. As my job was eight hours per day on a six day working week I had little choice in any sport. To get away anywhere was only possible by bike, therefore my activities were confined to my bike on my day off on Sunday, and in the Summer months swimming in the river.

A temporary opening for a job as post office delivery boy was offered which I gladly accepted. Twice each day I had to go to the local railway station, sort the mail and carry the mail bag back to the post office for further sorting before the town delivery.

The local station master, knowing I was the nephew of the railway clerk, asked me if I would like a job on the railway after finishing at the post office. My mother's father was the local railway ganger and every one of his nine children worked on the railway except my mother, and many times during our school holidays my older brother and I had spent time with one of the railway family relatives. The job was six months probation on no pay, then if satisfactory, a job as the lowest classification on the railway, a messenger at 7/6 per week. In April, 1937 I commenced work on the Tasmanian Government Railways, as messenger and no pay. Within three weeks, thanks to a transfer, I was appointed as a Lad Porter on 17/6 per week.

Working on the railway at that time meant transfers at a moment's notice. For the next three years I had several transfers around the state, until at Scottsdale in 1940 I requested unsuccessfully my parent's permission to join the navy as a cadet bandsman.

My father had been a member of the Deloraine Band for many years and as we grew up we were always at the concerts in the local park during the summer months. We helped Dad, the librarian, by handing around the music and collecting, after the concert. The town kids also including my brother and I made mischief throwing stones into the Meander River or playing in an old boat at the river bank. As my older brother and I grew up, we joined the band as learners, I played a bass and my brother played a flugel horn.

Early 1940 my older brother entered the army, and this prompted my effort to join the navy. My parents promptly refused their permission for me to enlist.

The railway clerical exam open to railway staff gave me an incentive to try for advancement. By setting aside a few of the pleasures in life and concentrating on study, with top marks in the exam I was transferred as a junior clerk to the Accountant's office in Hobart.

In early November 1941, just a month before the Japanese entered the Second World War, I volunteered for aircrew in the Royal Australian Air Force. In retrospect, more for the education and perhaps a little adventure, rather than through patriotism.

I was accepted and placed on the reserve to study under an Engineer, John Baker from Australia Post, telephone section. I studied with another reservist, Max, who had matriculated, and who was confident the study course would be very easy.

At first I made heavy weather of it. I was not very confident after the first few lessons as I had no idea on algebra, trigonometry or geometry.

As a practical person I could not understand why in algebra an X or Y could mean something else.

Other subjects of the course were also difficult for me, The instructor, who lived at Lenah Valley, a suburb of Hobart, was confident I would make the grade. He did his best on the two class nights per week to help me understand the lessons, despite me telling him I felt I was wasting his time. He was confident I would beat Max in the final exams, and I should keep on trying.

This period was a strain financially. The class at the instructor's house was three miles from where I was boarding, and I could only afford the tram fare one way. After the lessons I walked home.

In retrospect, I believe his confidence was the psychological push which finally helped me make the grade in reaching the desired level of education. My final marks after six months were 87% against Max with 74%.

These instructors who gave of their time to coach the reservists under the Empire Air Training Scheme, did a wonderful job, and if it hadn't been for their assistance many of the reservists like myself would never have made the necessary standard for aircrew. (On my return from overseas I made a very much appreciated visit, to my previous instructor to thank him sincerely, for having given his valuable time in helping me with my lessons).

From Scottsdale I had gained top marks in the Railway junior clerical exam and had been transferred to the railway Accountant's office Hobart in November 1940, and it was from this office that I had enlisted. I informed the Accountant that I had volunteered for service in the Air Force, and officially applied for leave of absence for the duration and twelve months thereafter.

Next day I was informed that I had been transferred into traffic as clerk, goods shed, within the week. As the traffic branch was a reserved occupation I would not be granted leave. This to me was a deliberate contravention of the law governing enlistment.

I protested and was sent to the Railway Staff Officer, Mr. Tom Barnes. He had transferred me to Scottsdale, following a glowing report of my work and my ability from Stationmaster Rolley Hill, with whom I had been working at New Norfolk.

Having put my case to Mr. Barnes he said "OK, you will remain in the railway Accountant's Office until you are called up, and your leave will be granted".

He went on to tell me he had been an observer in the First World War. When flying over the trenches and bombing the German lines, they had held the bombs over the side of the open cockpit, and when they thought their aim was right dropped them on the German trenches. Actually I was the last volunteer from the railway. The management office staff were not exempt, (The railway traffic section was classified an essential service with employees exempt from military service.) The policy was changed, and the junior clerks from the office management were transferred into traffic positions, thus making sure that no one else got away.

In order to keep me gainfully employed, the Deputy Paymaster (a most senior clerk) was moved out to my job as assistant to the Chief Revenue Clerk and I was moved in with the Paymaster.

A suggestion from Chief Revenue clerk, Len Rodwell, with whom I had worked over the previous year, was that if I failed to do the job, then the Accountant could still have me transferred out into a traffic job, and thereby have me exempted from war service.

The job in the paymaster's office was not difficult and the paymaster was very happy with the arrangement. He considered me as good an assistant as any he had previously had.

At the cycling carnivals at Christmas 1941 I rode 2nd in the Youths' cycling race over one mile at the Latrobe Athletic Carnival. At the Ulverstone Carnival on 28th December 1941, I won the youths' race of one mile, and was third in the "B" grade 5 mile scratch race. It was to be my last cycling race, due to a back injury suffered during the War.

On 19 June 1942, having made the education standard, I received my call up. My first posting was to No 1 Initial Training School (Aircrew) as part of 29 course at Somers. Somers, situated on the South coast of Victoria, overlooking Bass Strait, was ideal for an initial training school. It was isolated, bitterly cold when the winds were from the ocean, and had absolutely no distractions of any kind for the trainees.

Travelling from Hobart to Burnie by a special troop train at Deloraine my hometown, we stopped for refreshments and for the engine crew to top up the engine with coal and water. It was an emotional farewell to my parents, who were waiting at the station to say goodbye. We knew that flying involved aircraft, and as Australia had few warplanes, I would be headed out of Australia to a war zone. As the train pulled out of the station there was much waving from my parents up on the bank, and some tears were shed.

After a very wearying and rather long train journey of twelve hours, we arrived at Burnie. From the train station we crossed over to the wharf where we boarded the SS "Nairana" an old coal driven steamship sailing out of Burnie at 8pm. This was to be my first ocean voyage.

We had only been on board for a short time when with shouts of "Cast off for'ard" the ship's engines came to life. Slowly the bow swung away from the wharf, then with a ringing of the bell from the bridge the ship started to move forward. "Cast off stern" and the ship was under way.

As we cleared the wharf, which had been built as a breakwater, we steamed into the full force of the wind and the waves. Suddenly a wall of water hit us as we were broadside on to the towering white crested waves. Very slowly we turned, heading into what built up into the worst storm in Bass Strait in 90 years, making the old ship creak in every joint.

Wallowing in the trough of one wave, the next moment we were smashing into a wall of water as the next wave came tearing towards us threatening to roll us underneath. It was an effort for the old ship to raise its bow and struggle to the top of each wave.

The evening meal was an ordeal. If we didn't hang on to our plates and eating utensils they would go sliding away down to the other end of the table as each wave sent the old ship shuddering one way or the other.

We found this amusing at first as we joked we could take a mouthful as our plate slid by, but then we might catch our neighbour's plate in mistake.

After we had finished our meal, we headed up the stairs toward the open deck. Not being used to the ship heeling and pitching, we laughingly staggered one moment uphill then the next almost pitching forward at a run on our way to the top deck and some fresh air.

We hadn't long been there when a couple of the fellows said they were feeling a bit off. One of the other fellows pulled out a banana saying: "See this banana!" and peeled it down. Then, with a theatrical flourish he peeled it down a second time; three fellows headed for the rail where they were horribly sick.

We had steamed out into Bass Strait well clear of land and were feeling the full blast of a westerly gale blowing so strongly that we were heeling to starboard.

The thirty-fifty foot waves from the north, and the westerly gale caused the ship to heel to starboard as it slowly rose over the crest of the wave. Then as the bow dipped the propeller spun madly in the air before burying itself in the trough of the wave as the ship heeled to port. Sheltered momentarily from the full blast of the wind, the ship seemed to lurch forward as the wave raced away toward the stern. Then slowly the bow rose, whilst the ship, seemed to stand still and slowly, sluggishly, climbed the next wave shuddering as though it was ready to break apart.

The wind blowing a rainstorm of spray from the tops of the waves mixed with the sleet making the windward side of the deck untenable. A wellwisher had advised on the first rough sea voyage to get into the bunk early, with your head down. This method was said to save one from being seasick.

Heeding this advice I headed for bed about 9pm, but wasn't keen on the smell of the ship down below.

The ship was completely blacked out and all closed in, with only very dim illumination. Pitching and rolling made it difficult for a landlubber to move along the passageway, whilst the disinfectant used in the toilet area, and the musty smells evident in the shower area were nauseating.

Sleep was practically impossible and I lay on the bed fully clothed and dozing, listening to the fury of the storm as it seemed to be increasing within the ship pitching and rolling in its corkscrewing motion. The constant throbbing of the propeller interspersed by the wild spinning as it came clear of the water made the old ship shudder from stem to stern.

About 5 a.m. I rolled out of the bunk and headed for fresh air on the deck. The ship was still blacked out, and in the darkened companionway it was difficult to find the door out on to the deck. Finally, when I did find it, I had a problem in getting it open far enough to step through. Much to my horror, I stepped into surging water almost up to my knee, and quickly stepped back closing the door and latching it tightly. I thought the ship must be sinking.

Retracing my way back along the companionway I found some stairs leading up toward the main deck. The climb up the stairs was more of a stumble and thankfully at the top I found a door leading out to the deck.

The fresh air, whilst bitterly cold, was much more pleasant than the smell of the inside of the ship, so I stayed on deck until we had berthed in Melbourne. This was one of the slowest crossings of Bass Strait the vessel had made. The Captain estimated that 95% of the people on board were sea sick, including most of the crew. Being mid winter didn't help a great deal, as Bass Strait is a well known as one of the roughest areas of water in the world, especially during a wild winter storm.

An Air Force truck was waiting at the wharf, to transport us to the RAAF station at Somers, some 2½ hours away. With twenty of us loaded onto the back of the truck fitted with a canvas tarpaulin covering a frame over the top of the truck's tray, and bench seats so that we were able to sit down, we set off on the next part of our journey. The rough old truck didn't add a great deal to our personal comfort as every bump could be felt as a bone-jarring thud of our bodies. I was still feeling the roll of the ship, and wished that perhaps if I had been sea sick, maybe I would have felt better.

We were learning fast that the only comfort in the services was reserved for the senior officers.

CHAPTER TWO
ROYAL AUSTRALIAN AIR FORCE
Training School (Aircrew)

SOMERS Vic.

Arriving at Somers we were unloaded near the latrines for a comfort stop. It was a timely stop, but a bit of a shock. The buildings were not attractive and comfortable quarters with all the modern conveniences laid on, but buildings sheathed with galvanised iron and with fibro roofs. The latrine was something else; a row of pans along each side of an open hut and anyone occupying a seat had absolutely no privacy.

Next stop was the Mess overlooking the windswept parade ground. As we queued up at the Mess, earlier course trainees were chanting: "You'll be sorry!" together with other tormenting remarks. Inside the Mess were long tables, with wooden bench seats down each side. We Tasmanians reckoned they had copied the Mess seating arrangements from a convict settlement.

After the meal we were lined up outside by a Sergeant who told us he was taking us to the store where we would be issued clothing for "airmen for the use of".

We were issued a kit bag, in which we had to pack our clothing. The kit bag would be subject to inspection at any time and should only be used for our Air Force issue clothing. Into the kit bag went the issue boots, socks, underwear, including long johns, which were viewed with much merriment, but were much appreciated when we got into the colder climates.

We were commonly known as "Menzies' Blue Orchids" a name bestowed we believed by the Army. The issue of the distinctive best blues complete with the little forage cap, known universally throughout the RAAF by the name of portion of a female's anatomy, made us look more like a bunch of Menzies' Blue Orchids

Classified as RAAF Aircraftsmen class 2, we wore a white felt strip, inserted in the front of our caps, which signified "Aircrew Trainee". That little piece of white felt, perhaps the cheapest badge of classification in any service, was the most highly valued badge of attainment for many months by the aircrew trainees. In fact it was only removed when we had our Wings Parade, our Wing signifying our aircrew qualification and classification.

We commenced our training with a 6.30am parade in semi-darkness. The bitterly cold winter mornings had an ever present wintry blast blowing straight off the ocean. Tasmanians in the camp reckoned it was almost as cold and soul destroying as being a convict at Port Arthur.

On our first morning we lined up, the roll was called, and everyone was sorted like a pack of cards into flights according to surname. Having the name Woods I was in flight "H" the last flight, together with the XY & Zs.

When we were separated into flights on the parade ground, a big tough looking sergeant introduced himself in a very gruff voice as Sgt O'Byrne. He said we were his responsibility. He expected we would do our best, to lick ourselves into shape under his direction.

Thereafter our daily routine was basic training and rifle drill, 6.30am till 7.30am. Breakfast 45 minutes then lessons till 5.30pm. our evening meal time. Then back to the classroom for study till around 9.30pm. The basic training and the rifle drilling, whilst severe and pretty tough on rookies, I didn't find too bad as I had been playing in brass bands since the age of fourteen.

Learning to handle the rifle military style however was another story, leading to much fumbling until the correct drill was learned. In the process it had its amusing moments.

For the first few days some of the trainees did not seem to know their right hand from their left. Rifle drill was especially difficult for those who had never handled a rifle, and many times AC2 Pepler dropped his rifle. He just seemed unable to hang on to that rifle.

Warrant Officer Monty Parkes, in charge of discipline, was on the parade ground checking on how we were progressing, when AC2 Pepler dropped his rifle. The tirade from Monty Parkes, as he sent AC2 Pepler doubling round the parade ground with rifle and full kit, was too much for John Ward who was next to me. John had maintained he wouldn't be caught doing wrong, but couldn't help smiling at the tirade. Unfortunately Monty Parkes saw John smiling, and said, "O.K. you smart Alec! I'll make you wish your mother had never put a smile on your face when you were born. Round you go too". This was too funny for me, and so I was on the end of a pointing finger and a snarl of "That airman! You too! Round you go! Now any more comedians in this outfit?" It was the funniest sight, three of us in full marching kit and rifle, doubling round this rather large parade ground.

It was a prudent lesson; beware Monty Parks or "we would be sorry". Now we knew where the saying came from.

The next intake of trainees arrived at the mess right on lunchtime, on a Sunday, one month after our arrival. We were lined up, ready for lunch when someone started mimicking Warrant Officer Monty Parke's best parade ground voice "You'll be sorry! We'll make you sorry!" and soon everyone had joined in a chorus of "You'll be sorry, we'll make you sorry". Suddenly the man himself appeared: "They're not the one's who'll be sorry! You're the ones who'll be sorry! Take their names Sergeant and give them a special treat next weekend, cleaning and scrubbing the toilets, I'll make them sorry!"

The new trainees had to serve the first month in the tents, while we were promoted into huts for the remaining two months. When we were sure we were safe in the huts we had our little hate session about Monty Parkes, and how stupid we were to so easily get caught by him.

We reckoned it must have been his delight to catch the new recruits in the same manner each month.

At the first opportunity, I checked on the new intake to see if any Tasmanians had arrived. I met David Saunders of Hobart, and three or four others, giving them the run down on what experiences lay ahead, and how to avoid the problems as much as possible.

One amusing thing for me was, whenever I made a mistake on the parade ground, Sergeant O'Byrne and occasionally Warrant Officer Parkes yelled at me "AC2 Prosser! Do this or that", until after a few times I would stop and say, "Do you mean me Sergeant or Sir, I'm Woods".

I sometimes caught a twinkle in Monty Parkes eye, and sometimes Sergeant O'Byrne, but it always paid to be cautious.

Many times a demand of "That airman!" would stop us in our tracks wondering if we were "That airman" and what would be the penalty. Hands in the pocket, dirty boots, unshaven, buttons undone, you name it, we copped it.

With a new lot of trainees arriving, each month, it would have been hard for these instructors to keep track of names. I never did catch up with AC2 Prosser, so I didn't have a clue why I was often called Prosser.

We had just moved into the huts and in order to keep the huts free from any contamination we were told we had to be vaccinated. On a Friday morning we were lined up for vaccinations and inoculations against all the possible problems we might encounter in our service. Quite a few of the trainees, when they got up close to the vaccination point, fainted.

I saw a familiar face, Bill Moritz, the brilliant South Australian cyclist, known as the "Ajax of cycling". I was very pleased when he recognised me from the Tasmanian cycling carnivals at Latrobe and Ulverstone.

We had a short discussion as we waited in line. I was surprised when it came our turn to have the shots in the arm, and he fainted. Unfortunately Bill, a brilliant cycling champion and one of Australia's finest ever young sporting stars was one of the early fatalities of our course, being killed in an aircraft accident.

The next weekend leave was granted and a travel pass was issued for those who wished to head to Melbourne or home for the weekend. We also were dosed with some bromide in our food prior to the leave, supposedly to dampen our ardour. I had no reason to leave the camp, and I had agreed to do a mate's weekend detention duties. I was wakened about 2.30am by the pounding of military boots past our hut, as the various trainees "took short", and raced for the latrines. The bromide had a quick and severe laxative action.

Needless to say it was not long before we too had joined the rush in the darkness. This seemed to be a pre-leave treatment to dose with bromide, hotly argued by the trainees, and hotly denied by the station staff.

On Saturday I had agreed to do some duties to enable some of my mates to go on leave, and decided to go to bed early. I intended rising early on Sunday to wash my clothes and also those of my mate Norrie Wallace, an old feller of 32 years. I put the clothes in to soak and not feeling very well, I returned to the hut and lay on my bed.

The next thing I knew Norrie and a couple of others were fussing over me. They got me off the bed and up to the hospital, where I was admitted at 8.30pm with a high fever, 104° and I was bordering on being delirious. According to the Doctor I had a positive reaction to the vaccine. I remained in hospital over two nights before returning to lessons and study.

Physical fitness was high on the list of priorities, and a new physical fitness officer had just arrived. Known as "Oppy" he was none other than Pilot Officer Hubert

Opperman, World Champion long distance cyclist. Oppy proceeded to lecture us on physical fitness, and also staged a demonstration of his cycle fitness on rollers.

We regularly had sessions in the gym and during one of these sessions, we were practising somersaults. Ron Stenhouse, who was second in front of me, landed heavily on the back of his head with a sickening crack. Everyone was held up while they took care of him and carried him off to hospital with a broken neck where he died early next day. It was quite a sobering experience, and the first of many thoughts of who would be next.

To qualify for aircrew, we studied for 12 weeks, 33 subjects including maths, trigonometry, geometry, navigation and meteorology, map making, compass, electricity and magnetism, physics, theory of flight, morse code and semaphoring, airframe construction and mechanics, aircraft and ship recognition. According to our qualifying marks we would be allocated to the various flying musters. Failures went to the cookhouse or other duties.

In grading for the various training, we had to go before the aircrew selection board, consisting of senior officers and instructors. It seemed that at least one third of the trainees had failed and were being posted out into other categories of RAAF service.

My teeth were considered to be potentially troublesome so I had been lined up at the dentist, and all my top teeth removed. The dentist, must have been in a veterinary practice. He managed to break part of the jaw socket bone giving me much pain for some weeks, and putting me in hospital for three nights.

A few days later we had to front the allocation board, Queued alphabetically, as usual, we waited for the best part of five hours till they got down to the "Ws".

We all declared in the next war, we would change our name. To help pass away the waiting time, it became a game, who could beat a name like Abe Albert Abbott. We were all in a state of tension when we were called,.

All the selection board officers seemed to be very relaxed and keen to get this boring business over for the day, with very little regard on how they were shaping our future, if we had a future. I was nervous in the interview and without teeth I hadn't much control over the quivering of my top lip, making my nervousness evident.

1st Question: "You want to be a pilot?"
    Answer;   "Yes, Sir,"

2nd Question: "What sort of planes do you want to fly?"
    Answer;   "The fastest you have Sir,"

3rd Question: "I haven't got any", a bit of a laugh from the board. "Did you ever make any model aeroplanes in your younger days?"
    Answer; "No sir, only a few propellers."

4th Question: "Have you had any flying hours?"
    Answer; "No sir haven't had a chance yet."

5th Question: "Would you be disappointed if we made you an observer, as your result marks are so good you should be an observer?" (navigator/bombaimer/gunner),

    Answer,   "No sir I wouldn't be disappointed, but I still would like to be a fighter pilot."

"That will be all Woods." I was dismissed.

In later service I found aircrew, who doubted their ability, would volunteer as gunners but ended up as pilots.

Many "scrubbed" pilots (those who were not able to fly the planes or complete the pilot's course) would end up as gunners, so I wondered about the value of the selection board.

I believe in the Royal Air Force up until quite late in the war, each aircrew trainee was given up to 14 hours of pilot training in order to select them for the right category.

My marks, especially the higher marks in mathematics, earned me allocation for training as Observer, which meant Navigator, Bomb Aimer, Gunner and I was promoted to Leading Aircraftsman.

Most trainees wished to become a Pilot because that category always seemed to be the more glamorous and heroic. Many of us were disappointed not to be chosen, but as it was pointed out, pilots in a bomber needed expert navigators to tell them which way to go.

Before being sent home on leave, we were then issued with a summer uniform of khaki shorts, long khaki socks, and khaki shirts. Dressed in these summer clothes we were known as "Curtin's Cowboys".

In farewelling Sergeant O'Byrne, or "Froggie" as we had christened him on account of his gruff manner and gravelly voice, we found a very kindly sympathetic airman, who wished us well in the service. He expressed the hope that we would all meet again, which was a nice way of saying I hope you survive.

Before leaving Somers on our posting to Mt Gambier, the trainee observers were issued with flying kit, to commence the flying part of our training. With a five-day leave pass I took a taxi out of Somers to Frankston then travelling by train to Melbourne, was in time to catch a plane out of Essendon at 2pm arriving Western Junction 3.45pm.

After two days in Deloraine with my family I spent two days in Hobart. The plane on my return had been cancelled, due to rough weather. I returned by boat from Burnie to Melbourne.

Meeting with other members of my course in Melbourne, we caught the Serviceton express from Melbourne to Ararat, arriving at 1.25pm. Changing trains we travelled on to Hamilton where we boarded an Ansett Airways bus to Mt Gambier. Leaving Hamilton at 4.40pm we were on the road for a couple of hours, when one of the boys requested a "comfort stop" at a suitable spot. The bus driver stopped the bus opposite a lone tree, about 70 yards from the road. The fellow, watched by everyone on the bus headed for the tree, and after spending a moment or two behind the tree, he reappeared with a big smile on his face. As he headed back to the bus the driver, Reg Ansett, burst out laughing, asking everyone:"Wouldn't a quick visit round the back of the bus have sufficed. Does anyone else want to do the same before we move on?"

Arriving at Mt. Gambier at 7.30pm we were met by an Air Force tender and transported to the aerodrome arriving in time for the evening meal.

All agreed the Mt Gambier station food was much better and generally much better and more comfortable living conditions suggested our time spent on this station would be much more pleasant. The following morning we were issued with books and instruments, and were taken on a familiarisation tour round the station.

No 2 Air Observers School, Mt. Gambier,

South Australia, was a place to stir the senses. It was our first flying training school. My first sight of an aeroplane doing a night landing and my first RAAF flight in an aeroplane on the 28 September, 1942 flying in an old Anson, twin engined bomber, built with a light metal frame and covered in fabric.

Although slow, with an average cruising speed of 120mph they were a stable aircraft and reasonably safe, and we were now flying

In company with two West Australian trainees, we lined up beside the plane, with instructor Sgt Bennett as pilot. He held out a sickie bag to each one of us, saying: "It is no disgrace for an aircrew trainee to be airsick on their first flight". For the next hour he did everything possible to make us airsick. One of the fellows succumbed and held the bag out to me and yelled: "What do I do with this!" I pointed out the window not wanting him to upset my stomach by sticking his bag under my nose.

Suddenly I had a thought; I hope he doesn't jump out the window himself. I grabbed him, taking the bag from him and threw it out myself

To me the hardest part of flying in Ansons was the winding up of the landing gear after take off, and winding it down before coming in to land.

One of the more exciting episodes was a couple of Japanese submarines being reported off Adelaide.

In company with a half dozen Beaufighter night fighter/bombers (nicknamed "Whispering Death" by the Japanese, as they couldn't be heard until right on you), led by Squadron/Leader (Wiry Whiskers) McCormack, we were briefed for air searches out over Spencer Gulf.

What an exciting and exhilarating search. What if we spotted a Jap submarine? What if we called in the Beaufighters?

We would have a grandstand view of the submarines being blasted out of the water. What if they were surfaced and started firing at us? Could we get away quickly enough? We never did get an answer, excepting wait and see what happens first.

We flew over the sea on 12 October 1942 with Pilot Officer Lonsdale. We flew again on the 14 October 1942 with Sgt Barrett, flying a three-hour sweep across Spencer Gulf. What a disappointment. No sighting of any Japanese submarine.

Squadron Leader McCormack's wiry whiskers, twirled on the end, the imagery of the real fighter pilot stuff, with the tunic top button undone, proved too much for the station pilots and officers. After a drinking session they got the Squadron Leader down, cut off his moustache from one side of his face, and ruined his ego. He left Mount Gambier station as mad as hell.

One instructor at Mount Gambier was a dedicated meteorologist. Whenever we were changing classrooms or outside, he gave a lecture on the sky conditions and what pending weather could blow up within a day or so. Norrie Wallace, always a joker, asked him whether the feeling in his corns, when rain was threatening could be relied upon, for predicting the weather. His reply was: "If it helps in forecasting the weather for your purpose then it would be worthwhile."

The township of Mount Gambier was only eight miles from the airfield. On Sunday, with time off, three or four of us visited the Blue Lake where Adam Lindsay Gordon, the Australian poet, politician, policeman, sportsman, was said to have made his famous leap when out kangaroo shooting with a party of his friends. During the course of the hunt, the mettle of the various riders and the ability of the horses was discussed.

Adam Lindsay Gordon set his horse "Red Lancer" at a four rail fence with a narrow ledge on the other side and very little clearance before a 200 to 300 foot drop to the waters of the famous "Blue Lake". He had to angle his horse in the jump to prevent horse and rider going over the crater lip into the lake. Not content with that leap, Gordon jumped his horse back over the fence to the road, feeling sure that none of his companions would emulate his feat.

A couple of our class had cars, and blatantly sidled up to the instructors, inviting them into town for a ride in their car, with free beer at the other end. Whilst this was not our idea of how to attain good marks in the course, it certainly paid off for them, as they passed and were commissioned as officers at the end of the course.

Qualifying as an Air Observer meant studies of dead reckoning & theory of navigation, compass & instruments, maps & charts, meteorology, photography, reconnaissance, signals practical, aircraft & ship recognition. I was very happy, when the final results were posted, to see I had qualified as an observer.

Mount Gambier had been a very pleasant station. Possibly the flying had made it much more enjoyable. Also after the spartan conditions experienced at Somers in the winter time, the spring and early summer weather at Mount Gambier were delightful.

Bombing and Gunnery School at West Sale

Having qualified as an observer we were posted to No.3 Bombing and Gunnery School at West Sale in the heat of summer. My first impression was the poor quality of the food. The weather was very hot, over 100° Fahrenheit for three weeks on end.

The area surrounding Sale was cattle country and whenever we were on parade our backs were covered with bush flies and they had a nasty habit of buzzing round your face. On parade we had to stand to attention and to ignore the flies. The blowflies were a hazard and when sitting down for a meal in the mess it was usual to inspect your meat, to make sure it hadn't been flyblown.

The cook was unimaginative. Cabbage and rice were his specialties, or should I say seemed to be the only items he could cook.

One day I scored a raisin in my rice. The others at the table were envious, how did I manage a raisin in my rice when they all had plain rice. Being a little suspicious I uncovered it and found it was a blowfly.

At the neighbouring Bairnsdale aerodrome a couple of recent crashes occurring with several casualties, were thought to be as a result of sabotage. In view of these accidents, security was tightened up, with extra guard duty round the planes. The aircrew trainees had a four hour on, and two hour off, guard duty allowing us to have a two hour sleep, which coupled with our daytime studies, was a very heavy and tiring workload.

The guardhouse was also part of the station's electricity generating plant and the constant throbbing of the generator made sleep almost impossible.

In the daytime heat of around 100° Fahrenheit, the metal of the Fairey Battles would expand. In the coldness of the night, the metal would contract causing a creaking/cracking noise, very similar to a person trying to clamber on to the wing. As there were several planes standing together, this was a continual worry, and stretched the nerves of the guards. The creaking noise had the guards constantly looking for saboteurs.

One particular orderly officer was being very smart, sneaking up to see if the guard was alert. He very narrowly missed being pierced by a bayonet by a trainee made nervous by this creaking of the planes. The officer was instructed to cease this rather silly practice, or feel the steel in the belly.

Lessons were scheduled during the day. Lack of sleep, plus the heat made this period a very exhausting study time. As a consolation we did get some flying with aerial bombing and gunnery practice flying in Fairey Battles.

Fairey Battles were the all metal single motor bombers, used against the German forces in the evacuation from Dunkirk, when the British forces were driven out of Europe. Weighing eleven tons, a crew of three, (pilot, navigator, and gunner) was about as much as they could handle, but they still carried a small bomb load on operations.

It was apparent that the plane was grossly overweight, underpowered, and was a sitting duck for the faster more manoeuvrable enemy fighters. This was the reason they had been relegated to training.

In the Fairy Battle the bomb aimer lay on the floor with the bottom hatch partly open, in order to sight the target through the opening when dropping bombs.

With the bottom hatch open, the glycol fumes were sucked up through the plane, causing many breathing problems for the bomb aimer and the gunner. These fumes made me airsick for the first time.

One of our instructors, Pilot Officer Nichols, liked to see his name on the board. Not a day passed without some message, no matter how trivial it might be, being chalked on the board, signed, T.G.Nicholls Pilot Off.

These messages created a great deal of merriment from the trainees and also gave rise to some ribald remarks about the author and his little notes.

Graduating from Air Bombing and Gunnery School, was the ceremonial occasion of a "Wings" passing out parade, having our hard earned Observer's badge presented and pinned on by the Commanding Officer, Squadron Leader Mills-Thompson. Our badge was a single flying wing, with a large O with the wing off toward the left from the O. The large O in the badge also gave us a very uncomplimentary name, "Flying Arseholes" among aircrew.

On the way to our next posting at Nhill, in the far north of Victoria, I spent a couple of days in Melbourne with my older brother Ben, who was in an Army transit camp close to Melbourne, awaiting troop movement somewhere North.

We visited our father's great uncle George Grigg, who lived on St. Kilda Road in a most impressive house, complete with long drive and statues in the garden. The house had a large entrance hall, which was almost the size of the house in which we had grown up in, in Deloraine, Tasmania.

Nhill, No.2 Astro Navigation School, after the long grind of training, was a most pleasant change. Here was the final month of training and an anti climax.

Astro Navigation School meant more flying, this time in Ansons, mostly at night, as we had to study the stars. For accurate navigation we had to identify the individual stars, and be able to take a sextant shot, then, by calculating the angle of elevation in relation to the Earth transfer the result onto a flat map surface.

The final studies in our course, concentrated on meteorology, the stars in relation to the Earth's movement and applying that movement to navigation. It required a large amount of study to learn the stars and their constellations.

By taking sights of them with a sextant, we were able to plot our approximate position on a map. It thus enabled us to fly at night without relying on ground identification, or radio waves for bearings.

We were extremely fit and to keep up our fitness, we had cross country runs two or three times a week. We no longer had rifle drill or gym sessions. Although very hot, the heat was a clear dry heat, which wasn't too bad. There was usually a canvas bag of artesian bore water hanging on the wall on the outside of the buildings. I had the impression that after drinking this water for a few days, we had a faint body odour.

A "Pass" at Nhill carried promotion to the rank of Sergeant Air Observer. Then it was final leave and home to Tasmania, where I was married on 6th March 1943.

Returning to Melbourne from leave we had been posted to No.1 Embarkation Depot, Ascot Vale Racecourse, where I played in the Ascot Vale station RAAF band.

The band played in a big Navy march through Melbourne on 20 March 1943 and also led the Melbourne parade, March 31 to welcome the 9th division back from the Middle East on its way to New Guinea. Aircrew members, playing in the band were Brian Coates, Norrie Wallace, another aircrew member and myself. It was the largest march of returned men ever held in Melbourne.

The March was particularly memorable to me as I was playing a sousaphone, a large American bass that encircled the body and over the shoulder, whilst the bell of the instrument was way above the head pointing the way the player was going.

The crowd became so enthusiastic in their cheering, they closed in and I was trapped in the lead and had to use my instrument to bulldoze a way through this temporary block, otherwise the march would have come to a standstill.

Whilst in Melbourne I had permission to live out with my wife Marion, until she returned to Hobart on April 16.

Two weeks later we were posted to No 2 ED and travelled on the Spirit of Progress Express to Sydney.

As a railway employee, and one who has had a lifelong love particularly of steam trains, the ride on the Spirit of Progress was something I would have only dreamed about, before joining the Air Force. Having bid my wife farewell, here I was on the Spirit of Progress and headed out into the World, not knowing where the journey would take me.

I wasn't very impressed with the city of Sydney, but liked the harbour and bridge. We were camped at Bradfield Park for a week (sleeping on the floor with only a blanket, ("Who was the b............!, who said the Air Force had it good").

CHAPTER THREE

Heading overseas

On May 4 I was posted overseas, with embarkation to start as from 5^t May. (We were paid in Yankee dollars, but where are we going). We were on the train headed north in the afternoon, stopping at Kempsey at 2 am for a meal of sausages and mashed potatoes, with a slice of bread, but no eating utensils. Perhaps they feared we might eat the utensils as well, or pinch them.

Arriving in Brisbane early on 5 May 1943 we loaded on the back of trucks and about mid-day were taken through Brisbane to the Hamilton Wharves, where we went on board the cargo liner SS "*Willard A Holbrook*", an American ship of 14,000 tons.

The Queensland trains were shunting the wagons into position for transferring their load onto the ship. One Sydney airman said: "They are Q.R. Queer and Rattley." The way the wharfies worked with American loading machines was also very interesting. The ship's sleeping accommodation, with bunks slung in the cargo holds, was passable but later became very uncomfortable as we approached the tropics with much hotter conditions.

While waiting for the ship to be fully loaded, many of us leaned on the ship's rail marvelling at the size of the jellyfish, floating by in the crystal clear water. (The water 60 years later is unbelievably dirty and polluted).

On the morning of the 5 May, at 10.15am we sailed from Brisbane. It was a beautiful sunny day as we cleared the mouth of the river in the early afternoon.

Being at sea on Mother's Day May 9 was a new experience with an open deck service, which was enjoyed by everyone.

The majority of us had never been on a sea voyage, and the thought of it was very exciting. The sea was as smooth as a sheet of glass, not a ripple to be seen, only the wake of the ship disturbing the millpond effect. The ship lazily rose and fell, as we steamed eastward across the Pacific Ocean.

At night we seemed to enter a different world, with the waves filled with fluorescence, as the bow cleaved its way ever onward. The little wavelets back from the ship's bow were filled with an ever-changing glow of the fluorescence and it was fascinating to watch.

The weather was perfect, and at times the ocean was so flat, it seemed as though it could never get rough and stormy. There was little to remind us we were in the middle of a war, apart from the fact that the ship was blacked out, and all sound muffled except for the throb of the engine and the beat of the propeller as it thrashed through the water.

Next evening we were passed by the ingoing hospital ship "Centaur" which was ablaze with lights, painted white, with floodlights shining down the side of the ship. The International hospital ship identity number "47" was painted on the side of the bow clearly visible, and there was no way that this ship could have been taken for anything other than a hospital ship.

A four feet deep green band was painted along the side, broken in three places by great red crosses at least seven feet square. The funnel was yellow with the same size red cross on the side of it. These were the distinctive colours of recognition of a hospital ship under the Geneva Convention. The next day much to our horror, it was reported that the "Centaur" had been torpedoed with few survivors. How close was the submarine to our ship?

It was necessary to help crew the vessel with so many people on board ship and we were called to volunteer for crew duties. Some volunteered for duty as gun crews, whilst many volunteered for kitchen duties.

The American meals were a surprise to the Australians. We had a tray on which the food was dished up to each person. Instead of potatoes we had unsweetened macaroni, or rice, lots of spam, which we didn't consider to be as tasty as our own bully-beef.

Most of us ate the macaroni or the rice as a sweet and plastered it with sugar, much to the amusement of the Americans. The kitchen detail then had the job of cleaning up and putting the dirty dishes through the steam cleaning process before stowing them away.

Half way across the Pacific we had a scare, when all gun crews were called to report to their gun stations. An unidentified ship followed us all day, with only portion of the superstructure visible above the horizon. All very exciting but nothing happened and the gun crews were finally stood down until further orders.

Apart from an Australian boxing tournament challenge to the Americans, which the Aussies won, very little activity took place. Eighteen days at sea becomes a little boring.

On a couple of occasions we saw large numbers of flying fish, their silvery bodies gleaming in the sunlight as they rose above the surface of the water and skimmed across the water before diving out of sight.

On another occasion a whale came quite close to our ship. It seemed to be lazily keeping pace with us. Seeing it blow a spout of water when he surfaced, we guessed it was a "Good Luck" or "Bon Voyage" in its language. We were close enough to hear the spouting of the water.

We had been at sea sixteen days, when seagulls flying overhead indicated we must be approaching land.

A coastguard blimp flew over and shadowed us for part of the day, and we guessed we were probably no more than two days out from America. This attention after the Pacific crossing was very welcome. Next day after lunch an American destroyer met and started escorting us.

Early next morning the mournful sound of several ships' foghorns wakened us. With only a slight sea swell the ship was steaming at about a quarter speed and constantly sounding the foghorn. Going on deck we found we were in a bank of fog, with visibility down to about 200 yards.

Among the crew was an air of expectancy, as they guessed we were approaching America, and they were very confident the fog would clear in an hour or so.

San Francisco Due to the fog our speed entering the harbour was slow as we steamed slowly in the millpond conditions, toward the inner harbour. The fog visibly cleared about 10.30am: however it was mid-day before we were able to steam closer to our normal cruising speed. In front of us was the outline of the Golden Gate Bridge slowly materialising through the fog, but we were still a long way from it. As we drew nearer we could make out the traffic streaming across the bridge.

There was a great deal of shipping in the harbour and also some warships. A couple of aircraft carriers with three cruisers escorting them passed us on their outward bound journey. As we steamed further in to the harbour we had a grand stand view of it all.

Finally passing under the bridge at 8pm we anchored and bedded down not far from the prison island of "Alcatraz".

After an early breakfast next morning we disembarked on to lighters, and were ferried to Oakland, where we boarded an American train. We were informed we would remain on the train for six days crossing America.

Crossing America the troop train hauled by giant steam locomotives was a special delight to me. The engines were changed as we passed through the various divisions. As we climbed into the Rockies, the engines were changed for much bigger and much more powerful engines.

Awakening at Grand Junction, the high point of the Rockies crossing I was in time to see one of the monster engines being disconnected from our train. The massive engine was at least twice as long as the biggest Australian steam engine. After leaving the high point, we progressed mainly on level or falling gradients with much faster type engines, sometimes two double heading, as our train was eighteen coaches long.

Each day we stopped, usually on the outskirts of a city where the locomotive facilities were built for servicing of the locomotives. Whilst the servicing or changing of engines took place, and the coach tanks were filled with water we had a short route march to keep up our fitness.

While we were away on the march our black attendant collected for some of the boys a two bucket load of beer on ice. Returning from our march we could sit down to a very welcome drink. It was against all the rules, and all went well until on the second day our padre Flight Lt R.W. (call me Clicker) Clarke, was standing at our elbows watching us.

Norrie Wallace immediately held out the beer to the Padre saying: "Would you like a drink of our American lemonade Padre." "Yes!" he replied, "I don't mind if I do", and after a couple of good swigs at the bottle, stated: "That is a mighty fine lemonade boys, do you mind if I join you tomorrow".

"Padre we would be honoured!" said Norrie, so each day we had our session with the Padre, who was also good for a yarn or two. It had to be called lemonade otherwise he would have been obliged to confiscate the beer and forbid us from having it.

On most evenings the next coach porter visited our porter, and there would be a heated discussion on the American ball games. The discussion was carried on in the drawl from the south, which we loved to hear. Shamelessly we listened in, as it was as good as any radio show we had ever heard.

It was the journey of a lifetime. The scenery of the Rocky Mountains was magnificent. We threaded our way through the deep gorges, following the Colorado River, through the Glenwood Canyon, the outcrops of rock with massive boulders in some places seeming to tower almost over the top of us. It did not take a great deal to imagine them almost ready to roll down and crush our train.

It was awesome and we were intent in not missing any of this wonderful scenery, remaining glued to the windows for hours on end. After the more mountainous part of our journey we crossed the salt lakes to Salt Lake City.

Following our usual route march and change of engine we left Salt Lake City, our track descending for about half an hour of travel and then we travelled for many hours across the prairie, through Kansas City, Chicago, Cleveland and on to Providence, Rhode Island. It was a very interesting six days of train travel for everyone, and the magnificent new diesel electric streamlined trains, after the massive steam locos in the Rockies, made the Australian trains look like toys.

The superb motor cars and massive trucks were an eye opener as many of the models we had never seen. With much pointing and calling our mates attention to this truck or car or that model we very much enjoyed the route marches. Many of the buildings we saw on our daily march round the cities were awesome.

And of course, all the beautiful and not so beautiful ladies, all colours, all shapes, and sizes. One in particular in the outskirts of Chicago was an American negress, driving a big American "gas guzzler" car. She had stopped at the traffic lights, and sat there smoking a large cigar, casually with a disdainful look she flicked the ash out the car window. These unusual sights we had only seen in the movies.

Camp Myles Standish near Providence, Rhode Island was our staging destination and we were transferred in coaches to Camp Myles Standish where we remained until a full draft had been accumulated from training establishments in Canada, or from a further influx of Air Force personnel from Australia. Two months we waited for our draft to be completed for the next move, and in order to keep us fit we had a route march every day and played an assortment of ball sports. Generally we were bored with the inaction and wished to be on our way.

With little to keep us occupied in Camp Myles Standish we were given leave of three days in New York. What a thrill! On arrival with Norrie Wallace, and Bill, a Sergeant medical orderly who was going to England for service, we booked in to the Hotel Little New Yorker.

Bill and Norrie immediately headed for the bar. Being by choice a non drinker, I went walking up 5th Avenue then down Broadway, just soaking up the atmosphere. Here I was in New York at only 20 years old. What an experience! I would enjoy it while I could.

In gazing at all the wonderful sights and the immense buildings, I went to cross the road and almost stepped in front of a taxi. He was on the wrong side of the road. It gave me quite a fright.

Then I realised the traffic was all travelling on the right hand side of the road. Wake up, or I wouldn't last long in this rush and tear. I headed for Greenwich Village, an area I had seen on the movies and had admired.

After wandering through Greenwich Village, savouring the sights of the stalls, fruit barrows, and the different vendors offering their wares, I walked to Central Park where I sat admiring the hansom cabs and the prancing horses drawing them. The passengers were mostly elderly people out to enjoy themselves, and not interested in anyone else but themselves in their daily excursion in the open air.

I sat on a park bench looking at the apartments round the edge of the Central Park wondering who lived there and generally enjoying the scenes and the pleasant afternoon sun, when suddenly a lady came up from behind and sat on the seat next to me.

I smiled at her and said: "Hullo". She turned and looked at me giving me a frosty stare, as much as to say: "Get lost". After eying me up and down she said: "Don't try and pick me up young man! I'm not that type!"

"Please forgive me! I'm a stranger just arrived in New York and have been looking around, and wondered who would live in those expensive looking apartments, overlooking this Central Park". She looked me up and down again and then she caught sight of the "Australia" flash on my shoulder, and said: "Australia! isn't that one of the places down Texas way?"

"No! It is a country, part of the British Empire, over the Pacific Ocean where the US troops have gone to fight against the Japanese". She puzzled over my statement for a few moments then said: "You mean one of those countries in the South West Pacific". She reeled off a few names of residents of the apartment including Mrs Eleanor Rooseveldt, wife of the President of the United States. She then suggested that, as I was a stranger in New York, if I cared to see some of the city she would meet me here on the morrow and show me some of the sights. She turned and looking intently at me said "One thing puzzles me, how long did it take you to learn our language, and how come you speak it so well?"

This was an amusing question, so I tried to explain that as American was basically English, and Australian language was based on English we shared a common language. We had no difficulty understanding each other.

The offer of a guided tour was wonderful, and I thanked her promising to be there on the morrow. I headed back to the hotel where I found Norrie drinking with some female and suggested he was wasting his time. I wasn't impressed with her at all, and suggested to him she was only out for what she could get. He told me he would take all she had to give, and I should go and check on Bill in our room to see if he was all right. I found Bill spreadeagled on the bed as full as a boot

Not for me thank you. I wanted more out of my time in New York than that. It was now about eight o'clock. After telling Norrie that Bill was safe on his bed and sleeping, I walked out of the hotel and up the street deciding I would have a look at the sights and some of the shows.

After a very pleasant evening enjoying the sights and sounds of a very busy city, where it seemed busier at night than in the daytime I finally headed back to the hotel climbing into bed in the early hours. With only a couple of hours sleep, I was up, had breakfast, and was waiting in the Park at 10am.

The lady had told me her name was Helen Keller and that she worked as a private secretary for her father a very busy consulting industrial chemist. She didn't think it would be too difficult for her to spare some time to show me some of the more interesting sights of her home city New York.

She arrived as the clock was striking 10am and suggested we travel on the subway to the Bronx where we could visit the Zoo. It was one of the world's first zoos to introduce the open range method of keeping animals, and she felt I would find this interesting.

It was most impressive, and as I have always loved animals I enjoyed it immensely. After several hours at the zoo we then headed to "The Museum of Natural History and Painting Gallery". Catching a lift to the top we then walked down a circular ramp which seemed never ending and must have covered about six floors, viewing all the exhibits and works of art on the way.

By this time it was evening and as we were close by Radio City Music Hall Helen suggested a visit to the show of the world famous dancing girls "The Rockettes" who were performing at Radio City. She said I would enjoy their precision dancing, and also the sight of these beautiful girls who were much sought after as companions or in many cases as wives.

The girls had been chosen for their figures and beauty, and they were fantastic in their precision dancing. The presentation was a sight to stir the blood of any young 20-year-old, and I could quite imagine that they were a goal for any young beau who waited at the stage door in the hope of a date.

It had been a wonderful day, Helen wouldn't allow me to spend any money, but I was able to pay at the slot machines on the underground, as she usually didn't have any change.

We arranged to meet at "St. John the Divine Church" on 5th Avenue the next afternoon. This gave me some time in the morning to go exploring down Broadway and along 5th Avenue on my own. I found the church without much trouble and as soon as Helen arrived we went inside.

I was amazed at how richly the church was decorated. It was more a showpiece than a place of worship. After viewing this beautiful old church we then walked across on to Broadway, and into a nearby botanical park.

Walking leisurely through the park we arrived at one of the leading hotels on Broadway, where Helen had booked a table, for a dinner and dance evening.

There was no way that I would have been able to afford to be in this hotel and I told her so. She assured me it was her pleasure and not to worry about the cost. The table was in a prime position overlooking the dance floor.

There were a lot of young girls she called "taxi girls", as they could be rented for the dance. I would have called them budding film stars, as they surely were budding, whilst some were in full bloom.

It was a set-up right out of the movies, and I was enthralled, especially when she asked me if I would like to meet the orchestra leader, Guy Lombardo. After the introduction during the course of a dance, we returned to our table, which she had reserved conveniently close to the dance floor.

When the band had a break, Guy Lombardo came over and talked with me. I found him a very interesting and friendly person, and marvelled that one of the leading dance bandleaders should have bothered to come over to pass a few moments with me, and as we left gave me a wave.

Helen wished to know when I would have leave to visit Boston, as she would like to meet me there, and before leaving in her taxi gave me her phone number. She had attended a ladies finishing school in Boston and would be very pleased to show me the sights. I thanked her very much for the enjoyable sight seeing in New York and promised to ring.

Returning to Camp Myles Standish, we travelled by train to Providence, Rhode Island. then by bus to Taunton and as there were so many of us many were forced to stand. The amazing thing was that while standing erect, many were asleep on their feet. It sure must have been either a tiring leave or one where the aircrew fellows had burned the candle on both ends. Was it worth it? Yes, it was wonderful! an exciting city full of life. Oh, for another leave in New York.

The Officer in Charge for the journey to and in America was Flight/Lieutenant Goddard. We were told he was a Victorian pig farmer before joining the Air Force. In our opinion that is where he should have stayed. In order to impress himself with his own authority he was continually issuing directions on what we should be doing, how we should behave, and how we should show more respect by saluting the officers, who after all were fellow course mates with whom we had trained.

We retaliated by educating the U.S. Army fellows to salute the sergeants. We told the Americans the officers wearing the peak caps, were our baggage boys, and they should not think of saluting them. We really got the message across, as the officers appeared very similar to the baggage porters on the stations.

Our commanding officer decided to send us off on another period of three days leave, possibly getting rid of his problems for a few days. I decided to visit Boston, but when I rang Helen she unfortunately could not get away. I did my sightseeing in Boston on my own.

The thing about Boston I remembered most was going boating in a swan boat on Boston Common. It also was a very old city with many fine stone buildings, giving it an appearance of an extreme amount of wealth invested in the buildings, particularly in the areas surrounding the beautifully laid out parks and gardens.

The Boston people didn't seem to be as friendly nor as helpful as people in the other areas where we had visited..

On returning from our three day leave there was expectancy in the air. Trouble was brewing, F/Lt Goddard declared the camp closed and no passes were to be issued. With the inaction and the lack of direction from the commanding officer we didn't take kindly to being closed in the camp with nothing to do and no worthwhile activity to keep us interested.

Why should we just sit and do nothing so after some grumbling we decided on a mass exodus from the camp. We were some 300 Australian airmen and it was soon a case of "go for it fellers get moving or we will be stuck here all day". The Australians were being picked up, and returned to camp by the US MPs, who were continually patrolling the perimeter road in their jeeps.

After studying the situation with several of my mates, we waited in the bushes close to the fence about 10am. When the jeep went by, we raced to the wire fence, crawled under the wire and crossed into the bush on the other side of the road. We then split up and headed off to enjoy our day of exploration of the area.

I was hitch hiking to wherever, when an American picked me up and invited me home to lunch, some twenty miles out of Taunton. It was a pleasure to be riding along in the latest American convertible, and conversing on many topics. He was very interested in Australia, and I had many questions to answer. After a very pleasant drive we arrived at his house, a bungalow style standing in a wooded area, with a few close neighbours.

Following a very pleasant lunch which lasted a couple of hours, the father suggested that the daughter might like to leave a couple of hours earlier and on her way to work take me to their weekend holiday shooting lodge. It would be a nice drive in the country and I would see more of the surrounding countryside.

She would drop me off in Taunton on the way back, as it was not far out of her way and it would be no trouble. The holiday home, about a half hour drive away nestled in a secluded forest setting, some fifty yards from a lake which was about half a mile across. The father had the lake seeded by the fisheries Dept., when he first bought it twenty years previously and it was now providing extremely good fishing.

The daughter, an attractive young lady of 19 years made me feel rather uncomfortable as she was showing me through the holiday home. She seemed intent on the bedroom, remarking there was no one to disturb honeymooners or lovers in this secluded and wonderful hide away, and didn't I think this would be a lovely spot to spend a few hours.

Being a newly married person and rather shy I wasn't about to be seduced. Feeling very guilty I made excuses to return early to meet up with my mates. She was a lovely, curvaceous young lady full of energy and youthful enthusiasm for life, and what it had to offer and I was severely tempted. She was a little reluctant to leave. However, with some prompting she finally drove me to Taunton, The holiday home although only used occasionally would be a wonderful home Next afternoon for any family.

I had hardly stepped from the car after saying goodbye when a jeep pulled into the kerb and I was picked up by US Military Police, and taken back to camp.

Next day everyone was paraded, and we were read the riot act. There were complaints from the American Officer in charge of the camp as to why his MPs had brought in over 300 Australians. He only had a record of approximately 230 RAAF personnel listed.

He asked why were so many of them called Wing Commander Swan (W/Cdr. Swan was with us and took over the draft for the final sector to England) or F/Lt Goddard, our CO, or F/Lt A.R. (Clicker) Clarke, our padre. He also complained of the slovenly way the Australians appeared in the camp. There was, he said, a definite lack of discipline.

W/Cdr Swan, who had now assumed command, called an urgent parade, stating there would be no charges laid regarding the AWOL.

Instead of charges being laid he expected that we put on a fine display of marching on the next day, when we were marching out of the camp, then by train headed for New York.

If we were heading for New York then that meant we were at last on the move. Embarking on a ship, the destination would have to be England. So on the morrow we turned on the works for a march past with the US Commander taking the salute.

Afterwards we received a message from the Commander to say it was the best march past of any troops he had ever taken the salute from, and he wished us safe journey and God speed.

At Sea - "Queen Elizabeth"

On Monday, 5 July 1943 we travelled by train from Camp Myles Standish to New York, boarding the RMS *"Queen Elizabeth"* bound for England with 23,000 troops on board. In the berth next to the *"Queen Elizabeth"* was a memorable sight, the burned out, capsized hull, of the one time Atlantic record holder SS *"Normandy"*

On the *"Queen Elizabeth"* each cabin had 24 bunks, and these were allocated in such a way, that one third of the occupants got out of bed and off to breakfast. After the first lot had moved out of the way, there was room for the second lot to get out of bed and off to breakfast, making room for the remainder to get out of bed. My breakfast period was No. 3 sitting at 10.15am and the evening meal at 7.15pm. With only two meals a day, the canteen was soon sold out.

This was not a pleasure cruise on the world's largest ocean going liner, but a cruise of necessity, with as many troops crammed on board as possible.

There was only a token regard for safety should the vessel sink, but then there was a war on, and personal safety didn't really count. If any of these large troop carrying ships had been sunk, very few people would have escaped.

The top decks were closed in as sleeping quarters where thousands of American black troops slept on their bedroll on the deck. I remember on one occasion, when looking for the way out on to an open deck, I stepped out into one of the sleeping decks. It had a closed in foul air smell.

On the third night out from New York, our ship heeled hard over, almost tipping us out of bed, and wakened us a few minutes after midnight. The ship then immediately started to vibrate as the turbines increased to maximum speed, of around 35 knots, the equivalent of approx. 40mph (64 kilometres per hour)

The Captain had ordered a change of course 90 degrees to Port and as we were too fast for any ship, or submarine to catch, had immediately ordered full speed.

After maintaining this speed for twelve hours, we then reduced to normal cruising speed, resuming our original course. It was much more pleasant cruising without the vibration set up by the faster speed.

When questioned, one of the crew officers told us, we had almost run into the middle of a pack of submarines. The safest evasion strategy was a considerable change of course, then a good period at full speed. At full speed we could outrun any ships or submarines and had a good chance of escaping in case torpedoes were fired at us.

On the afternoon of the fifth day out from New York, two destroyers joined us as we rounded the North of Ireland. After keeping station with us overnight, they departed early the following morning. They heeled over as they turned and with some screeches on their sirens raced off in a fine display of speed.

With a final couple of hoots on their sirens they departed behind us. Bloody Royal Navy showoffs, they probably knew we were all Air Force and US Army.

We made landfall just after mid-day and were soon steaming up the Clyde River viewing the little white thatched cottages all along the northern shoreline with the gently sloping green hills in the background providing a wonderful first view of Scotland.

On the foredeck sitting on the massive spars, which are used for unloading the cargo from the holds, we had a marvellous view of the shipping in the Clyde, including a goodly number of warships of different types.

Then out of nowhere came our first sight of a Spitfire flying low down on the starboard side. He was flying past the ship, many feet below where we were sitting.

With a wave from the pilot he did a steep turn out in front of the ship, then came back at us, head on, and passing down the port side. No one but an Aussie fighter pilot would be bothered giving us a welcome, so he had to be one of us.

There was a great deal of excitement. It was our first sighting of a Spitfire, a plane we were all to become very familiar with. Some of our group would probably fly this type of fighter plane in the future, whilst others would become very familiar with the plane's silhouette in the air.

CHAPTER FOUR

ENGLAND AT WAR
1943

Berthing at the wharf late in the afternoon, we unloaded on to a train and left almost immediately for the overnight run to the south of England and Brighton.

Unlike in America where we had a troop train for our rail movements, in England we shared the seats with the civilian travellers. In our compartment we had a couple of people who had just arrived from Ireland.

Everywhere the country was blacked out and this was something we would now have to get used to. It was mid summer, and with two hours daylight saving, it was not dark until almost midnight. There was plenty of interest to see as we steamed south.

As a precautionary measure, the trains were slowed considerably from the pre-war speed and travelled at 40mph maximum. The railway companies had slowed down the trains because of the dangers of track damage by intruder bombings. The slower speed had been found less dangerous.

This was an exciting part of the journey; everywhere seemed to be a hive of activity. The railways fascinated me so it was no wonder I hardly had any sleep.

As we passed through London we could see plenty of evidence of bombing. Further south of London the countryside was looking very fresh and green, a little similar to Tasmania and I had the feeling I would feel more at home in these surroundings.

Brighton was a surprise, a lovely city full of old buildings with very fine architecture. It was situated right on the south coast of England. The Australians had just been moved from their staging station in Bournemouth to Brighton, awaiting further posting to RAF stations.

Lord Haw Haw had just announced the Australians and New Zealander aircrews who had just moved from Bournemouth into the Grand and Metropole Hotels in Brighton, over the last couple of days could expect some nice friendly visits from the German Luftwaffe boys. Sure enough in our first four nights in Brighton, we had three nights of air raids.

To see and hear the gunfire, and the roar of the aero engines, as our night fighters searched the night sky for the German planes, was really exhilarating.

Quartered in the Hotel Grand and the Hotel Metropole, on the esplanade along the seashore, we were hanging out of the windows watching all the excitement without thought of falling bombs or stray bullets. There was barbed wire along the Esplanade in front of the hotel, and behind the barbed wire, gun emplacements and searchlights.

To see and hear the multiple 20 mm Bofor guns, each firing 800 rounds a minute, blasting away at the enemy intruders, was something out of this world. The ack-ack going up into the air was a wonderful and somewhat exciting sight.

Watching the fireworks that night, I don't think many of the boys realised in a very short time the German guns would be blazing away at us with much more ferocity. The station orderlies were doing everything possible to get us down into the air raid shelters, but without success: we were not going to miss the fun

Suddenly a few hundred yards out over the water, the searchlights fastened on two German fighters. One of our fighters, directly overhead, opened up with his cannons and we could see the tracer bullets disappearing into the blackness. We realised later they were hitting the German plane. With a flash of flame, followed by a delayed explosion, the sky was lit up by the exploding German plane and we could see, momentarily, the winner, a Spitfire. A great cheer went up, as the show closed for that night.

On one of our first weekends in Brighton we were given leave. In company with Ian Vickers, a fellow Tasmanian, with whom I had trained on the same course at Somers, we visited London.

Many of the places like Victoria Station, Trafalgar Square and Nelson's column, Westminster Abbey and the tomb of the unknown warrior, became fact as we headed from place to place taking in all the sights.

In the evening we decided on the show at the Palladium seeing "Maxie Miller" England's funnyman, "The Cariolli Bros" musical clowns, and many other famous acts.

With a bed at the YMCA Hostel, in Arundell St., just off the Embankment, we were on the spot to look over Capt Scott's ship "Discovery" in which he had sailed to Antarctica.

A little further along the Embankment was 'Cleopatra's Needle" erected in Egypt 1500 BC and presented to England by the King of Egypt 1879. It was lying where it had fallen in the desert and whilst it was being transported to England from Egypt, the needle was abandoned in the"Bay of Biscay" during a storm. It was later recovered, and erected in London, near Waterloo Bridge, in memory of Admiral Lord Nelson and General Sir Ralph Abercrombie.

We then headed down to Thread Needle Street to see "The Old Lady of Thread Needle Street" as the Bank of England headquarters was known.

It was then only a short walk to the Tower of London. The building itself was very interesting, and the age was apparent. As it was being used as a service establishment, it unfortunately was out of bounds.

From the Tower we crossed to St Paul's Cathedral, where just inside the door on the left, was Lord Kitchener's tomb and monument, all done in white marble. We were not allowed anywhere near the Cathedral's famous Whispering Gallery, as an unexploded bomb was in the process of being removed.

Early next morning we walked through Hyde Park to the Archway leading down Piccadilly. We were lucky here. On the one side was a police station and one of the officers took us inside, and up onto the roof of the archway. The whole top of the archway was taken up with a statue of the state chariot of "Queen Boadicea" being drawn by four horses. It was so large it was possible to walk beneath the horse's bellies without having to stoop.

Across the road was Apsley House, the home of the Duke of Wellington. Looking in the other direction we were looking down into the back of Buckingham Palace. It was only a short walk down the Mall to Buckingham Palace, where we arrived in time to join the crowd which had gathered for the changing of the Guards. The Band of Scots Guards was playing, and the Scots Guards, were being relieved by the Coldstream Guards.

As soon as the changing of the guards finished we headed to Victoria Station to catch the train. We had only just reached the station when the air raid sirens sounded. A warden warned us to take shelter but we remained outside to see the action. The searchlights had zeroed in on two German fighters, and the ack-ack gunners were very quickly shooting at them. We were amazed at the manoeuvring of the planes as the pilots twisted and turned to evade the lines of tracer going up.

The manoeuvring as seen from the ground, was very exciting to watch. We discussed the benefits of all the twisting and turning,. The raiders remained high over London because of the barrage balloons. After our hectic weekend of London sightseeing, we had forty winks in the train on the way to Brighton.

In settling us into England, a system of home stay had been arranged. The idea was to register the part of England you would like to visit, and if it could be arranged with some family. Then away you went visiting.

The lady asked me what area I would like, and I said Sherwood Forest, being an avid fan of Robin Hood. She said the Robin Hood story was only a fairy tale and she didn't think there was any of Sherwood Forest left.

"That is the only place for me", I told her, "if you can arrange something, it would suit me fine". Two days later I had a message to see the lady. She had found me a place near Newstead Abbey with a doctor and his wife, and suggested this might suit. My visit was arranged and off I went headed for Nottingham, where the doctor's wife Mrs Patricia Green, would meet me at the railway station.

As an Aussie arriving in uniform it was easy for me to be found. I had hardly stepped from the train, when a lady spoke, asking me if my name was Laurie Woods. She introduced herself as Mrs Patricia Green, "Just call me Pat". First stop for lunch was at the pub set in the ground level of the rock on which Nottingham Castle stands. Called "Ye Old Trip to Jerusalem" it was so small, even at 5 feet 7 ½ inches, I had to stoop to go in the front door.

Reputedly the place where King Richard formulated the plan for the crusades, it was England's oldest pub, and was appropriately named. Inside it was similar to most English pubs where you could have a game of darts, while waiting for the very English baked dinner of roast beef, carrots, onions, potatoes, and Yorkshire pudding.

After a delicious meal we headed for Pat's home, which was only half a mile from Newstead Abbey, on the way Pat stopped at the Abbey gates and pointed to an old oak tree, which was right in the middle of the entrance, just clear of the gates. A large metal plaque on the tree stated that under that tree the Pilgrim Fathers had gathered, and decided they would arrange an expedition to leave from that spot, to go to America, and set up a settlement. They successfully did this and settled in America founding the colony of Plymouth, near Boston.

From the Abbey gates, it was a short drive to the Doctor's home where I met Doctor Green. He was in his 70s and had almost given up his medical practice, only carrying out house visits to his long time patients, with patient clinics on three mornings a week.

Pat, who was in her early forties, an attractive ex-nursing sister, acted as his assistant. She would be available to escort me round and show me the area, and she said that if there was anything I wished to see, please tell them. I told them of my wish to see Sherwood Forest and anything to do with Robin Hood.

As the local market at Mansfield was on the next morning, we headed for there remembering that the Mansfield market and archery contest, were part of the Robin Hood folklore. The market was a real social gathering out for trade, socialising and just for a talk.

On the way back Pat dropped in on neighbours Mr and Mrs Brooks. They had migrated to Canada, returning to England 5 years later. In their early fifties they were good fun, so much so, that I walked to their home on a couple of occasions. They invited me for tea to meet their two children who would be home in the evening. A most enjoyable dinner with some mead to round off the meal had everyone in a jolly mood.

After discussions on many topics and answering many of the questions asked about Australia, they told me the track I used from the Green's, was part of the old Roman road, which passed through to Mansfield. Many ghost stories were told of people walking on the old road around midnight, hearing the coach and horses going by, and of the sound of the driver's whip cracking.

Being close to midnight, they suggested another mead for the road, and asked if I needed company along the old coach road. Not being one for ghost stories I assured them I would be OK. I left and started out along the road but I did glance behind a couple of times as I walked.

I suddenly stopped. I had distinctly heard a sound like a tinkle of harness. Unbelievably an animal's head was showing up in the mist. I didn't know whether to run or what to do. Finally, I became brave and walked toward it. As I got closer, I could see the head was sitting comfortably on the rest of a cow, and realised it was only the thick ground fog which had prevented seeing the rest of the cow. After this little scare I arrived home safely.

Doctor Green was a keen pigeon fancier and proudly showed me his loft of birds. He told me he had acquired most of his pigeons from some of the most famous English lofts, and was a keen student of their breeding. He also had his share of good race wins. As a pigeon fancier I admired three or four of his birds which pleased him a great deal as he considered they were some of his best birds.

He told me they had had a couple of Royal Australian Air Force aircrew come to stay with them before, and he thought one of them had become a little too familiar with his wife. He thought this was a little beyond what good hospitality was about, and this particular fellow would not be welcome again.

He suggested perhaps that I might like to accompany him, collecting some honey from his bees in the forest. A small remnant of Sherwood Forest, it was not very thick, more an open wood.

On arrival the doctor set himself up with nets over his head and shoulders, gloves and a smoke puffer and started smoking the bees before removing some honey from one of the hives.

I walked over a little way toward his beehives, and he suggested that I should get back as his bees were wild. As I retreated one of the bees stung me right on the bridge of the nose between the eyes. He told me not to touch it, and when he had finished he very gently removed the sting (with a bit of liniment), so as not to squeeze the poison out of the sting. He was successful and It came out with no swelling or discomfort.

After lunch Pat suggested a visit to Newstead Abbey, and she would show me what remained of the cliff dwellings.

Newstead Abbey had been a priory of "The Order of St John of Jerusalem" until the order could no longer afford it. They decided to sell and Lord Byron, the grandfather of the poet then bought the Abbey. The grandson, Lord Byron, the poet, gloried in drinking parties with his friends, and during one of these parties, they dug up a portion of the monk's graveyard, recovering a monk's skull, which they cleaned up. They then used the skull as a drinking cup for their more lurid toasts, when it would be filled with wine and passed round the table, for each person to sip the wine.

Another fascinating item was a marble table. A young Italian craftsman, on finishing his apprenticeship, commenced building this table completely of marble. Even the tabletop was inlaid marble and a wonderful work of art depicting a garden scene. The artist died at a young age, having completed only the one project. Lord Byron had purchased the table whilst in Italy for £20,000 and had it transported back to be placed in his home at Newstead Abbey.

From the abbey Pat suggested we walk down to the lake where I could see the remains of the cliff dwellings. On arrival she kicked off her shoes and dipped her toes in the lake, "Oh goodie", she exclaimed, "let's have a swim, we don't need any swim suit, no one will disturb us".

I declined, making excuses that I felt I was in for a bout of flu, but she should go ahead with her swim while I looked over what remained of the cliff dwellings.

She had slipped very quickly out of her clothes and stood in all her womanly beauty. She was sure a lovely sight to see, and very tempting, beautifully rounded breasts, well proportioned, nicely matured. It was difficult to refuse, what I felt was being freely offered.

Not wanting to abuse the old doctor's hospitality I headed round the other side of the cliff dwellings looking at nothing in particular, but feeling guilty that I felt so tempted.

Pat made me promise not to reveal to her husband about her swim. She said she was so sorry I felt as though I was in for a bout of flu, but should I come again to visit them, we could enjoy plenty more of this type of outing.

On the next day she dropped me off at the train station, and after a long lingering kiss goodbye, suggested I would be more than welcome to come again. She would like to share the pleasure of more of my company, and me. "Whoa boy", I thought, "Take it easy, one visit to Nottingham is enough for me".

Back at Brighton during our route marches, I used to enjoy studying the architecture of buildings we passed. It took one's mind from the spit and polish put on by the Sergeant who was detailed to oversee our marches.

Whenever some young woman was nearby this sergeant, with moronic regularity, would start yelling orders of "Straighten up your dressing", "Swing those arms", or more annoying calling the step:" Left' right 'Left' right" with some further: "smarten it up" etc.

The word went round, whenever this Sergeant opened his mouth, everyone change step, and then tell him in no uncertain terms to get into step, to lift his marching skills, or whatever. To overcome this and to save face he would march us round a couple of corners, then break us off to have some morning tea in one of the little cafes or coffee shops, before marching us back in time for lunch.

We were often stood down for the rest of the day and I walked around Brighton looking at the lovely old buildings, marvelling at the architecture.

On one occasion I hopped on the bus and went to Lewes, where I visited an old castle. Forty five years later I found that my mother's great grandmother's birthplace was Lewes. She had lived there until convicted and transported to Australia in the 1840s.

On the return to Brighton I saw a lot of bomb destruction along the waterfront at Hove. A couple of days later with nothing to do I decided to make the walk along to Hove and have a closer look. Viewing the remains of the buildings left me with very mixed feelings.

Here was an example of what the air raids were doing all over England, with much loss of life to the civilian population. The whole end of a city block of top class residential conjoined houses, spreading from the corner for 100 yards along the waterfront and 100 yards back into the block, had been flattened.

The only protection against German aircraft coming in from the sea would have been the air force fighters overhead, and the ack ack batteries spread very thinly along the front.

As I stood looking over the shattered remains I heard a window slide open and looked up to see a young woman saying something. I couldn't hear very well, so I stepped onto the bombed site, to get closer to her window.

She asked me if I was interested in what had happened to these buildings. I replied that I would be, and she invited me to come in, as she and her mother were just having a cup of tea and would I care to join them.

The mother was the wife of one of the Chief Inspectors of Scotland Yard. She wasn't keen on London with all the raids and every opportunity she loved to head for Brighton, spending some time with her daughter, Rhonda, who was 27 years of age and had been educated at one of England's leading schools for young ladies. As well as medium length brown curly hair, a beautifully proportioned body and lovely legs, she was also blessed with a vivacious personality.

We had a most enjoyable discussion, as they were both lovely ladies and their company and conversation made me feel very comfortable to be sharing some time with them.

Suddenly the daughter turned to mother and said: "Mother it is time you went home, it is getting close to my bedtime, and we must get to bed early you know. Laurie is staying the night". Although I had not expected something like this to happen I did feel it would be more than a pleasant way to spend the night than back in our barracks.

After the mother left we sat at the table. With light classical background music and the soft glow of candlelight and a glass or two of wine we discussed many intimate details of our lives. She was married, I was married, what were we looking for, and what did we hope the future may hold.

I told her what the service life was like and my impressions of England and the English people.

79

Rhonda was very surprised at my remarks regarding the average English servicemen, especially Royal Navy types we had met on board ship, and how they were full of their own importance. They considered the colonials (Aussies, Kiwis, and Canadians), as someone they had to put up with, and generally they didn't want to pass the time of day with us.

This feeling that colonials were a little inferior seemed to be fairly general, even though we had left our own countries to join England in their fight for freedom. I told her we loved the English ladies, as they seemed so feminine with lovely lilting voices, a charming accent and a pleasure to hear speaking. Last but definitely not least, was their lovely skin and complexions. Possibly due to wartime rationing their figures were generally very fine, with very very nice curves, much admired by the Aussies.

Another amusing revelation was our medical officer's lecture on VD and how he advised us to be extremely careful, be honest, and if we had any doubt or discharge, report sick immediately.

He had told us if we must have a woman, either choose a married one, or a professional prostitute. They were most likely to be disease free, but beware of the enthusiastic amateurs.

This, Rhonda found very amusing and her reply was: "I'm married, I'm not an amateur and at the moment I'm very enthusiastic. Sorry there is not room for you in the shower, but let's shower and then we can hop into bed". She was a very beautiful young woman with her dark lustrous eyes, and as I took her in my arms, she pressed her body into mine in a most insistent and inviting manner. As my arousal grew I started feeling for the fastenings and managed to undo several before she suddenly pulled away and headed to the shower.

After my shower I stepped out of the bathroom and by the light of the shielded candlelight I could just make out the bed. Needing no invitation I slid in beside her lovely warm body. She smelled good, and she felt terrific as my hands began exploring and our bodies were merging. I was in no hurry as my hands wandered slowly over those curves. When I had reached the breasts they felt as though they were swelling and feeling firmer. In fact they felt so good that I could not resist the temptation to play round with them and then tasting them.

There was no particular hurry we had all night but Rhonda was soon curling her legs over me and I felt the urgency of her embrace pulling me into her. The rhythm of her movements and the pressure of her arms clasped so tightly round me, were an invitation to the joys of pleasuring each other. She was trim, taut, and terrific, we enjoyed everything the other had to offer.

It was a long time before we settled down in each other's arms to a spasmodic sleep because, as Rhonda had said, she was very enthusiastic. What a glorious body she had, I couldn't get enough of her.

Early next morning before leaving, Rhonda was insistent that I come again in the evening. I promised faithfully I would be back as I had had a wonderful night with her and would be most anxious to resume where we had left off. On the way back to the hotel where we were billeted I bought an early morning paper as though I had been out for that purpose.

The evening walk to the appointment with Rhonda was one of the most enjoyable walks I experienced. It was made all the more enjoyable by the anticipation of looking into those dark lustrous eyes, and to see the gleam of mischief there. The joy of feeling the smoothness of her skin, of running my hands over her, and of the little squeals, and of the wriggling, to get a lot more of the same passionate embraces, and in pleasuring her infinitely was very rewarding.

Unfortunately the arrangement didn't last long, and it was disappointing to be posted off to Whitley Bay, not quite four weeks later. Rhonda was not very pleased and wished I could get out of the posting. I pointed out it was only for a period of six weeks and then I should be back. I promised to call as soon as I returned

Whitley Bay, a suburb of Newcastle-on-Tyne, had been chosen as a base set up for commando training. Staffed by a Grenadier Guard major and Guardsmen NCO's, the commando course had become an unarmed combat course in August 1943. In the last few days of the course, with a very bad dose of flu, I was admitted to hospital where I remained for six weeks, putting me behind all my original mates.

On my return journey to Brighton the train passed through Chesterfield and I was most intrigued to see a church steeple which had a distinct twist in it. The timber used in building the steeple had been green and as it weathered, had dried out and shrunk giving the steeple the appearance of a corkscrew.

Arriving in Brighton I excitedly made my way to Rhonda's flat, intent on expectations of the joys, excitement and pleasures of my previous visits. After several knocks the concierge answered. She was sorry but the lady had moved out three weeks previously, and had not left a forwarding address. What a disappointment. I felt as though I had been abandoned.

While in Brighton I had joined the Royal Sussex Regiment Home Guard Band and spent many hours with them at practice and concerts.

In September I was promoted to the rank of Flight Sergeant.

CHAPTER FIVE
Service in the RAF

No 4 (O) A FU West Freugh, Scotland

On 9th November 1943 our batch was attached to the RAF and posted to No 4 (O) Advanced Flying training, at West Freugh, out from Stranraer Harbour in Scotland.

A few days before Christmas I met and talked with RAAF Padre Wood who had made an official visit to West Freugh. He had a reputation for his wonderful work with fliers. His personal contact had been very helpful to those with a breakdown in nerves, or where the rest of their crew had been killed, and they were not able to carry on. He told me he periodically visited the stations where the bulk of the Australian aircrew were stationed, and sometimes found men with problems. If he could help then he felt his visit had been worthwhile. A few days after returning to London he was killed by a German bomb exploding near him as he was going to the Boomerang Club for lunch.

Flying in winter in Scotland was dependent on the vagaries of the weather, with many recalls to base on account of deteriorating weather. On December 10th whilst out on a sea patrol, we flew near and were challenged (a convoy of approximately forty ships). On the way back we passed close to the convoy again, and also passed over a friendly submarine moving along on the surface.

Our training was now becoming very challenging and once we started flying most of us were looking for more. On December 16 we had an exciting night firing exercise with tracers on the gunnery range.

The target was a mock up plane, with faint glowing light, moving quite quickly on a track across our line of vision about 100 yards away.

The tracer (every fourth bullet fired) enabled the gunner to adjust his aim and was wonderful to watch, burning green a little way then turning red, finally, burning out at 600 yards.

Accuracy in our navigation work was becoming very important and was continuously being impressed on us, as one degree out in a calculation would put us one mile off course in every sixty miles we travelled. In low level flying one mile out on a dark night could mean life or death if we were flying near mountains.

After landing from a training flight on 20 December the accuracy factor in navigation was brought home to us. An American Flying Fortress B17G, the very latest top secret Yankee heavy bomber, brand new off the American assembly line was standing on the tarmac in front of the control tower. The crew had flown across from America, headed for Preswick, become lost, and landed at the first drome they saw. They were 100 miles south of where they should have landed.

Fortunately it was Scotland and not the continent, otherwise the Germans would have been delivered the very latest weapon being used against them. Security on the base was also very slack.

The American airmen were nowhere to be seen and had left the hush-hush Flying Fortress unattended so we climbed inside and examined all the secret equipment at leisure, especially their latest highly secret bomb sight.

Flying from West Freugh several Australians were killed crashing into the mountains in the inclement weather, often encountered in the West Freugh area.

On 22 December 1943, with F/Sgt Wallace we were forced down with engine trouble landing at Valley, in Wales. It was a dark cloudless night with reasonable visibility and not a very pleasant place to have engine problems among the mountains.

We were twice recalled to base because of weather closing in. On two occasions our bombing exercise was cancelled by bad weather in the target area. On Christmas Eve flying was also cancelled on account of the weather. Our last flight in Scotland was on the 30 December 1943.

We were then posted to No. 27 Operational Training Unit at Lichfield, near Birmingham, where we would be flying Wellington twin engined bombers. I had just passed 150 hours flying.

After a few days leave at Glasgow and Girvan, the birthplace of Robbie Burns the famous Scottish poet, we left West Freugh heading for Lichfield. It was a long cold journey with several changes of trains on the way. Standing on those cold station platforms made me think of the lovely warm weather in Australia, which we are inclined to take for granted. For me the delays in changing trains put me in a box seat to see all the different train movements.

Birmingham, where we had a two hour wait changing trains, seemed to be one of those cities one reads about. The dirty industrial city serviced by a massive network of railway lines, and a continual haze of coal smoke covering the place. I wondered whether they ever had a nice day, a day when they could clearly see the sun and feel its heat?

It was extremely cold on arrival at the Lichfield railway station late in the afternoon of the 5 January 1944.

No 27 OTU Lichfield, Staffs.

Our group of Australian airmen consisting of pilots, gunners, wireless operator air gunners, and the observers. The observers were doing their tour as navigators, or as bomb aimers, whichever they chose.

Arriving at Lichfield in such numbers, it was some time before we were picked up. Looking at our massive pile of luggage for approximately 250 aircrew, each airman had an extra large kit bag of flying gear, a second kit bag, not quite so big for uniforms and underclothing, and most of us had an overnight bag for change of underwear, toiletries etc. It was a massive job transporting aircrew from station to station as they completed their training.

Finally our transports arrived and were given a few cheers plus some desultory remarks, taken in good humour by the airmen and air women drivers. A twenty minute drive to the station where we were dropped off at the long crew huts and told take any bed for the night and we would move in with our crew after we had crewed together the next day. Operational Training Unit No 27 meant stepping up the tempo of our final training for operations.

The aerodrome was much bigger than West Freugh as the bigger Wellington twin engined bombers needed longer runways in order to take off. The dispersals were also more scattered in case of enemy raids, or in case of accidents should the live bombs fall from a plane and detonate with a likelihood of damage to other planes.

The extremely long Nissen huts, our sleeping quarters were also dispersed, for safety in air raids, and were quite a distance from the flight office. Because of these distances, everyone was advised to purchase a bike and to mark it distinctly otherwise it would soon be stolen.

It was at this stage that everyone had to "crew up" with those persons they wished to fly with. We were paraded in a big hall, on 6 January and given a welcome by the CO and then told to sort ourselves out into crews. This was quite a tall order. Where did one start? The only people I knew were those with whom I had been training and we were all navigator/bomb aimers trained in the same category. In a life and death situation, how can anyone just walk into a room and from some 250 aircrew pick those persons, with whom to risk one's life?

I was approached by an older pilot, quite dapper looking, with his little penline moustache, and accompanied by a young navigator officer, taller than myself. They asked me if I was doing my tour as a navigator or as a bomb aimer and was I looking for a crew. Would I like to join them as their bomb aimer, as almost everyone else had crewed up? Liking the look of them and their manner, I joined them.

The pilot was Ted Owen, aged 29, from Warrnambool, and the navigator, Don Hudspeth, from Hobart, son of the Headmaster of the Hobart Technical College.

Together we met a wireless air-gunner and a rear gunner who seemed not to be wanted by anyone, and was quite happy to join us. So we became a crew. A crew almost of leftovers, as most had crewed up with their mates, whilst we were a crew of complete strangers.

Almost immediately I received word that my wife had given birth to a daughter on the 9 December 1943, and her name was Gillian Margaret. This called for a celebration in the crew, but I didn't drink. They wouldn't agree that a suitable celebratory occasion had been honoured, unless I had a shot of whisky. I agreed on this occasion as it was special.

The crew was lucky in that the pilot, the navigator and myself didn't drink and made sure no one in the crew did so, especially when flying was the order of the day.

The crewmembers were;

Pilot,
      Flight/Sgt. Ted Owen,   Warrnambool, Victoria,
Navigator,
      Pilot/Officer, Don Hudspeth,   Hobart, Tasmania,
Bomb/Aimer, Front/Gnr,
      Flight/Sgt. Laurie Woods,   Hobart, Tasmania.
Wireless/Opr Gunner,
      Sgt. Steve Turner,   Red Rock, N S W
Rear Gunner,
      Pilot/Officer, Dick Bates,   Roma, Queensland.

Our study now called ground school, as distinct from flying duties, kept us very busy and we were also getting to know our crewmates.

On completion of the concentrated study we were given the next day, 21 January off. With the address of a cycle store in Birmingham, we headed out on our first sortie as a crew together to that city to purchase a bike.

In order to identify mine I christened it after Dad and Dave's racehorse "Socks" and painted the name on the guards and frame. It was effective because my bike was never stolen. Any free time we now spent on excursions riding our bikes round the countryside.

Our W/Op Steve Turner, we soon found was fond of a drop of the "doings" and after a few drinks became a happy, inebriated airman. When under the weather he became a real Casanova type. He would tell all the girls how beautiful they were, and how he would love to become their escort. We kept a close eye on him to make sure we got him safely home.

At Lichfield I joined the station band, and enjoyed playing the spare baritone and the relaxation of the weekly practice with the boys. A Salvation Army concert party visited the station while we were there and gave a performance, with the station band playing a few items.

We had our first experience of snow on 27 February 1944. It snowed all day and apart from a snow fight, and some photographing we stayed inside by the fires. The runways were snowed up preventing any flying. Our physical training changed slightly next day. We were given a shovel, or a broom, for three days of shovelling snow off the runways working from daylight till dark.

Even though it was hard work, there was a lot of tripping, pushing, skylarking and snow fighting especially on the long 15-20 minute walk back to the airfield perimeter. When we were finally able to fly, we were much happier.

I contracted flu and reported sick. The receptionist WAAF took my temperature and told me to take a seat. There was a commotion, something about an airman walking through and being hit by a spinning propeller at Church Broughton, a satellite airfield and the whole place was in a flap.

I couldn't be bothered waiting and headed back down to the flight section to see if we were flying. There was no flying, on account of the weather. I started a game of darts with a couple of the other airmen when in walked a service policeman and called my name.

I was escorted back to the hospital, and immediately into the doctor. He "tore strips" off me for reporting sick and then walking out with a raging temperature. Wasn't I aware that the local cemetery was full of Australians, who contracted flu in the First World War, and ended up in the local cemetery?

"No, I wasn't and I didn't want to miss out on flying with my crew"
"Well that's O.K. Flight Sergeant Woods you can do just that after at least a week in hospital, if you have sufficiently recovered".

Without any further ado it was into hospital, where I found myself in the bed next to the Australian airman, who had walked through the spinning propeller of a Wellington bomber, and was still alive to tell the tale.

The propeller must have been spinning at 1050rpm idling speed and he hopped out of the plane, to try and direct the pilot to their parking spot in the dark. He accidentally walked backwards through the spinning blades of the propeller, being hit on the back of the head and thrown forward. The doctor stated, had he walked into the propeller frontwards, he might have lost his life, as the leading edge of the propeller would have probably sliced him in two.

Early next morning he was stirring and I could see he might fall out of bed. I called the nurse and they put a restrainer strap over him. He came-to just before the medical officer rounds, and wanted to know what he was doing in bed, he wanted to be with his crew.

The doctor said:"Do you know you walked through a spinning propeller? You were hit on the back of your head throwing you forward. You could have been cut in half or decapitated by that propeller, so just quieten down. You will be back with your crew as soon as possible. You are the luckiest airman alive that you are not leaving here in a box". My sojourn in hospital lasted ten days and I came out fighting fit to rejoin my crew.

Our third flight was under the command of Flying Officer John Holmes, CO of "C" flight, a pilot who was to become a good friend with the crew generally and with skipper Ted Owen, and navigator Don Hudspeth, in particular.

With this "real dinkum" Aussie pilot who had already done one tour of operations, we dropped 11 pound practice bombs from 20,000 feet in a group of 12, all single drops in twelve passes over the target.

With a 200 yards average error John Holmes thought it was not too bad. A few days later John Holmes was promoted to Flight Lieutenant.

As our training progressed we were sent on a flight across the country, to drop a couple of bombs, and then drop an aluminium sea marker in the target area in the Wash for some air-to-sea firing. This was rather exciting, as we were able to do some strafing type runs. I enjoyed this very much as I was always a good shot. After a couple of sorties when, as the front gunner, I blew the seamarker to pieces before the other gunners got a chance, I had to rest on my laurels and leave the practice shooting to the mid-upper and rear-gunners.

Flying in Wellington twin engine bombers at Lichfield our training was concentrated on bombing accuracy and on night flying we were told we would be later converting to a larger, faster and more up to date type of plane

We started on night circuits and landings on 8 March 1944. I flew separately from the crew with pilot F/Lt John Holmes on 11 March inspecting sodium lights on the approach to the flarepath at Lichfield.

On our final night of circuits and landings on 12 March 1944, the constant speed unit on the starboard motor failed, causing the motor to go to 4,000 revs, turning us on our back at 1,200 feet.

Ted our pilot, who had trained on fighters until suspected stomach ulcers put him into heavy bombers, was able to haul us out of the dive, feet from the ground. As we were climbing, Dick Bates, the rear gunner, reported the Lichfield Cathedral spire estimated between 100 and 150 feet, just above him, which means we were very close to the ground, almost crashing into the cathedral.

After landing, F/Lt Holmes, hearing what had happened, stood us down for the night.

It was Air Force policy that in case the pilot could not fly the plane, then another member of the crew must have the fundamentals of flying the plane. At Lichfield I did 20 hours training in a Link Trainer, a flying trainer simulator. The instructor was of the opinion that I should immediately re-muster as a pilot. As my training was almost complete, I decided I would have my tour of operations first, and, if I survived then I could consider a re-mustering to pilot.

Now we added a mid upper gunner, Sergeant Frank Mayor, a very broad accented, nondrinking companion, from Lancashire. Although Frank had practically no flying hours he was a dour Lancashire lad, who took what came and never seemed to worry or get excited.

His very broad Lancashire accent was hard to understand but after he had been with us for six weeks, he went home and his parents couldn't understand him, "because he had been mixing with those Aussies and sounded more like a foreigner".

In moving from county to county, in England, we found the language or local dialect changed a great deal. We would only just be able to understand the locals, when we were moved on to another place, where again we had to sort out the local dialect.

Frequently we explored the countryside on our bikes. It was a means of keeping fit and also if we happened to be shot down over the continent then we might be able to get hold of a bicycle to help us get to freedom. It was on one of these forays, that I visited the village of Epworth.

Badly in need of a haircut I stopped off at the local hairdresser in Epworth where I was surprised to meet my first female hairdresser, Cynthia Johnson, a little shy, but a very friendly young lady. As it was her lunch hour when she finished my hair, she invited me to have lunch with the family, as she felt they would be very happy to meet an Australian airman.

Their house right on the junction of two roads was named "East View" and opposite was the grain merchant and carrier, where her father Frank Johnson worked.

With a family of girls, he was pleased to have another male to talk with. As I was leaving to return to Lichfield, they invited me to come and spend the weekend with them sometime. Later on during a weekend visit Frank arranged one of the truck drivers in his firm to take me on a delivery, once to Coventry, and once to Hull. The bomb damage at both of those cities was unbelievable.

This friendship with the family endured for as long as I was in England. Occasionally I was able to spend a few days with them.

(In 1993 I called again at Epworth and when inquiring at the local seed merchant found Cynthia was the only remaining family member still living in the village, and was his wife. I told him, who I was, and wanted to surprise Cynthia. I asked for the address, but told him not to warn her I was coming).

As I walked round the side of their house she was coming the other way, and I was able to instantly recognise her. She stopped and for a moment looked and then smiling said: "Goodness me, Laurie Woods! What a long time since I saw you! It must be almost all of fifty years"

I introduced my wife Barbara. We then spent a couple of very pleasant hours with Cynthia catching up on her family news, before bidding her farewell. I expressed once again my heartfelt thanks for the kindness of her family, in looking after me so very well during the war.

An American Liberator drome was near Lichfield and many skirmishes occurred in the village between the Aussies and the Yanks. In the hope of stopping these skirmishes our station commander considered making Lichfield out of bounds. He finally decided after consultation with the American commander, that his men should attack our drome and we would defend it. It was assumed that if fist fights developed it would be too bad.

We waited, and waited, and waited, until the word went round the Yanks had got lost and the exercise was off. For a long time they didn't show their faces in Lichfield so there was no more Aussie vs Yanks fighting.

On the night of the 18 March 1944, we carried out, what was described as a diversionary raid to a position 54°20'N 02°10'E that was well out over the North Sea. After we crossed the coast we commenced dropping an immense amount of window (strips of foil to make it appear on radar as if there was a greater raiding force, heading on the way to northern Germany)

We had just turned homeward from this position when our squeakers picked up what appeared to be a convoy close to our course. We were well out over the North Sea when suddenly a great amount of flak began bursting closely around us apparently from some escorting naval ship. It was sudden and quite frightening; we were not expecting any ack – ack in this area. To see the flashes of the explosions, and hear the immense crack of the exploding shell spelled danger. The strong smell of burnt cordite from the bursting shell indicated it was awful close, and the thump, which in addition to being heard could be felt as an immense thu---m---p.

We were on the receiving end and being shot at for the first time from the barrage, which was short, but very severe, and much too close for comfort.

We didn't argue but headed for home. Suddenly a plane swept head on over our plane missing us by around six feet. A calculated guess by the gunners, that it was a Mosquito night fighter bomber, had gone close (much too close) almost skimming the top of our plane. We returned to base with no further frights.

When flying in the Wellington twin engine bomber the flexing of the wings up and down whenever we hit an downdraft was fascinating to watch.

At last the big day came! A leaflet raid on Paris on the 22 March 1944. It was an exciting thought to be actually flying over German occupied territory.

This was what our training had been preparing us for, and we were like horses primed for a race. We were rearing to go with little thought of what dangers we might encounter over enemy territory.

We were taking off at 8 minutes after 7pm and were expecting to be dropping our leaflets at about 9pm just in time for the French people to be reading them as they sat down to their supper.

After take off we headed south to be at 8,000 feet over Reading then setting course to be over Beachey Head at 12,000 feet. Maintaining this height to cross over the French Coast we were almost coned by a small bunch of searchlights as we crossed the coastline. They attempted to zero in on us but were behind us.

The searchlights usually worked in conjunction with the ack ack batteries but in this case the light ack ack fire was being fired quite independent of the searchlights. It was very accurate and came far too close for comfort.

Unloading the leaflets in heavy cloud over our dropping zone on the designated time with accuracy not too demanding was a rather good exercise. It demonstrated to the aircrew that if all courses flown, and if timing was good over the target it would give each plane a measure of protection in passing over the target as a group rather than singly. Through a timely break in the clouds we were able to get a successful photograph.

Soon after turning onto our new heading out of the target area we were rather disconcerted by small shell bursts, which lit up the clouds for up to 30 seconds, as they exploded and then came chasing toward us.

The shooting stopped just south of Dieppe, and we could see heavy ack ack coming up and bursting about a half a mile to starboard, probably one of our planes straying off course and slightly below us in the cloud. We could certainly hear the crack of the explosions, warning us to keep a sharp eye on the bursts

Crossing the French coast the heavy ack ack coming up over London and the British fighter flares, were clearly visible. Jerry was carrying out one of his heaviest raids for quite a while. Not far behind us we could still see the Jerry fighter flares still bursting just above the clouds. The lesson was clear, drop your load, don't lag behind, and once on the way out from the target, get to hell out as quickly as the briefing allowed.

The Intelligence Officer was quite amused at the looks on our faces, when he informed us we must have been hunted by a pack of German nightfighters. They were not shells we had seen, but fighter flares dropped to light up the clouds, to help them find the intruders.

He was quite surprised, when we insisted that they seemed to chase us. A few days later we were informed that the Germans had developed a new heat seeking missile. They became known as" Chase me Charlies"

Heavy Conversion Unit, Blyton
Lancaster Finishing School, Helmswell

Our next posting was to 1662 Heavy Conversion Unit, Blyton, where we would be converting on to four engined Halifax bombers.

In accordance with the latest RAF policy, which deemed the skipper of a plane should have a commission, Ted, our skipper, was promoted to the rank of Pilot Officer, and moved into the officers' quarters, and henceforth ate in the officer's mess.

On arrival at Blyton we picked up the last member of our crew, Flight/Engineer, Sergeant Peter Odell. Peter only had six hours flying experience when he joined our crew. At this stage Ted, Don, and myself had 250 hours up. Our wireless operator and gunners had considerably less flying experience.

Peter, quite excitable, was a young lad from a village in Bedfordshire who had joined the Air Force as a flight engineer because of his knowledge of engines, also to get away from his father.

He was a bit fond of a drop of the doings, and I think he was not very happy at being picked up by an Australian crew. He and Steve our wireless operator, became drinking mates, and on occasions had to be kept in check.

On 31 May 1944 flying a cross-country exercise we flew into a thunderstorm. It was very rough flying in the Halifax and to escape the worst of the storm we climbed to a height of 21,000 feet. We were diverted and landed at Leeming, the home of No 429 Canadian Halifax Squadron. Next morning we returned to base in very rough flying conditions.

During the day we were briefed to fly out over the North Sea on a diversionary raid, dropping as much window as we could to give the German defences the impression we were part of a raid heading towards Northern Germany.

Flying in the very rough weather conditions to a position at 57°20N 02°00E we then returned on our planned route to base. The Halifax performed creditably on this uneventful exercise.

From Blyton we moved a short distance to Helmswell's No. I Lancaster Finishing School, a peacetime drome with much better accommodation, and generally better living conditions.

We were surprised to find several Polish airmen were converting on to Lancasters and wondered how some of the Aussie instructors could get their instructions across to them, as many did not understand the English language.

One of the Aussie flying instructors, Gerry Bateman from Perth WA, had an exciting flight when his pupil was almost ready to lift the Lancaster off the ground with "George" the automatic pilot engaged.

This meant the pilot would have no control over the plane, and would be unable to climb away unless he realised quickly enough to start trimming the aircraft in the hope it would remain airborne.

The control for engaging "George" was to the left of the pilot and it was almost impossible to get to the control across the front of the pilot. Gerry, a very worried airman, had to get the message across in an extreme hurry somehow to the pilot who didn't understand English.

Fortunately keeping his cool he somehow managed at the last moment to disconnect "George" and save them crashing.

On 10 June we excitedly lined up in our flying gear for our first flight in a Lancaster. The Lancaster was the ultimate heavy bomber and here we were on the verge of going flying in this wonderful machine. It seemed to take a lot of instructions and going over of the cockpit drill before we were ready to taxi out to the runway and line up for the signal to take off.

The sight of the green light was the signal for the throttles to be advanced to take off power. (Later on operations the throttles were advanced through the gate to maximum full power when taking off fully loaded, or evading German fighters, or to get quickly away from searchlights) Within a short space our tail was up and we were rolling down the runway at an ever increasing speed and soon we lifted into the air and up came the undercarriage with a bump. As we climbed away from the aerodrome there were smiles all round the Lancaster was more responsive and livelier aeroplane in the air, and the four Rolls Royce Merlin engines had a good healthy powerful sound to them.

After several flights and 10 hours flying converting to Lancasters, we were very happy to be flying in them for our operations as they impressed us more than the Halifax and we were quite happy also at being posted to Binbrook, No 1 Group, Bomber Command, the home of the senior Australian No 460 Lancaster Squadron. The idea of being among mainly Australians was almost like a homecoming.

CHAPTER SIX

460 Squadron, (Australian) Binbrook

Tuesday, 13 June 1944 together with six other crews we arrived at Binbrook, in Lincolnshire, the home of the senior Australian Lancaster Squadron No. 460. No 1 Group. We totalled 49 airmen, with only 9 airmen from the original 49 airmen surviving five months later.

Our first sight on the aerodrome was a battle scarred Lancaster bomber complete with a nose drawing, of a naked lady with winged feet, similar to the drawings of "Mercury". She was holding a bomb ready for dropping. A 20mm. cannon shell, had hit right in the centre of the roundel, painted on the aircraft side, leaving quite a large hole. The shell, complete with an exploding head, had hit the midupper gunner in the stomach where it had exploded. There was little left of the poor gunner and they needed the firewagon, to hose out the remains. We moved over closer as the firewagon arrived but were hunted away, as the area was declared out of bounds, and a guard placed on it. The sight was very sobering.

Ted, a "scrubbed" fighter pilot, took to flying our Lancaster as though it was a Spitfire. The Lancaster, powered by four similar engines as the Spitfire and with empty power weight ratio close to a Spitfire, responded almost like a fighter, being fast and very manoeuvrable.

At Binbrook I caught up with several of my original course mates. It was sobering news to hear of the loss of many others on 460 squadron. In a letter, which travelled to Australia in "G" for George a course mate, Geoff Tallents, at the end of his tour, described to perfection the bomb aimer's job in the crew.

Arthur Hoyle navigator, of Bob Wade's crew very kindly gave us a bit of a run down on squadron life. *"Returning from Berlin on the night of 16th December, 1943 "We found the low cloud and fog had reduced the visibility to not much more than 100ft above the airfield. Searchlights were shone from the airfield on the base of the cloud but, flying above the fog, it was difficult to see them unless we were nearby.*

Casualties had reduced the battle order to 20 crews, many of them new or "sprog" crews as they were known. Tired, and with fuel running low, the sensible thing would have been to divert them to another airfield which was still clear of fog and low cloud.

A scene of terror and destruction ensued. Flying at heights of between 300 and 500 feet above the ground those aircraft which had found the searchlights flew in a tight circle so as not to lose the airfield. Everyone, joining in the circuit was trying to find the correct end of the runway not daring to descend too low in case of hitting a hill or another aircraft which had found the searchlights and were also circling in as tight a pattern as possible. The fear of a collision was in everyone's mind as we flitted in and out of cloud. Our bomb aimer was lying prone in his compartment, peering out the front of the plane, when suddenly he yelled, "Pull up, quick, Pull up, Pull up quick. Bob, our pilot responded instantly and, as the stick came back, we climbed away into the cloud and night sky. A few seconds later Vic, the bomb aimer said over the intercom – "Jesus, that was close! We were right on the deck and there was a cyclist in front of me!"

More worried than ever, we circled as close as possible to the searchlights, then just before reaching them, we dived and suddenly broke into the clear some 80 – 100 feet above the main runway. We joined two other Lancasters, who had just done the same thing, in a mad race around and just above the perimeter track. Banked hard to port to stay in sight of the ground, with our port wing tip only feet from the field, flaps down and the engines at 2,850 revolutions, we flew just above the heads of the groundcrews who were laying flat on the ground in the dispersal areas bathed in a curious blue glow as the searchlights reflected back from the clouds.

It seemed like an old fashioned air race only now it was dark, the aircraft were huge and they were nearly out of fuel. On the ground the red obstruction and yellow runway lights twinkled in the gloom.

Suddenly under the controlled hands of Bob "J²" stood on its wingtip in the tightest of tight turns – as though it was a Spitfire – a few seconds later we straightened up and touched down at almost the same time. It was a superb piece of flying. We realised after how much we owed to Bob's skill and judgement. Other aircraft reached the vicinity of Binbrook but could not find the airfield.

Flight Lieutenant Eric R. Greenacre, after escaping five separate fighter attacks over the target, which holed the fuselage in many places and shot away the hydraulics and turret pipes, headed for the emergency landing field at Ludford Magna, where coming in low, suddenly was on the ground on top of a small round green hill, breaking the propellers off. Greenacre, the pilot, shut off the power and, when the aircraft slithered to a halt, the crew stepped out unhurt".

(After finishing his tour Eric Greenacre later returned to 460 squadron to do a second tour. His plane was shot down on his fourth operation. see target report on Emmerich raid).

"The next plane flown by Ken Godwin, had lost an engine crossing the Dutch coast on the outward journey but decided to carry on, bombing the target on schedule. On their return to base, and unable to see the ground Godwin asked permission to bale out as he was almost out of fuel. Permission was refused and shortly after the plane hit the ground disintegrating and injuring some of the other crew members.

The third pilot Flying Officer F. A. Randall circled for three quarters of an hour awaiting an opportunity to land coming down so low on one occasion the aircraft hit a tree as it descended, climbed again they lost the airfield. At 2348 he called up Binbrook control to say he could not see the airfield that he was firing off Very cartridges. This was the last message from him. A few minutes later the aircraft crashed into the bomb dump at Market Stanton and all the crew was killed. Another case of the policy to save the aircraft and no concern for the crew. Altogether 29 Lancasters were lost on the return to their base".

"Late in January 1944, Bob Wade and crew, again on the way to Berlin in "J²" take off 1700 hours, after taxying slowly around the perimeter track, turned onto the runway and waited for the green light from the caravan. When it flashed, Bob and Harry, the engineer, together opened up the four throttles and "J²", laden with 10,000lb of bombs started to lumber forward. After running about 400 yards along the mile long runway the port outer engine suddenly lost power.

The aircraft immediately swung off the runway on to the grass at an angle of about 25 degrees. Instead of aborting Bob pulled the throttle back and pushed it forward again. The motor came back to full power and we continued across the grass.

With such a rough grass surface "J²" was slow to pick up speed. We raced over the perimeter track and then tore down the slope through the dispersal area where B Flight aircraft were normally parked, with our wheels thumping on the grass but still firmly on the ground. It now seemed nothing could save us, and in a couple of moments we would disappear in a great explosion.

I could hear Bob, our pilot, saying "Get off the ground, you bastard, get off". Then at the very last moment, the wheels hit a hedge and bank, flanking a sunken road, and the aircraft was bounced into the air. Beyond the sunken road the ground sloped away quite steeply into a valley. We staggered into the valley and gradually picked up flying speed enabling us to climb away".

Arthur goes on to say, "By this time we had done 13 operations and were one of the few experienced crews on the squadron. In the face of the continuing losses, our early confidence that we would survive a tour of operations was slowly melting away.

On this trip I could hear the engines coughing into life and although I knew what I had to do my feet were reluctant to move. My mind kept saying to me, if I entered the plane I was *going to my certain death; although I believed I would survive. When we returned to Binbrook after the raid, some eight hours later, I felt my time was not up, and I would survive and that in future I could face death with some courage and some dignity".*

Arthur carried on, "Late on the night of 26 April, 1943, 25 Lancasters from 460 squadron headed for Essen in the middle of the Ruhr. Almost over the target, Vic. Our bomb aimer took over and began the familiar, "Left, left, steady, right, steady, bomb doors open, steady, right, steady, bombs gone, steady for photo". When the 14,000 lbs of bombs fell away the aircraft leapt upwards as it was relieved of the weight.

A moment later, with the bomb doors still open and the aircraft steady on course, the plane rocked as a shower of bombs hit us from a Lancaster just over our heads. Fortunately, the 4,000 lb bomb missed us or we would have been blown to Kingdom Come. We were hit by a shower of incendiaries which immediately knocked out one engine and badly damaged another so that it was useless and the propeller could not be feathered, greatly increasing the drag on one side of the plane. A third motor was hit but kept going on reduced power. Another incendiary damaged the starboard fuel tank but did not set it alight. Yet anther smashed the hydraulic system which operated the bomb doors, undercarriage and flaps. By a miracle no one was hit.

The Lancaster had started to dive away to port and the pilot and engineer struggled and brought the plane under control. With limited control and lack of speed giving us a much reduced airspeed, the skipper opted for a direct flight to base, even though we would be on our own across Germany.

Losing altitude as we approached the Dutch coast we decided on the long sea crossing hoping to maintain enough height to make England. As we crossed the sea in the early hours of the morning the aircraft gradually lost height. With the bomb doors wide open, the bomb inspection covers had blown off and an icy gale whistled through the cabin. On two motors and the third propeller uselessly windmilling adding to the drag, we could go no faster than 140mph.

At 0345 we crossed the darkened coast of Lincolnshire at 1500 feet and turned for the short leg to Binbrook. In sight of the base beacon the third motor stopped. Bob, at once, feathered the engine and we began to lose what little altitude we had. We were now down to 600 feet above the Wolds.

Bob called up flying control and asked for an emergency landing. To our incredulity and disgust, we were refused and told to go away to an emergency airfield in East Anglia.

Because we were arriving at the same time as the rest of 460 squadron aircraft flying control didn't want the runway blocked by a crashed aircraft. Bob Wade, with an understandably temper outburst at this callous unconcern by flying control for a Lancaster in such dire straits, told flying control with a few Australian adjectives included ignored the instructions and continued the approach telling Harry to operate the emergency lever to lower the undercarriage.

Only the right wheel came down and when an attempt was made to retract it, it remained down. With one engine working, one propeller windmilling, the bomb doors open, no flaps and one wheel up and one wheel down, and too low to bale out our only option was to ride the Lancaster to the ground.

Not wanting to block the runway, after telling control he was coming in whether they liked it or not, Bob lined up some 300 yards to the right. Even though it was very dark off to the side of the runway, he began the short final approach with no flaps to maintain lift at our low speed and holding the right wing low to counter balance the dead engines.

The Lancaster "B²" touched down on one wheel and ran along the grass at about 100 mph while Bob fought in the dark to keep the left wing up as long as possible. Gradually the wing sank lower and as the speed dropped shut off the last throttle. Suddenly the left wing tip touched the ground and immediately the aircraft ground-looped violently, spinning across the grass and finally coming to rest in the middle of the runway, right in the path of another Lancaster which was on the point of touching down.

As our aircraft came to rest their was a wild scramble to get clear in case the damaged fuel tank caught fire. First man out got stuck in the escape hatch but was quickly shoved out by those following.

Scrambling down the fuselage we ran for our lives. In the glow of the searchlight, the fire truck and ambulance raced across the grass, but we did not hear them because of the shattering roar of the engines of the Lancaster which had just touched down. Faced with a wrecked Lancaster in the middle of the runway, the pilot gunned his motors to emergency power and slowly struggled over our heads to safety. As the roar of the climbing aircraft died away, even though I was about 40 yards away, I knew Bob was still alive as I could hear him cursing and swearing as he turned off the switches.

Without any respite from our recent frightening experience, we were briefed for a raid on Koenigsberg, capital of East Prussia. With the briefing over we trooped to the mess for our "operational meal" where the men usually tried, to cover their fears, which they were unable to admit, with laughter and banter. We had reached our planes with some motors already ticking over when the order came through to stand by for one hour. After one hour the raid was scrubbed on account of the weather expected on the return.

Emotionally and physically geared up for the operation we retired to the mess to while away time before retiring. Suddenly there were two explosions in quick succession. Outside we could see the glow from our C Flight dispersal area where the planes were standing fully bombed up. We soon discovered our aircraft had been loaded with delayed action high explosive bombs set to go off four hours after they were dropped. The armourer who had loaded them had been careless and had broken one of the delayed action capsules, setting the fuse in train. If we had set off on the raid, somewhere over the North Sea the bomb would have exploded and we would have been killed instantly. The armourer was court-marshalled and given a long sentence in a military prison".

We were assigned to "C" Flight at one end of the aerodrome whilst "A" Flight seemed miles away down the other end. The flights were separated or dispersed as a protection should we be attacked by enemy fighters or should we cop an enemy bombing raid.

The crews from the different flights only met up in the mess at meal times, or for a special parade. To settle us down and to get used to the routine on the squadron we were rostered to fly a couple of cross country training flights in Lancaster "D2".

An air firing training was our next exercise in "J2" over the sea in the Wash area. The Lancaster had to attack a drogue being towed behind a plane and the gunners had to fire as the Lancaster flew past the drogue. We attacked several times until the gunners had used about 400 rounds and then we broke off the exercise to return to base.

On the return journey Ted asked me to take over the controls, to judge whether I could handle a Lancaster, after my limited link training. The Lancaster "J2", once I got the feel of it, responded to the controls well, and I felt it flew beautifully. The only trouble my lesson only lasted about ten minutes.

Our next flight was a five hour night cross country in "A2" taking off just before midnight. Having successfully carried out this exercise, we were declared ready and we were rearing to go.

There was a measure of excitement in the crew when we were allocated "K2", "Killer" as the plane we would generally be flying. It was the planes 34th raid, and our wish was that she would do a hundred trips, and in the process carry us safely through our tour.

On the side of K2 "Killer" was a big yellow swastika with a hand holding a dagger, the dagger piercing the heart (red) of the swastika, with red blood dropping out of the wound. Underneath were the letters "Killer" in yellow with red blood dripping off the letters.

The design on **K2 "Killer"** was very striking, having been drawn up mainly by Bill Gourlay, navigator from Launceston, Tasmania. Bill flew in Vic Neal's crew and they had commenced flying this new aircraft on operations on 15th March 1944 on a first raid to Stuttgart, 2nd and 3rd to Frankfurt, 4th to Berlin, and 5th to Essen. What a blooding in operations for any aircraft or crew. Vic Neal and crew flew 23 trips in K2 "Killer", whilst Bill Gourlay flew an extra "Killer" trip with W/Cdr Douglas.

From Flying Officers, Vic Neal, Pilot & Bill Gourlay, Navigator, we had a good report on what to expect, as they described to us their experience in "K2" on the raid to Mailly-Le-Camp, on 3rd May 1944. They both felt lucky to have escaped any serious problems, and thought the raid was a bit of a mess up.

As they described the raid:
"Situated 80 miles east of Paris, the Mailly-Le-Camp had been a French army permanent camp, taken over by the German force. It was believed at the time to be holding up to 10,000 men from the German panzer units. Later reports confirmed 218 killed and 156 wounded mostly Panzer Division N.C.O.s. Many barrack buildings, vehicles, ammunition and tanks were destroyed.

The moon was right for a raid, by Nos. 1 & 5 Group led by Wing Commander Cheshire. He was flying a Mosquito, together with three other mosquito bombers, to mark the target. The raid was timed to start at midnight, to catch all the troops in camp.

Taking off at 2200, "K2" was in the first group of aircraft from Binbrook. Climbing to 2,000 feet, Vic Neal set course climbing on track to rendezvous over Reading.

From Reading, the course was over Beachy Head, to Dieppe. Then we crossed the French coast at 12,000 feet with perfect flying conditions on a beautiful night, not too much moon, providing good visibility. From Dieppe, the flight plan was to descend at speed to arrive at the target at 5,000 feet. With a Lancaster descending at speed, some German fighters would not be very much faster.

We could see the German fighters were intercepting, as we passed Compiegne. The Germans were not having much success, as we didn't see any bombers being shot down. We did see three fighters go down, which was a welcome reversal of fortune for us.

The red target markers had gone down on time but W/Cdr Cheshire, marking from 1,500 feet was not satisfied. He called in his deputy, Squadron Leader Dave Shannon, who dived his Mosquito to 400 feet and marked accurately".

Neal and Gourlay in the second wave carried on *"when they arrived at the orbiting point they were surprised to see other Lancasters still orbiting over the yellow marker, fifteen miles out from the target.*

There was also some chatter going on from the crews, on the R/T when suddenly one spoke out:

"Come on you markers; pull your bloody finger out!" Soon there were several remarks too rude to be printed.

Then an English voice: "Cut your chatter and wait for the order to bomb!" With a lot of planes orbiting, the German fighters started picking off the bombers, and several were seen to blow up, or go down in flames".

Suddenly a voice obviously a pilot requested:

"For Christ sake shut up and give my gunner's a chance!" the chatter still carried on when suddenly we heard an English voice;

"For Christ sake! I'm on fire!" answered immediately by an unmistakable Aussie voice, "If you're going to die, then die like a man, quietly!"

"We were still waiting instructions to bomb, and some planes had flown out wider to get more room in orbiting, and several Lancasters had been shot down".

Some Lancasters in desperation turned toward the target, and Vic Neal steered "K2" to follow suit, far better to get rid of their bombs on the target, before they were shot down.

The ack ack around the target was not too heavy as they bombed, from 5,000 feet. With a "Cookie" 5,000 feet was a bit close, they were more used to bombing from a higher altitude.

As our bombs dropped from the Lancaster it felt as though the plane was bouncing up a set of stairs. The blast from the bombs gave quite an *exciting ride through the target and of course when the cookie dropped we bounced up a good 2/300 feet.*

"Leaving the target did not get rid of the fighters, as we saw many more planes, shot down". A report later stated that the German fighter plane pilot named Dewes, had shot down five Lancasters in 40 minutes, taking his total to 45 bombers.

An upward firing gun position built into the fighters and a twin 30mm MK 108 cannon

installation, angled at 15° and still not known to the Allies, was doing most of the damage. It was codenamed "Jazz Music" and fortunately for the bomber crews on this raid not many German planes had been fitted with this gun arrangement.

From underneath the bomber in a relatively safe position from the bomber's gunners, the Germans were able to fly close in under the bomber, as close as 70 metres, fire the incendiary cannon shells into the bombers petrol tanks, and in this way shoot down many bombers".

In 1944 the Germans shot down 3527 RAF bombers, killing almost 25,000 aircrew

The German fighter pilots using "Jazz Music" also favoured attacking the bombers after they had dropped their bombs. With no bombs left to explode, they could attack much closer, without the fear of explosions also killing them. Out of 346 Lancasters that took part in this raid 42 failed to return and two were so badly damaged they were scrapped. 460 Squadron lost five.

"Flight Sergeant George Gritty, of 460 Squadron, was attacked by an FW 190 who made no less than three passes, setting the Lancaster on fire.

In the bright moonlight three parachutes were seen to open. The FW 190 cheekily flew just behind, and watched as the Lancaster exploded.

The master bomber's radio communication had failed, but there was no way these sorts of problems could be fixed in the air. By firing a Verey pistol with pre arranged colour, visual bombing could have been set in motion".

This account from Vic & Bill of "K2 Killer" raid on Mailley-Le-Camp sounded like they were shooting a line, but as we soon found out, the unexpected could always happen, and the best laid plans on any raid could always bring unexpected results.

To add insult to injury, because this area was only credited as one third of a raid, the crews in view of its severity and the losses, demanded a reassessment. This was a miserable deal on the part of the authorities.

How could one raid be counted as a third of a raid. Of course it was easy to see that although a tour was 30 raids, by counting a raid as a half or a third, it could extend the tour by several more raids.

The lifespan of the crews was not even considered, on this raid alone 294 airmen were lost.

Vic and Bill went on to say *"they were all bombed up and ready to go in K2 on the Nuremberg raid, when number 3 engine was missing revs and at the last moment they were changed to the spare aircraft which happened to be "G" for George"* (which is now the star attraction in the Australian War Memorial in Canberra)

The Nuremberg raid became famous as the raid on which Bomber Command experienced its heaviest losses. A total of ninety five heavy bombers lost, most of them shot down by fighters. This result was a loss of 665 flyers in one raid sending a bit of a traumatic shock wave through the operational airmen and also the airmen who were getting close to operational flying.

The results from the Nuremberg raid were uppermost in the airmen's minds and were often mentioned in a cautionary note even by the briefing officers. The photo of Vic Neal leaning from the pilot's window was taken a short time before **"K2 Killer"** was flying over the landing area 11 minutes before the actual D - Day landing.

Vic and Bill also told us of the end of Lancaster AR-R JB 662, when on the 18 April 1944 sixteen aircraft were detailed for operations, but only eight took off because JB 662, piloted by Bob White caught fire whilst taking off and eventually blew up, rendering the runway unserviceable for several hours.

"According to Bill when accelerating to be airborne, the plane suddenly swung badly and hitting a light at the side of the runway, crashed on to the asphalt and burst into flames. The rest of the squadron, lined up, each crew waiting its turn to go, were horrified witnesses to this event, which was quickly followed by a massive explosion of the bomb load.

Operations for the night were immediately cancelled and sadly we taxied slowly back to the dispersal points and gathered up our gear wondering what about the poor crew?

After putting their flying gear away, they moved down to the mess, then what joy, for there sitting around, white and shaken, were all the members of the crew. Bill said to his good mate Ken

Tweedie, (navigator) "However did you get out of it?" and he replied, I have no recollection of my movements at all - I only know there was a crash and the flames and then I was about 100 yards away, face down behind a low mound, watching the explosion."

The staff Medical Officer (Dr Roberts) had grabbed a vehicle and rushed straight out to the scene, risking his life trying to get near the burning wreck to give help. He returned to the control tower and reported, "It was no good the whole crew has been lost."

Later Ken told Bill that "I had no recollection of getting out of the Lancaster, but after a beer or two, supplied free by those who didn't have to fly, thanks to us, the sequence of events did come back to me.

When the flames started Bob, the skipper ordered us in no uncertain terms to get out. I used the escape hatch in the top of the fuselage, then onto the wing which was touching the ground, then off.

Bob checked us all getting out and hadn't seen me. He called out "Where are you Snowy?" My voice from 100 yards away reassured him I was OK. We all broke every record in the books, and luckily were safely away sheltered from the explosion".

Col Wheatley, a member of Dan Cullen's crew, reported: "We were in the take off line about two aircraft behind, so we just had to switch off and go and lie on the grass, waiting for something to happen. We all expressed approval at the speed at which you vacated the "burning deck". So athletic.

After watching the ammo go up and the other pyrotechnics, we heard the big bang - what a beauty - followed by a hail of engines, turrets, guns, all hissing like a big bag of snakes, so they must have reached a great height. As far as I know' none of the hundred or so of us lying around were hit."

ON OPERATIONS

Armed with a short history on what to expect and some friendly advice on how we should be careful to make sure everything was right before we were given the green light to start our take off run from Vic and Bill we were listed on the battle order on Friday, 30^t June 1944, for our first operational flight.

The railway yards at Vierzan Ville was the target, and we were carrying a bomb load of eleven 1,000 lb. and four 500 lb. bombs. Taking off at 2220 meant we had our pre flight meal at 1700 hours, then off to the briefing room. The crews gathered for the information of the target, the weather, the bomb load, the petrol load, take off time, the route, expected ack ack danger spots on the way, the expected number of searchlights and number of guns at the target.

The responsible officer then gave each section of information. On the end wall was a large target map. This was only unveiled when everyone was seated, and the door locked and guarded. The route out and back was indicated by a ribbon pinned on each turning point, and we were routed to dodge any known ack ack positions and to steer clear of known night fighter dromes.

To be addressed by our station commanding officer a living VC winner Group/Capt. Hughie Edwards VC. DSO. DFC. at the briefing was rather awe-inspiring. When he called for an extra No.1 Group effort to make this a successful raid and show the other groups what we could do, we clapped him.

The town of Vierzon was only small however the railway yard were considered an important target. It was an area where marshalling of traffic carrying supplies, headed for the Caen area in support of the German frontline troops, was carried out.

On take off we were to fly on a heading away from Reading till we reached 6,000 feet then back, to be over Reading, at 12,000feet at rendezvous time. This kept the bombers organised in a stream and prevented flying in confusing circles with the ever present risk of collisions. After all our training we were now approaching time for take off.

A full load of bombs, a full load of petrol, full of apprehension and full of suppressed excitement tinged with a considerable amount of nervousness for a first time crew. How would we react to full war conditions? Would "K2 Killer" carry us safely through? Would the load be too heavy for us to climb safely away after take off? We had always been flying an empty plane and now we had a bomb load of 13,000 lbs. of deadly explosives.

Then Ted checked the crew one by one on the intercom. "Skipper to Bomb aimer are you ready", "Bomb aimer to Skipper, everything O.K. Skipper". And finally "Skipper to crew, ready to roll, on your toes boys, and good luck". The engine beat suddenly quickened and we slowly crawled forward and joined the queue of planes on the perimeter track slowly inching forward.

Each Lancaster, with engines increasing in power, started rolling forward and then gradually up came the tail as with full power and increasing speed it rolled down the runway, and then, with a slight lowering of the tail, finally lifted off.

Imagine the belching noise and fumes as they disappeared momentarily and then appeared again slowly gaining height on climbing power, taking the war into Germany.

The English people went to bed in safety, quite happy that the 45 minute procession of noise and power was assisting in keeping them safe and helping to keep the war as far away as possible.

It was our turn to run forward and line up in position. With brakes full on we waited for the green light from the control van at the end of the runway. A final quick check, on all crew members, the green light signalled, the engineer increasing the power (as Ted released the brakes) then pushing the throttles and boost through the gate to maximum power.

With a surge of power as 4 Rolls Royce "Merlin" engines opened up to full throttle and a final wave from the WAAF and airmen well wishers at the end of the runway, we are away. Slowly rolling forward, and then gathering speed with every yard **K2 "Killer"** leaps into life, with tail up and the engines roaring at full power we move along the runway, the engineer holding the throttles fully forward 90mph, 100/110, and 120mph. the skipper holds her on the runway till the 2,000 yards are almost used up (to get as much air speed as possible before lifting her off the deck), then he gradually trims her back till she flies and then we lift off and slowly, slowly, seem to be fighting our way upwards.

A bump as the undercarriage retracts and we are safely in the air. With engines throttled back slightly to climbing power, the crew settle in their stations with everyone on the alert for other aircraft in case they fly too close.

Fear and excitement is now replaced by the professionalism of doing the job, for which we have been trained.

With a full load it was a slow climb to 6,000 feet and then turning on a course to be over Reading at 12,000 feet we were being joined by bombers from other squadrons all converging. The crew had to keep a sharp lookout for other aircraft to avoid any possibility of a collision.

What an amazing sight over Reading. A stream of heavy bombers converging behind us and a stream of bombers in front of us on course on the first leg of our route to the target.

It was a new experience to be flying in a stream of aircraft, and to be rudely shaken if by chance we were caught in a bomber's slipstream, which on occasions would give a few nasty bumps and shakes, and had been known to turn heavy bombers upside down.

At briefing the ribbons stretching across the map from Reading indicated our route, stretching to three turning points on the way to the target, and nine turning points on the way back, the idea being to dodge and also confuse the German defences into believing the raid was heading for a special target. This in some cases sent fighters off at a tangent, when in fact the bomber stream had changed course and was heading for a target in a different sector.

On the run in to the target, a Lancaster was shot down just to port of us. With a mighty flash the plane had received a direct hit and had blown up and the remaining sections arced over and fell toward the ground. It would take about one and a half minutes before hitting the ground but the crew were already gone. On my visual report to the navigator, the time was logged, and the position recorded where the Lancaster was shot down.

The target flak was very heavy, the air seemingly alive with the almighty crack of the bursting shells all around us and the bright flash and telltale black puff similar to a mushroom unfolding as the lighter ack-ack shells exploded sending their splinters of death in all directions.

From approx. 50 ack ack guns concentrating their fire directly over the railway yards it was an awesome display forcing us to fly through the barrage as we dropped our bomb load.

The planes that were being shot down just round us and were easily identified as a blinding flash as the plane exploded or just a flash of an exploding shell with the plane firstly a small red fire growing almost instantly into a larger red ball of flame. Then a diving curve heading down into a final vertical dive with fire streaming behind, sometimes the plane breaking up as it dived to earth, and sometimes remaining intact until the final explosion as it hit the ground.

The concentration of getting rid of our bombs made it impossible to keep a check on these planes as they disappeared out of the sky, but the incident was momentarily flashed into one's mind like a photograph being imprinted on a film as these incidents became imprinted on the mind.

There was a concentration of about twenty searchlights, which were like huge glowing cones with their shafts shooting skyward ever searching for a target among the raiding aircraft. After our photo was taken we cleared the target area safely. Two fighters flying as a pair, closed in on us from the port rear quarter, the skipper quickly turned to port and although the fighters fired several bursts thankfully their shells flew a little wide, and no damage to our plane. Having managed to evade them they disappeared looking for other targets.

The shells and bullets were loaded usually with every fourth one being a tracer that could be clearly seen, enabling the gunners to correct their aim. Of course if you were on the receiving end, for every tracer shell you could see there were usually three more in between.

Seeing the ack ack coming up at our plane was rather frightening. From the bomb aimer's position lying on the floor in the nose of the plane with a clear view to the front and all around underneath, most of the shells heading toward the plane seemed to be headed for my stomach. They only turned away or dropped behind at the last moment.

After much practice it was possible to judge, which ones to dodge and which ones were not too close. Perhaps if we were lucky, we would pick the correct one to dodge.

It was a new experience to realise these gunners were in deadly earnest, and to survive we had to be wide awake. Bomb quickly and efficiently, and then hope our luck held and we could clear the target without a collision as this was the most dangerous spot for collisions.

This was the favourite position for the fighters to carry out their attacks to get a good shot at the planes. We raised our hats to those German fighter pilots, and the risks they took flying through their own ack ack in the hope of getting a victim or two.

They were intent on getting us, flying through their own flak. They realised they had an easier killing over the target as the bomber was intent on flying straight and level on the bombing run. Additionally there was a lot of illumination from searchlights and the bursting flak.

We couldn't relax for a moment as our lives depended on being wide awake and alert. Woe betide anyone who strayed from our course on the way to base. Any stragglers were usually very lucky to get home, the wayside ack ack, or fighters, were on to stragglers very quickly. The fighters quickly picked them off as they were on their own and did not have the protection of the guns from the rest of the bomber stream.

Having cleared all the target hazards we always hoped to get a good run home, with no guarantee of a safe passage. The results from 118 Lancasters bombing this target were excellent. However we lost 14 Lancasters, which meant 98 highly skilled men. It was not hard to understand how so many could be lost considering the ferocity of the attacking fighters and the heavy barrage sent up by the ack ack gunners.

The Intelligence Officer had told us at briefing that many of the ack ack gunners were women and they were hell bent on getting their man, dead or alive.

Flying bomb installations at Oisemont was the target on our second operation. It was with some trepidation that we loaded up our gear on 2 July and checked the equipment, paying particular attention to our guns. Flying in daylight we knew we could be an easy target if we were attacked by fighters, and also the ground gunners would have a clear view of their target. This raid was in "B2" on her last operational flight with 460 squadron before going to 626 Squadron.

The target area was covered by 10/10ths cloud and we could only rely on the markers as our aiming point. Take off time near mid-day 12.20 gave us a quick taste of raids in daylight. Lining up on the runway with heavy cloud overhead and slight drizzle of rain made us wonder what if the weather worsened over base. How would we find our home base on return. The weather man had forecast a lifting of the cloud base but then his forecast had been wrong before and after all it was our life at most risk.

The green light and the increasing sound as the engines were opened up to full throttle put all thoughts of weather and cloud to the back of the mind. We were on our way to another job. We climbed away with a cloud base at approximately three hundred feet and climbing in cloud we continued on course, emerging at 7,000 feet into bright sunlight. It was rather exciting to see the planes gathering like a giant flock of birds.

Wheeling like a flock onto the new heading we were being joined by more planes and as we crossed the coast of England turned slowly on to a new heading. With so much cloud we only had an occasional glimpse of the Channel waters as we headed toward the continent.

The brief glimpse of the white caps on the water down below indicated our wind speed and direction were very close to the wind speed and direction the meteorological officer had given us at briefing.

The run to the target was quite quick and I was soon giving the order to open bomb doors. On the run up we were peppered with mainly light ack ack fire, and some planes returned with 303 calibre bullet holes, indicating that rifles were being used from the soldiers on the ground against us.

Being daylight it was very satisfying to see our bombs exploding on the target and the thoughts from the crews of "take that you bastards for these cowardly and indiscriminate flying bomb attacks".

The raid was successful and uneventful. Our bomb load was 11 X 1,000 lbs. and 4 X 500 lbs.

Third operation was to fly in our newly assigned Lancaster "K2" "Killer" ND 615, complete with the Swastika motif and 34 daggers representing one raid for each dagger. Taking off at 2230 on 4 July we were to fly Base - Upper Heyford gaining height all the way to join the bomber stream at 12,000ft our rendezvous point briefed height. Reaching our rendezvous point over Lynie Regis we set course toward our target, the railway yards at Orleans.

We had been briefed to change course four times in order to confuse the German defences. A considerable wind change, which we hadn't picked correctly, resulted in us being last plane over the target.

Even though it was a lovely moonlight night with very good visibility the wind change made it rather difficult for bombing. We were running late as we came in closer I reported one bomber blowing up to starboard, then about fifteen seconds later another bomber coned in searchlights, then a direct hit by ack ack and the plane was going down in flames.

Our own tracking through the target had to be corrected to compensate for the wind error. Many corrections were necessary, and my last correction was an immense 30° to starboard. Just as we started to turn the Germans momentarily coned us with searchlights and the glare was so bad it was impossible to see clearly and we got a frightening taste of their ack ack, bursting all round us.

It was imperative to get out of the searchlight immediately so I reported "bomb aimer to skipper, dodge searchlights, side-slip to starboard". We were not a moment too soon, as we had been targeted. Immediately followed the crack of the exploding shells, right where we had been a moment before. The smell of the cordite from the bursting shells was very strong, something we hadn't experienced. We were lucky our turning and our sharp side slip got us out of the searchlights and saved us from damage, as normally the bombers flew straight and level when dropping the bombs then waiting for the photograph of the target to be taken.

Depending on our height, the camera flash was set to explode after so many seconds fall and to get our photograph as an accreditation of bombing the target. We were ordered to fly straight and level till the photograph was taken and we often wondered how many planes were shot down in this straight and level time whilst waiting for the photo. Almost immediately after the photo was taken we usually had a change course.

From the photograph it was possible for Intelligence to plot where our bombs hit the target area. As the time was also recorded it was possible to plot the other planes' bombs and where and when they fell in relation to our bombs. Even though we were still banked and turning I dropped the bombs and was able, with grim satisfaction, to visually see them exploding right in the middle of the target. The raid was a good one from our view, with a good concentration of bombs in the middle of the target.

Fighter flares were dropping very close around us, as we left the target, and Ted clapped on full power. We raced for a bank of cloud at 240mph and with a bit of weaving and heavy banking we had just reached and were entering the clouds, when one searchlight, which seemed to have a bluish tinge, caught us.

Almost immediately about twenty searchlights swung their beams toward us trying to cone us. We breathed more easily. We had dodged both the searchlights and the fighters. It was commonly believed the bluish tinged searchlight was a master and the other searchlights would lock onto the master and once coned a bomber rarely escaped as all the guns would fire madly at it until they shot it down.

Keeping as much as possible in cloud as we headed for home, we were tracked by fighters. Their tactic was to drop a flare on the edge of the cloud on our track. We countered, as soon as a flare showed we changed course right away from the flare.

This worked well a couple of times but suddenly we came out into clear air with a few minutes ahead of us to the next bank of cloud. Without any warning "mid upper to pilot, dive, dive, attack from starboard" and then "Gee that was close he has gone over the top, watch out to port" the fighter dimly visible in the light from his previous flare had crossed over the top of us and as he turned in for another attack Ted turned to port and flew in under him, luckily for us into the cloud. It was too quick for the gunners to get a shot at the fighter.

The cloud lasted almost to the French coast where we had some more ack ack thrown up at us. Putting the nose down and clapping on full speed to get through the flak very quickly and at the same time a 30 degree change of course we cleared the area and returned safely to base. We had dropped a bomb load of 18 X 500 lbs.

A crew meeting was held after that trip, and everyone was urged to make every effort to pick up any wind changes, or position identification points. That would help to give us a definite fix, which in turn would enable us to calculate our position, as well as check our wind speed and direction. Hopefully this would get us over the target on time.

No one wanted a repetition of the treatment we had received on our late run through the Orleans target, as we all knew how terribly lucky we had been in being coned by searchlights twice and getting away with it. Also as a single plane being chased by two fighters we realised it was only the cloud cover which had saved us, and we had been very, very lucky to get home safely

Next night 5 July at 2116 we were once again in the air with K2 "Killer" for our longest trip so far, just over 8 hours to Dijon railway yards, almost at the Swiss border.

The object of the raid was to create as much damage to the railway yards as possible, and hold up the movement of trains through Dijon. There was a reasonable cover of cloud, affording planes a measure of protection from enemy fighters, and also from any visual firing from the ground. Since leaving school at fourteen years of age I had worked on the railway and I preferred them as a target, they were easy to identify, and were clear of residential buildings. Because of their importance in transporting of troops and war equipment it was more satisfying to see them put out of action.

The enemy concentrated their fire power over the railway yards and to get at them we had to run the gauntlet through this concentration of ack ack

This raid with 154 Lancasters of No 1 Group was one of the very, very few raids carried out where no planes were lost. The ack ack was concentrated but compared with our previous targets it was very light with possibly only about ten guns firing.

Dijon was an exception in that we did not encounter any fighters, perhaps they were concentrating in another area or on another raid, so we considered ourselves lucky not to have the fighters to contend with. As we left the target I discovered we had a 1,000lb bomb "hang up" which had failed to drop. The release mechanism had been fired and the bomb could come loose at any time.

The safest way was to get rid of it over enemy territory as it would be a potential hazard if it came loose. I reported to Ted, "Bomb aimer to skipper, Bomb hang up, we can go around again but there's no guarantee, that I would be able to drop the bomb on the target. Why not head home. If a target shows up that we could dive bomb and try to shake the bomb loose."

"Skipper to bomb aimer". "OK, Good idea"

We were about half an hour from the coast when I suddenly saw a target. From my railway experience I realised a steam loco was ahead as the firebox door had been opened, to feed coal into the firebox of the loco. The light was fanning out from the firebox door. "Bomb aimer to skipper, train loco ahead. Bomb doors open. Left, Left, 5degrees, steady, --- ready to shake loose, dive now, -----shake, shake, climb' --- No luck skipper, bomb doors closed -----------bomb still hung up"

This manoeuvre was carried out perfectly. With a steep dive, followed by a sharp pull up into a shaking climb, but the bomb didn't shake loose. By putting my head down into a bulging cone of perspex I could look back into a portion of the bomb bay but apart from seeing the 1,000lb. bomb sitting there I could see no reason for it remaining hung up. I wonder if the crew of that steam engine ever realised how close they were that night to collecting a 1,000lb bomb right on top of them.

This inspection opening, in addition to viewing back into the bomb bay, was where the bomb aimer released the aluminium strips of foil, which as they floated earthwards reflected the German radar signals making it appear as though a much larger force of bombers was headed their way. I had discovered the opening was very good for having a pee with the slipstream sucking the wee out. The only problem was it was often so cold I had a fear that the stream of liquid may freeze into an icicle stuck to my most valuable possession.

On this raid we had taken off in daylight, flown through the night and were crossing the French coast on the way home when dawn was breaking.

Over the English Channel we tried a couple more times to get rid of the hung up bomb. We were not successful, and brought it back to base. With the cloud base down to 200 feet on arrival back at base we had some trouble landing as there many Lancasters in the circuit from approximately twenty seven from our squadron on this raid all wanting to get down as quickly as possible.

The thought of this bomb, in the bomb bay, was a little bit of a worry. If we landed too heavily the extra weight of the hang-up bomb could cause a tyre to burst, and this could easily be disastrous. The other worry was if the bomb dislodged itself with the bump as the wheels touched down then it could possibly cause us some problems. Our worries were unfounded as the bomb remained hung up and had to be removed by the armourers, which also gave them the opportunity to check why the bomb had remained hung up.
Bomb load was 8 X 1,000 lbs. 3 X 500 lbs.

In the late evening of 7 July we lifted off at 1950 in K2 "Killer" for a raid on Caen military installations timed to catch the Germans relaxing in the evening. That is if they ever did relax in the frontline.

Our route was across the English Channel and in over the beachhead where we saw hundreds and hundreds of ships, including the battleship H.M.S. "Rodney". There was very little to see of the front line apart from hospitals and aeroplane landing strips.

We had a good bombing run and had just dropped our bombs when we flew into heavy flak. A shell bursting just in front of us blasted a piece of shrapnel into the perspex nosecone just in front of my head. A piece of perspex blown out hit me a sharp stinging blow in the centre of the forehead.

Oh no, I thought, "I've been hit". I felt the spot, but there didn't seem to be any blood. I felt again and held up my hand, no blood on my hand.

What a pity! I didn't have a battle scar! The flak was particularly heavy right at our bomb release point and it was a mixture of heavy with plenty of light flak thrown up as well.

Over the target W/O G.E.M. Lindenburg's plane was badly damaged. In his words *"We had just finished bombing when the port outer engine stalled. I ordered the crew to put on parachutes, and swung to port out of the main stream. Immediately, the ack ack concentrated on us knocking out both the inner engines.*

The one remaining engine gave us just enough power to put down in a belly landing in a wheat field." He landed behind the Allied lines in a field much too small to even attempt to fly the plane out again. Later the plane had to be dismantled in the field and salvaged. Bomb load, 11 X 1,000 lbs. and 4 X 500 lbs.

During WW1 aircrews were not allowed to take parachutes into the plane with them as it was considered much better to save the plane. WW11 aircrews were always being told it was far better to stay and try and save the plane if in trouble as there was a much better chance of survival, and also the RAF was always short of planes.

This staying in the aircraft and trying to save the plane in effect cost many RAF aircrews their lives. On the other hand the Americans were short on experienced aircrews, so their orders were to save themselves by bailing out as the planes could always be replaced.

After we landed, we were picked up by a crew transport and taken in to de-briefing by the Intelligence Officer and other section officers.

We were read a message sent to us by the Commander in Chief of the 2nd Army congratulating us on the very successful raid. It made us feel worth while as the commanders were realising some of the value of close liaison with Bomber Command.

They were slowly learning that a softening up by the heavy bombers helped considerably in dislodging the enemy. The Air Force was also doing a terrific job of softening up the enemy forces when called to provide some assistance when the army was copping it tough or when it was bogged down and unable to advance.

Group Captain Hughie Edwards, VC., DSO., DFC. officiated at the Commanding Officer's parade, on the morning of the 7 July. All those who were not actually flying had to turn out for the parade.

I believe that in the five months on 460 Squadron we only attended two parades. Following the parade everyone joined in a cricket match, and we were surprised to see the Group Captain as excitably playing the cricket as any of the younger airmen, but of course on reflection he would only have been just over 30 years old. Rank didn't matter. It was everyone in for the game and a bit of fun and exercise.

Our crew were now settling down to the hard grind of flying discipline with a stern captain, no idle chatter on the intercom, as it could endanger the safety of the aircraft, crewmen to be addressed by their position in the crew, not by name. All reports to be concise and logged. Strict attention to duty at all times.

Although we were new at this we were beginning tio realise as young men continually running the gauntlet of thousands on thousands of ack ack shells, that would burst showering countless fragments of vicious shrapnel, which tore through the thin aluminium skins of the aircraft as though the skin was as soft as butter, we were on a life and death mission. These fragments of shrapnel were white hot messengers of death and did so much untold damage killing and maiming, or perhaps striking a vital component or fuel tank, or line, turning the plane in a flaming coffin hurtling in a screaming death dive for plane and its occupants, to the ground far below.

On the way into the target we were often passing by an area where comrades had been blasted out of the sky, and on the return homeward journey passing by the same area running the same hazards over again. It is impossible to describe what it was like in experiencing a trip in a bomber flying through the concentrations of the defences of the ack ack and searchlights on the ground, the concentration of the shells bursting in the air with the vicious shrapnel flying unseen in all directions. Not only these hazards but the continual fear of being caught in searchlights or to have fighters attacking out of the blackness of night at any moment. The sense of aloneness, which was so real if our plane was the one being attacked, the stomach sinking fear that the next moment may be our last.

There was always the fear that you may be seen to be afraid by your crew members thereby destroying their faith in you. The noise, the cold, if you bare skin touched metal it would immediately be stuck frozen on the metal, the lurching and jolting and the bumping of the aircraft was enough to upset many stomachs. The smells of the mixture of petrol, dope, chemical-toilet fluid, mixed with the smell of the burnt cordite from exploding shells that came too close, or from the firing of our own guns when engaging the fighters, became etched in our memory. We had a job to do and in doing so, would endeavour to stay alive by every means with fear subjugated to the back of our minds. These fears were ever present from the time of briefing, whether waiting to take off or whether waiting for the weather forecast to be favourable over the target area or more importantly on the return to know that you would be able to see the ground to be able to get down safely, or until the raid was postponed and all crews stood down.

A training and testing flight in K2 "Killer" was made on 8 July testing of "Y" a new navigational and bombing aid, to be used in Bomber Command. The "Y" sent out a radar beam, which reflected off any raised section, such as a shoreline of water, or of buildings, or any raised objects. It was then received back in the plane and reflected on a cathode ray tube.

The reflection showed the difference in the time of the beam being received as an outline on the screen. If water or any completely flat area was being reflected any change in height on the ground was shown as an outline on the screen. Even the outline of buildings could be seen and in the case of a city, the streets could be defined as a grid.

From a scale it was possible then to calculate a time and distance from any point showing on the screen. The "Y" was able to penetrate through cloud when we had no chance of seeing the ground, which made it very useful and invaluable for navigation purposes.

ACCIDENTS AND INDECISIONS

Heading down the runway under full power with our tail up on July 12 we were off in K2 "Killer" at 2130 for a raid on the railway marshalling yards at Tours, carrying a bomb load of 11 X 1,000 lbs. and 4 X 500 lbs.

With the deafening roar of the four engines, propellers turning under the thrust of full power, everything vibrating madly as though we would shake into pieces, we raced down the runway, gaining speed.

Almost at the point of lift off, there was an audible thump followed by a rush of air as our parachute hatch dropped out of the plane. It fortunately fell clear, landing on the edge of the runway.

Too late to abort the take off, we were soon airborne, with wheels and flaps up, and once settled on climbing power, we surveyed our options. After inspecting the bomb aimer's compartment, where the parachute escape hatch, which measured 23 inches wide and 26inches long, and was basically most of the floor section.

I suggested to the skipper that with my parachute on, with luck I could manage to drop our bombs on the target. I could straddle the opening and if I fell out, I would have my parachute, and have a chance of survival.

The other alternative was, with our safety landing weight only 56,000 lbs. and we were at 64,800 lbs. should we fly out over the Wash to jettison our bombs, and miss on the raid.

Ted reported to control, which instructed us to circle at 2,000ft and await instructions. With light cloud conditions we had a marvellous view of the action as the rest of our squadron planes became airborne.

It was the first time we could observe the control van the green light from the air and watch the Lancasters still on the ground start to move on their take off run.

As they applied power, slowly increasing their speed we could see the glow of the exhausts as they heated up under the engines full power.

Then ever so slowly, up came their tail. Finally, when there was no runway left, the Lancaster lifted off and was climbing. After the last Lancaster became airborne, control ordered us to land with extreme care.

We were all aware of the dangers of taking off with a full fuel and bomb load. We had a very, very narrow safety margin. Landing with this same load was another story, not yet written. We were also aware that we were about 8,000lbs overloaded. Even a blown tyre had occasioned the collapse of the undercart of a Lancaster, with the plane crashing and blowing up.

It was only a short time since Dan Cullen returning from a raid on Hasselt had ballooned when landing due to a surface inversion creating lift near the ground. Finding himself short of further runway, Dan had turned off the runway only to have his undercarriage collapse in a shallow drainage depression, with the Lancaster damaged beyond repair. All crewmembers scrambled madly to get clear of the plane in case she blew up. The stand in engineer in place of Don Gray who had been wounded on the previous trip, is reputed by Dan Cullen, to have climbed up over Dan's back to get out before Dan had time to move. Thankfully everyone got out safely.

Squadron Leader Chad Martin walked over to Dan and said, "What happened Cullen" and the reply, "It was piss poor flying, Sir" with which the squadron commander turned and walked away. It was only later in the mess that it became known that Squadron Leader Martin had also ended his landing in the same ditch as Cullen.

Sometimes crew members had managed to escape before the plane exploded, and sometimes they didn't. With these thoughts in our minds, and a full load of fuel and bombs on board, we were in a very dangerous position.

Usually WAAFs and airmen gathered to wave us a good journey as we went off. As we came in to land, they were scattering and running in all directions away from the edge of the runway. Despite our pilot's experience, and in keeping the speed and power on, to correct any possibility of a stall, we did stall a few feet off the deck, and landed heavily.

Fortunately the forward movement helped take the major weight off the undercarriage, which did not collapse. Our parachute hatch was waiting for us when we arrived at the end of our run. I took it from the mechanic and this time made sure it was clicked properly in place.

The skipper opened up "Killer" downwind and we raced back to the take off point so fast that at one stage we thought he was trying a downwind take off. Finally airborne 45 minutes late, we climbed on track to catch up with the rest of the bomber stream. Passing 10,000ft the engineer had to switch the petrol feed from the main tanks to the outer tanks to use those tanks up first, keeping the inner tanks which were puncture proof, till last. We had reached 12,000ft in the dark by the time he had to switch the petrol feed. Unfortunately he switched the petrol feed on to empty tanks.

Hearing the engines start to miss a beat I raced back over our main spar obstacle course, checked and seeing the switches in the wrong position on the empty tanks I quickly switched back to the main tanks, in time for the motors to pick up. Once the revolutions were steady, I switched the petrol to the correct positions. We lost about 3,000ft in the episode.

Our luck was still not with us. Climbing through 12,000feet the mid upper gunner Frank Mayor reported one of his hydraulic lines had burst, and he was covered in fluid, but could still operate his turret manually. He was soaked in the hydraulic fluid from the waste down, until we got home some four and a half hours later.

Forty five years later I caught up with Frank, and he was suffering badly from dermatitis, caused by the soaking in oil.

We were still twenty minutes from target time when we saw quite a vicious barrage open up over the target, and some dozen searchlights waving round looking for bombers. We didn't see any planes shot down.

The barrage had ceased, and the searchlights out, as we approached the target. The crew was keyed up and there was dead silence apart from the roar of the motors, as we seemed to crawl toward our aiming point.

In everyone's mind was the question could we sneak through without being shot at. Within about half a minute of our bombs being dropped, all the searchlights came on. In no time we were coned, and the guns were madly shooting up a barrage. The smell of cordite from the exploding shells was overpowering.

It was too late to dodge, "Bomb aimer to pilot, steady as she goes skipper, put the nose down and go like hell, I can drop on the run". With our bomb doors open and at full speed on our bombing run, the shells were bursting all round, so close the ear splitting explosions were quite terrifying and although experiencing severe buffeting from the explosions, our bombs dropped away safely.

"Bomb aimer to skipper,----------- bombs gone, -------------- close doors and dive! Dive!"

In true fighter pilot style, Ted put the nose hard down and we dived at somewhere around 400mph, levelling out in the moonlight, at about 500 feet from the ground with the ack - ack guns shooting almost horizontally along the ground at us.

When the firing ceased we eased up to 2,000 feet, changed course 30 degrees to starboard for fifteen minutes then a 60 degree change of course to port for fifteen minutes before resuming our normal course home. As a protection against any fighters who might be lurking looking for stragglers we stayed low for the rest of our journey back to base.

Safely home, landed and back to dispersal, where the groundcrew, led by Sgt Bill Young, were always waiting, asking the usual question: "Any damage?" and the answer, "You fellows have got some jobs to do. We must be covered in holes!" and the reply, "You bastards! You never look after our plane. You bring it back full of holes and expect us to fix them up, so you can go out, and get another lot of holes and damage for us to fix. No wonder we don't get very much sleep!" The aircrews reply "O.K. stop your bloody whingeing and get to work fixing it!".

Amazingly there was not a scratch on "Killer" and the ground crew gave us a torrid time over what they termed our make believe shootup.

When returning for our parachute hatch, we had landed with an all up weight of 64,800lbs despite the RAF official Lancaster safety landing weight of 56,000lbs. Bomber Command issued a new safety landing weight of 64,000lb after this episode.

The crew had a serious meeting immediately after. The whole incident seemed to have arisen from too much alcohol before flying, thereby reducing concentration. The crew being mostly teetotal agreed that anyone, coming on board in future with any sign of having consumed alcohol, would be severely dealt with. Everyone was in total agreement.

With no respite, our next briefing on 14 July was for a raid on the Revigny railway marshalling yards near the Swiss border. Take off time was 2130 in K2 "Killer" We were to climb to an operating height over Bridport, and join the bomber stream at 12,000 feet climbing on track to 15,000 feet for the flight across France.

It was a beautiful moonlight night, with a fair amount of scattered cloud. The moonlight added a fairylike glow on the clouds. It was really magical to view but we realised it made it easy for the fighters to pick up the bomber silhouette more easily, so extra vigilance was the order of the day. Had our flight not been on such serious business, then we could have lingered longer, admiring the picture in all its heavenly beauty.

On the last leg to the target, we were flying south, directly towards the moon, and as we approached the target the railway lines were glinting in the moonlight, reflecting the moonlight, and showing up like strips of highly polished silver, giving us a perfect sighting of the target.

The master bomber could be heard talking to his deputy:
"Deputy can you see the target, I cannot pick it, too much cloud".
"Deputy to Master Bomber cannot identify, suggest orbit".
This was too much for some of the pilots who broke radio silence.
"We have perfect sight of target can we bomb visually, no need for markers".
"Master bomber to Stream, hold your bombs, are you there Deputy, stand by, I'll come round again".

Suddenly there was a burst of ack ack and an explosion out to port followed by a view of a Lancaster going down in a ball of fire, and exploding on impact on the ground. Immediately a stick of bombs was dropped, exploding over the downed plane.

"Deputy calling Master Bomber, Deputy calling Master Bomber" followed by pilot's question,

"Permission to bomb? We have perfect visual sighting!"
Then an Aussie voice: "Shake it up mate; we can't hang round here all bloody night!"
"Attention! This is the Deputy, hold your bombs, I repeat hold your bombs! Cut the talk and orbit a rate one turn ".

For the whole of the bomber force to orbit was to fly round in a circle at approximately a 15-degree bank commonly known as a rate one turn.

This was something nobody wanted, a stream of bombers to orbit in the dark, risking collisions, and being exposed to night fighters or ack ack or searchlights in the target area with no possibility of being able to dodge for at least fifteen minutes.

Those extra minutes over a target could be an eternity and lead to eternity and we knew it. All attention would be in avoiding other bombers whilst we were turning. With such a perfect view of the target, the orbiting was ridiculous but we had no alternative but to follow orders.

Lined up on the target again and once again with a perfect view of the target, the Deputy was told very forcefully by several who broke radio silence what we could see. Despite this he ordered "Sugarplum!" "Sugarplum!" the code for the attack to abort and return to base with all our bombs. His Lancaster was found later crashed on a hillside close to the target.

What a waste of a long trip when with a perfect view of the target. We were not allowed to bomb because the master bombers could not sight the target. We were not very far from the target when the fighters became very troublesome. We were attacked a couple of times but managed to evade in the clouds.

If it hadn't been so serious this would have been the most fantastic viewing of Lancasters drifting through clouds, and of fighter flares being dropped, of the shadowy planes both Lancasters and Me 109s flitting in and out of the clouds, being lit up by the fighter flares. It seemed just when a fighter flare exploded and lighted the area, the Lancaster was disappearing into cloud. Sometimes with a thin patch of cloud, one could pick out the shadow of the plane.

Everything seemed suddenly so startlingly close.

Our rear gunner reported: "Enemy fighter attacking! 600 yards port, closing in --- closing in ------ 500 yards port, prepare to dive port!"

We dived all right, into some cloud, and immediately Ted cut the power, hoping the fighter would overshoot.

The cloud lasted longer than usual, and when we emerged the fighter had gone.

We were not left too long before another fighter was lining up: "Rear Gunner to Pilot, fighter about 800 yards! Closing in --- closing in ------ 600 yards closing in --- closing in ------ prepare to dive port, prepare to dive".

Then without warning the ear splitting roar through the earphones as the rear gunner's four guns hammered away each gun firing at 1150 rounds a minute, a burst of maybe 10 secs.

The horrific noise was followed by a nervous silence, then, from Dick Bates, our rear gunner "Got you, you bastard!" Because no one was witness to this kill it was not recognised and therefore not credited. Not long to wait and we had another attack, and Ted altered course into a patch of thick cloud. A moment or two later there was an explosion directly overhead as a fighter flare burst almost on top of us. We came out of the cloud on a new course flying wingtip to wingtip with an Me 109. The German fighter pilot must have got as big a surprise as we did.

For one moment, we had a clear view of his startled very white face, in the reflected light from his fighter flare. Before the gunners could get their guns lined up on him, he dived away to starboard, as we entered the cloud again.

Usually the run home seemed longer than the outward journey. After the journey to and through the target and the tension over the target the trip home seemed a let down and the crew tended to relax, but not this raid.

The running battle with the fighters had lasted for 90 minutes, but from that point on we had no more trouble. We crossed the coast of France and were within a few minutes of home when the fog closed in with zero visibility preventing us from seeing the runway.

We were diverted to Waterbeach, No 415 Squadron known locally as "Yo Yo" squadron, because of the number of times the planes were loaded with bombs, and then a change of target. It was bombs off the planes, then reload, and again bombs off. We told them we also had the same problem.

Waterbeach was also an American Liberator bomber base. They asked us what sort of planes we were flying, and all sorts of questions about, how fast they fly, what sort of a bomb load would they carry, where had we been, and why did we land on their aerodrome?

We were taken to the mess, where we had a very good meal, much better than we were served in the mess at Binbrook. Perhaps the change made the food seem so much nicer. It was one of the heaviest raids to date with just on 1,000 Bomber Command aircraft.

One of the 7 Lancasters who failed to return was that of P/O W.A.H. Vaughan from 460 Squadron.

We were told to settle in the mess, as there were no spare beds. Most of us slept on the floor, whilst some were lucky enough to get an armchair.

We were all pretty tired so had a reasonable sleep. We were out early to get our breakfast, as we had to head back to the squadron, as quickly as we could. This we found impossible, as the Yanks hadn't refuelled the Lancasters? It seemed that they didn't know where the "gas" went in. Being the bomb aimer I opened the bomb doors, to check that our load was safe before take off. The Yanks stood with open mouths and goggle eyed, looking at all the bombs we carried, and the size of the bay, which took up most of the underside of the plane.

Our bomb load was double that of the Liberator as they stated "Our Liberators carry eighty hundred pounds of bombs", (80 00) which actually was (8,000). On this raid we only carried 9,000lb, taking up only half of the Lancaster bomb bay. Our usual load was 16,000 lbs.

As we were taxying round the perimeter track, ready for take off, Yanks were lined up in their dozens, and every one of them had a camera.

What a wonderful opportunity to get photos of a fleet of British bombers, and their insignias painted near the nose. Leaving Waterbeach at 1215 we were home in thirty-five minutes

At this stage we had been briefed, loaded and ready to go on 21 raids in fourteen days. We were beginning to lose track of time and also which day of the week. Just imagine the work that entailed particularly the ground crews and armourers. Due to the uncertain weather we were experiencing, we had only flown seven raids.

The continual briefing and then standby for further orders, sometimes after we had reached our plane and were ready and waiting to start our motors. When the stand down was announced, it was tough on the nerves, as we were on standby at all hours of the day or night.

OVER THE NORMANDY BEACHHEAD

Our next raid was the military installations in the Caen area on 18 July in K2 "Killer" with take off at 0335am.
Flying in over the Normandy beachhead was always an awe inspiring sight. The ever changing parade of ships, roughly 1,000 of them, many of them coming and going, whilst other ships had flotillas of landing craft, either clustered round the ships, or shuttling back and forth to the beach.

We were being escorted by a swarm of Spitfires high above us and also a few flying quite close to the stream of bombers. The morale boosting effect of some protection from our fighters was welcome. However the fighters were soon forgotten as we came in over the fleets of ships. Over the beach at dawn, we split into four sections to raid military installations in separate sectors, almost like a dawn patrol, except that we stirred the German defences to blaze away at us with the ack ack.

We were directed down to 3,000ft for our bombing. At this low height, we realised why the safety bombing height for 1,000lb bombs had been set at 4,000 feet.
Flying through the target, was an extremely rough passage because of the blast effect from our own bombs. With so many explosions, the planes were flying as though someone was hammering at them from underneath, trying to shake them into little pieces.

One of our squadron Lancasters from "C" flight returned to base with a nosecone from one of our own 1,000lb. bombs embedded in his starboard outer engine.

This was reported as one of the most useful army support raids carried out, and severely affected a German Luftwaffe Division and a Panzer Division. They were caught at breakfast time and hopefully ended up with either a cold breakfast or no breakfast at all and something apart from cream in their coffee.

On our way out we were dodging in and out of the incoming stream of bombers. With over one thousand bombers on target it was an amazing sight to be dodging the incoming bombers as we were coming out of the target area.

We cursed such inefficient routing of bombers back through the stream of incoming fully loaded bombers. Such inefficiency could have caused a real catastrophe but miraculously there did not seem to have been any collisions
Our bomb load, was 11 X 1,000 lbs. and 4 X 500 lbs.

From a later report on these raids Bomber Command with 942 aircraft in the four raids had dropped 5,000 tons of bombs on the German emplacements in just a few minutes whilst the Americans also bombed the targets dropping another 1,800 tons to add to the damage.

A HELL OF A FRIGHT

The same night taking off in K2 "Killer" at 2300 for our ninth raid on oil installations at Gelsenkirchen, had us realising how tired we were. We had taken off in the morning at 0335 which meant we had started our preparations and meals before midnight, and yet here we were again airborne at 2300 hours. After take off we climbed for a height of 12,000ft at our rendezvous point over Mablethorpe.

We had on board our first loading of the block buster 4,000lb bomb, known and easily identified as "Cookie", The total bomb load was 1 X 4,000 lbs. and 16 X 500 lbs. filling all possible bomb stations.

The 4,000lb Cookie had a thin casing, which increased to four times its normal size then exploding. This factor created the blast effect. It was also dangerous, as had been proven when the bomb dropped from a plane to the ground in the dispersal. The bomb had exploded wiping out the plane and also damaging adjacent planes.

If hit in the bomb bay by a piece of ack ack, and the cookie exploded there was nothing left after the blast. The crew was always very happy when the Cookie had been dropped. It always felt so much safer, not having it riding just under our feet, with only a thin aluminium floor between the bombs and us.

This was our first block buster "Cookie". It was for maximum blast effect in the oil installations, and hopefully this would cause a lot of property damage.

It was also our first raid into the Ruhr Valley, and we had been briefed to fly on a route avoiding bad ack ack locations.

Flying a circuitous route from Mablethorpe to 53°00'N 03°00'E to 52°35'N 04°35'E to 52°20'N 07°05'E then the target Δ (marked in our log books thus) then 51°38'N 06°20'E to 52°20'N 05°20'E to 52°20N 03°00'E then Cromer – Mablethorpe – Base.

These different courses were set up hoping to confuse the German defences and the fighter controllers, for a little while. We always hoped that the ploy would work and keep the fighters away, but we seemed to attract fighters like bees to a honey pot. It was a deadly guessing game.

Which way was the raid heading, and where was the best place for the fighters to intercept the raiding bombers? It was a constant battle to see who could outwit the opposing forces, and gain an advantage. We had been told to expect a concentration of about 300 searchlights, with a possibility of around 500 ack ack positions.

The numbers didn't mean very much, excepting it sounded like, and turned out, a terrific amount of defences.

How can one describe flying into a rainstorm of ack ack shells bursting all round us, of violent explosions in the air, of explosions on the ground. The fighters and heavy flak 105mm and 128mm guns, bursting just around and above us as the gunners got onto our height.

The radar-guided 88mm guns which fired predicted flak and could pick off individual bombers at considerable heights. The lighter flak guns of 50mm, 37mm and 25mm, with their red green and yellow tracers arcing up toward us as though it was water being sprayed from a fireman's hose.

All guns being fired as fast as the gunners could load them. It was quite a sight as rings of shock waves, came up out of the inferno on the ground, as the Cookies blasted many into eternity. These shock waves were like circles of shimmering light, ever widening, rising through the smoke and fires.

I was absolutely petrified. How could anyone survive this fusilade of death and destruction? Someone had said when you are really frightened get your mind on to something else. I started saying to myself

"Into the valley of death, rode the six hundred, guns to the right of them, guns to the left of them".
"Yes, I'm thinking, what about the guns below them, and the ack ack shells curving upwards at my belly".

There goes a plane down in flames to port and another one underneath us. I grabbed my parachute putting it between my legs, and lay on it, at least perhaps I could preserve my manhood. This felt fine, and so my rolled up parachute was used on many more raids, for my personal comfort and protection.

With perhaps five minutes left on the run into the target, all sorts of jumbled thoughts flew in and out of my head.
"The Lord is my shepherd I shall not want, He leadeth me beside still waters".
"Into the valley of death rode the six hundred, and he will protect us".

There go another two planes. They must have collided in this air alive with flak.

"Surely goodness and mercy. Have mercy on us".
How could we possibly survive? The flak was unbelievable.

I was shaking like a leaf and my thoughts were jumbled. I was beginning to wonder if I could drop the bombs because of my shaking. This waiting and watching and seeming to crawl up to the target was dreadful.

My thoughts were becoming more jumbled the closer we got to bomb dropping. Suddenly there was a blinding flash less than 100feet above us accompanied by a shocking blast which shook our plane and then the mid-upper's voice: "Gawd, he's blown up, and his engine, white hot, just missed me as it went down between our wing and our tail plane!"

Ted had swung hard, when the explosion occurred and this had possibly saved us from the engine, which just missed the fuselage of our plane.

It was time to bomb and suddenly, after this violent manoeuvre threw me against the side of the plane and the blast of the explosion, I was as cool as a cucumber.

"Bomb aimer to Skipper, bomb doors open".
"Left, left, 20 degrees".
"Steady------------Steady-----------Right five degrees---------
Steady-----------Steady----------bombs gone.
Close bomb doors-------hold for photo ------- hold------OK photo taken". I always tried to have the bomb doors open for the least possible time. I felt safer with them closed.

The fires and the explosions on this raid were awesome and unbelievable. On the run up to the target there was a terrific explosion and flames shot up 4/5,000 feet, so bright that the searchlights were blotted out momentarily. It appeared almost like day for about fifteen seconds.

A smaller explosion, a minute later, indicated considerable damage had been done to the oil storage. As we flew out of the target area the German fighters were diving in among the bombers and the tracer bullets were flying in many directions. On the ground the fires were lighting up the whole area, and it was satisfying to see we had hit the target area good and hard.

Everyone was on tenterhooks with reports on fighters too close for comfort but, fortunately for us, they were not attacking us. Tracer bullets were flying from some of the planes and we saw a couple of fighters firing their cannon shells into one unfortunate bomber. After receiving two or three sustained bursts of fire the plane suddenly blew up, heeled over on its side and went down in flames. It all happened so quickly and the shell busts on the plane were so deadly that the crew didn't have a chance of parachuting.

On our return to base, as we climbed into the crew bus to be taken to interrogation, I heard one bright spark say "The flak was so thick we could have put our undercart down and landed on it". I was in silent agreement.

Another crewman passed an opinion that those German fighter pilots sure had guts as they risked being shot down by their own flak over the target in their hunt to get a shot at one of the bombers, as well as risking being shot down by one of the bomber gunners.

Of course we all knew that over the target in the bombing run flying straight and level the bombers were at their most vulnerable. However we would raise our hats to the German fighter pilots and to their courage.

When the aircrews came into the light at interrogation and again in the mess, they had a queer look about them. It suddenly struck me that their cheeks were sunken, and they were sullen with none of the usual spark and light chatter. Their eyeballs gave the impression of sticking out of their heads, and they were listless and moved like old men.

The two raids took 27 hours without a rest or sleep. The continual roar of the engines hour after hour, the nervous tension, and long hours were having their effect.

The next morning making an inspection of our plane in daylight, Sgt. Bill Young and Cpl. Jack Hill (Melbourne) "K2" chief groundcrew climbed into "Killer" and came out looking very subdued when they discovered most of the top of the pilot's canopy had been blown out by the explosion.

With 34 individual holes in the top of our plane Bill Young's comments were "Jeez what happened last night, you poor buggers, don't worry, we'll soon have her fixed up like new!" and they wanted to know what had happened. Miraculously no one was injured, except for the awesome fright of our young lives.

On the return, many airmen didn't attempt to get food but headed to their rooms, where they just flopped down clothes still on, too fatigued to undress and get into bed.
Most aircrew found it impossible to sleep after these raids. The mind seemed to go round in never ending circles, and we were only able to doze. The deafening roar of the engines was still with us for many hours.

Still in our clothes, after 3 to 4 hours dozing, some of us drifted back to the mess for some food. Others had a pick at the meal. We all drank a lot of fluid because flying above 12,000 feet, we had to use oxygen which had a very drying effect on our bodies. We then usually headed back for a shower, mainly looking to moisten our bodies. Only then were we able to lie down and get some sleep.

Without oxygen at 20,000 feet, we were told we could only survive for four minutes. Therefore its use was absolutely necessary. Crew members always had to be alert at all times, to make sure none of their crewmates were suffering from lack of oxygen.

When asked by the new crews what it was like over Germany, this raid became our measuring stick. "Wait until you raid Gelsenkirchen, then you will know how tough it can get", became our standard reply.

Speaking with Bert Uren, navigator in P/O G. Stone's crew he said they had Group/Capt. Hughie Edwards as their skipper on the Gelsenkirchen raid and the crew thought they were extremely lucky to survive. On the run up to the target almost on the point of bombing the mid upper gunner reported a bomber just above and he felt they might be hit by the bombs which he could see in the open bomb bay just above them.

Group/Capt Edwards in his true "press on regardless manner" ignored the warning and when the 500lb bombs were released one bomb just missed the leading edge of the wing and the next bomb just missed the trailing edge.

Almost immediately a plane just in front of them received a direct hit and with a blinding flash blew to pieces. It was so close they flew through the debris from the plane which had been blown apart. How lucky can you be?

On another raid P/O Stone and his crew were flying "J2" which was in the next dispersal to our "K2". Without warning when closing the bomb bay to commence taxying in readiness for take off, their cookie dropped to the ground. Bert Uren, the navigator, suddenly realising he was alone in the aircraft went to the door to find out what was happening and swears the majority of his crew were 500 yards away and running fast enough to win the Stawell gift. A ground crew man standing next to the undercarriage said 'Don't worry matey, if she was going to blow up we'd be in heaven now".

We saw all the commotion and our skipper did the next best thing. He opened up the motors on "K2" and we shot out of dispersal like a scalded cat, much to the amusement of the crew with comments, "Hang on skipper! We need a bloody runway and a green light before you think of taking off!"

The Duke of Gloucester, the Governor General designate of Australia, was visiting the squadron on 20 July, and after briefing and checking over our plane in dispersal, we had to stand by to meet His Royal Highness. It was all very exciting to be meeting up with royalty. Fancy him coming to see us. As time drifted on, we cursed HRH who was delayed in the officers' mess, and on shaking his hand in front of our K2 "Killer" we realised he had enjoyed some of the Australian hospitality served in the mess.

It wasn't until 0005 that we lifted off to raid the railway marshalling yards and a triangle junction, at Courtrai. It had been a long day. Over the target we were not happy when three fighters attacked us.

We had a fighter flare dropped almost on us, and then a JU 88 attacked. The flare must have blinded the German pilot as he came in. Ted had dived K2 "Killer" to port and the centrifugal force had me frozen in space almost suspended under the front turret and it flashed through my mind I was being thrown about like a puppet on a string. We were diving fast to evade, when the JU 88 suddenly appeared about 30 yards off our wing tip, he must have been just underneath getting ready to blast us, or perhaps there were two of them hunting as a pair, but we didn't know and we didn't wait round to find out

He would have been a real sitting shot for our gunners, but it happened too quickly for them to swing their turrets round. He broke off the attack, and disappeared.

Suddenly another JU88 attacked from starboard astern. The rear gunner reported, "Enemy fighter attacking from starboard side, prepare to dive starboard. 600 yards--------500 yards ------prepare to dive ------ dive!"

This time Ted dived at the same time ordering 15° flap, undercarriage down, as he simultaneously reduced power to idle. The fighter overshot us like a rocket, almost hitting our wing, and disappeared into the night. Miraculously, after another attack and one short burst, which went wide, no further shots were fired and the German fighters disappeared as quickly as they had appeared.

The target was absolutely devastated, with a terrific amount of damage to the railway yards. It was estimated that it would take many days before any trains could get through. Bomb load, 11 X 1,000 lbs. and 2 X 500 lbs.

On our return to base, our area was blanketed in fog, and despite all crewmembers keenly searching for a break in the fog or a sight of the ground we couldn't sight anything and were diverted to Lindholme. Only about six planes managed to land, before the fog closed in on Lindholme and the remaining planes still in the air were diverted to Leicester East. The fog on occasions closed the dromes so fast we were getting a little bit worried. What would happen if we were not able to land. What then? Others were not so lucky, as 9 Lancasters were lost.

We went to bed after supper at 6am and were called at 12 noon. I navigated home, while Don our regular navigator climbed into the rear turret to get a feel of what it was like on the tail end of a plane, and to see the scenery. After formalities at base and a meal we climbed into bed for more rest and sleep.

Awakened at 1830pm and dressed at 2030pm. Frank, Steve, Peter and I walked to the village hoping to find something to eat, but no luck. On return we were lucky enough to get some food, and a cup of tea, in the mess. Then back to bed catching up on sleep.

From this raid P/O R.H.Jopling and his crew failed to return.
Jopling was shot down on this raid, and had some fun evading capture after baling out over Dixmude.

Harold later told me of his experience when approaching the target. *"He was flying in the front group enjoying the flight with no flak, and no fighters, when suddenly all hell broke loose, with flak bursting all round. Hit by flak as the bombs dropped, he was attacked by a JU88 with upward firing canons, their shells exploding in the starboard wing knocked out his two starboard engines.*

With half his starboard wing and tailplane gone and fire in the wing, the wireless gone through the roof, the navigator's table collapsed and crew members wounded, he lost control of the plane at 12,000feet as it commenced spiralling down to earth.

He fought desperately to regain control and at 2,000feet with partial control and with the remainder of the starboard wing glowing white hot and only the port outer motor operating he ordered the crew to bale out. The mid-upper gunner froze in the back door, and to speed his exit from the plane, the rear gunner gave him a kick in the backside to send him on his way.

The bomb aimer had difficulty in opening the front escape hatch so jumped on it and as it gave way he went out with it.

Jopling, when boarding the Lancaster at base, had foolishly thrown his parachute inside the door instead of carrying it up front to the pilot's position, and when the wireless operator, Sgt Don Annat, reported all crew were out and it was time to go, Harold told him he couldn't because his parachute was back just inside the rear door. The wireless operator somehow scrambled back over the debris and the main spar, difficult to negotiate at any time, collected the chute, came forward and clipped it on Harold's chest and said "Right let's go, Boss".

Jopling holding the stick hard over to lessen the spiral, eased himself, with a great deal of difficulty, out of his seat, and then following the wireless operator made a flying dive out the front hatch, which was a feat as the escape hatch was not particularly easy to negotiate at the best of times. Estimating his height at 700 feet he was extremely lucky that as his chute opened his Lancaster exploded and with the force of the explosion he was blown much higher. The minimum safe height for baling out was 3000 ft.

Landing safely in a village he quickly cut the top off his flying boots, got rid of his parachute, and was just in time to join a German troop who were looking for him so he joined them looking for him. They spoke to him in the dark but he just gave them a wave on and seeing a lane to one side, he ducked down the lane, and as soon as he was alone, he ran for his life. Once clear, he walked at night and hid during the day. He found a vegetable patch where he lived the next few days on raw carrots, raw potatoes and his escape kit.

While he was walking he met an American flyer, a Captain who had commanded a Flying Fortress squadron. When asked what happened the Captain stated his Fortress was running short on fuel and presuming everyone was also getting short on fuel he ordered the whole squadron to bale out. Harold got away from the American as quickly as possible.

On arrival at Ypres he was contacted by a member of the Belgium underground forces and taken to a café where he was given what he described as "a beaut feed of bacon and eggs".

The Belgian underground people took his uniform, dressed him in civvies and took him to a farmhouse near Boezingst, where they kept him under armed guard while they checked to make sure he wasn't a German masquerading in order to trap them. When they were satisfied he was taken by bicycle to Chateau Zonnebec where he lived in the upstairs of a farm shed. He had to haul the ladder up while he was up there.

Each evening the baroness would arrive with the meal of the day and from his hideaway he could watch the Germans doing their drilling, as they were in occupation of the chateau, using it as their headquarters".

A summary of a post war report from Mr Oscar Joos, 26 rue Camelinat states:

"On July 20 1944 after the bombardment of Courtrai, we have taken an Australian, Aus 410065 Pilot Officer Jopling, R.A.A.F. Not being well he was also nursed by Dr Bolvin.

Our district was always searched by the Gestapo who have taken several patriots, so we are anxious about our Australian and we used two hiding places, one for the days under the weaving looms, the other for the nights in a spring mattress, hiding places quite undiscoverable.

During the clearing of the Germans, this officer, helped by an American Captain, rendered us great service in putting in front of our house a big S.O.S. Allied aeroplanes saw it while we were shaking an English flag to obtain aid. - we went to our place of fighting with the Australian who seeing the first English motorcyclist went to the Anjot Staff to explain the critical situation at Halluin.

Mr Joos, member of the resistance, fighting in Lille Street, brought back home with him, the English cyclist, a doctor and his orderly. Tanks had been asked for Halluin, they arrived the next day and we saw our Australian on the turret of the first tank. After the liberation, Mr Joos, took the Australian dressed in a new suit, to the Major Staff at Lille, as well as his friend, Kenneth J. Butler, Engineer, taken by Mr Oprien

Nollet a retired policeman 238 Lille Street, Halluin"

Jopling was then taken to Menin where 3 girls took him to the French border and engaged the guards in a flirtatious discussion thus allowing him to cross. Two of these girls were subsequently caught and later shot for stealing ammunition for the villagers after the resistance had taken on the fleeing Germans who were in full retreat.

Jopling joined the resistance in some forays, whilst he was in the area. He finally got through to Lille where he joined up with the Allies and before his repatriation was organised he had the pleasure of hanging out of the top of a tank as they drove through the village where he had spent some time. He was then taken by a British truck, picking up several evaders on the way, to Paris.

Arriving in Paris they were stoned by the locals who at first believed them to be enemy. Next day they were airlifted back to England in a DC3.

On returning to 460 squadron Jopling pressed for a decoration for the wireless operator Don Annat. His action, at an extreme risk to his own life, in going to the back of the Lancaster to retrieve his skipper's parachute deserved an award. It had been a foolish action to throw the parachute just inside the entrance door and leave it there when boarding the plane. It almost cost him his life.

Jopling was asked "who else witnessed this action by wireless air gunner Annat" but could only answer truthfully that as all other crew members had already bailed out it left only him and Don Annat to bear witness. His claim was disallowed. As Jopling was listed by the Gestapo he was not allowed fly again over enemy occupied territory".

From Peter Firkins book "Strike and Return":

The mid-upper gunner, Sergeant Mills, was not so fortunate as the following account of his experiences reveal: *"My Lancaster was hit by flak over Belgium when we were returning from bombing Courtrai and we all baled out successfully. It was about 0130 hours when I came down and quite dark, I landed in the centre of a cornfield near Roelcappelle, about 10 miles north of Ypres.*

The corn was about 4 feet high and I pulled in my parachute and discarded my harness which I hid. "*Wanting to get to France as soon as it was light I made off south-west, crawling through the fields and walking by night. By dawn the following morning I reached a cement road which led roughly south-west and wanting to make some speed I followed it. It had rained incessantly the night before and I was wet through.*

"After about half a mile, at a crossroads, I came to a statue to the 18,000 Canadians who were the victims of the German gas attack during the last war. Here I made my first contact, a man who was clipping the bushes of the large garden

surrounding the monument. "In English he told me to avoid main roads after the curfew and I stayed with him until evening, when he brought me some food, tobacco and coffee.

He showed me a secondary road which was not on my escape map and which led to a small place on the French frontier.

It was getting dark when two Belgians on bicycles caught up with me and took me to a small wayside café. They said they were evading being sent to work in Germany, and took me to a disused barn about three-quarters of a mile away saying the 'Captain' would come to see me in two days' time." I slept there and they brought me food and civilian clothes.

On a Monday, about four days after my landing a taxi drew up to the other side of the road and two men stepped out and went to the café leaving the driver behind.

A child came from the café to call me and I went across. The cafe owner introduced me and the two men took me in the car. I was taken to a house about a mile from Ypres on the main road where two sisters of one of these men lived. The other man was the 'Captain'. They gave me some better clothes and food, and the two men took me in the taxi to Ghent.

I spent a week in various houses and cafes and was then taken back to the house near Ypres where I stayed for about three weeks. The two *men often took me out in the taxi to see various friends of theirs and I gather they used to ask for money.*

At about 0400 hours on 21 August 1944 I was woken by the two men who told me to get up quickly as we were all going to Dunkirk then to England. A taxi was waiting and we drove off, but a mile down the road half a dozen German military police were waiting for us.

We were taken to the German Field-Gendarmerie H.Q. at Ypres and about two hours later the café proprietor was brought in, badly beaten up. The Germans tried to make him say he knew me and also tried to get my admission that I knew him, but without success.

Various other people that I had called upon were also arrested. Either the man at the Canadian memorial or the 'Captain' were indiscreet or unfortunate, or else they could have been double agents".

Mill's escape, although unsuccessful, revealed the hazards and the nervous tension involved in these bids, and also the risks taken by the Resistance Movement members themselves.

A similar situation befell Flight Sergeant Don Dyson, shot down when returning from Hasselt on 15 May. After baling out he landed in a lake, and getting ashore, he walked for days in his cold wet clothes before making his first contact. After numerous moves he finished up in Brussels, awaiting the arrival of the allied forces.

When Dyson walked into the Boomerang Club in London a few days after his liberation, one of his former ground crew was standing just inside the door. As nothing had been heard from McLeery's crew since their loss, the ground staff man thought he was watching Dyson's ghost. It was some time before he was assured all was well.

The German flying bomb attacks were being intensified on London and the East Coast centres including the main RAF bomber bases in East Anglia and headquarters had ordered an increase in the attacks on the sites in the Calais area on the coast of France.

Although the raids, were successful in putting the launch sites out of action, it did not take long before the launching sites were back in action launching the deadly flying bombs against the English targets. It was a constant battle to knock them out of action even if only for a short time.

On 25 July the take off time was 0700 in K2 "Killer" for raiding flying bomb installations at Coquereaux. Flying in over the Normandy beachhead there was still a very large number of ships. Flying lower than usual it was fascinating to see the activity of the boats, either heading for the shore or returning to the ships but we were over the ships too quickly to see much.

The enemy fighters who waited for us at night could have had some good target practice on the ships but of course they would be running a gauntlet of very heavily defended targets.

We reported to intelligence a satisfactory result and a very successful raid with the launching site destroyed. As the bombs rained down there was a tremendous upheaval of dust and debris and launching ramps were being thrown about like a toy train set. The area surrounding the ramps was being churned up by the explosions. It would therefore be unfit for any activity and would take sometime to clean up.

Our bomb load was, 11 X 1,000 lbs. and 4 X 500 lbs. and clusters of **J. Type incendiaries.

Our crew missed out on a raid, as we were on leave on 7 August when a force of just over 1,000 bombers raided several targets in front of our advancing troops. F/O Don Tardent flew "K2" on this trip.

The Canadians in the Caen area had been specifically warned against advancing or ignoring the instructions issued about the bombing, and of the dire consequences

Having no German resistance in their sector they advanced. Although 1019 aircraft were raiding the target, only 660 aircraft bombed, before the error in the colour of the day was discovered and a stop called on the bombing. A lot of Canadians were killed because of the doubt.

Our very young Wing Commander Douglas led the force from 460 Squadron. He was a brilliant and dedicated pilot and the youngest Wing Commander in the RAAF at 22 years of age. He was a leader in the bombing of the Canadians as he had been scheduled to bomb in the early wave.

He was reduced in rank to Squadron Leader and posted to 467 squadron as a flight leader. Group Captain Edwards was not happy with the treatment of Douglas and tried unsuccessfully to keep him on 460. Douglas was killed in early 1945, when leading his new Squadron on a raid.

The Canadians claimed they had advanced because of no enemy opposition and had immediately laid out signals, which should have been seen by the Air Force.

** Footnote: *"J" Type incendiaries an experimental pack clustered and primed to burst open spreading them more effectively.*

Their signals were reportedly the same colour as the colour of the day's target indicators causing problems for the attacking force of bombers.

Ferflay flying bomb installations was our next target on 10 August in K2 "Killer" with take off at 1020. Due to bad visibility and heavy cloud formation, we descended from 9,000 to 2,000 feet and although we circled several times we were unable to identify the target through the heavy cloud.

It was a little hair raising to be circling in cloud in company with many other planes and always with the fear of a collision. The one consoling factor, if you did collide it would happen so quickly you would not have time to think about what would happen. Finally, to everyone's relief we were ordered home with our bombs.

Something we didn't like was having flown the raid and then to return home with a lethal full bomb load, and to face the danger of landing with the bombs still on board.

Any miscalculation resulting in an accident on landing and the crew and plane would be lucky to survive. It was much more satisfying and much safer for the crew to release the bomb load on the target,

We were only a flying aluminium platform, and we were sitting on this enormous load of dangerous explosive of death and destruction. It was no wonder we always breathed a sigh of relief when the bombs had dropped.

BULL'S EYE - NO RECOGNITION

The railway marshalling yards at Douai, Northern France, was our next target. Our crew had settled down into a well disciplined unit with each crew member having confidence and respect for the other members of the crew. There were no orders given, but plenty of laughing and joking between each other.

We all knew our jobs and we had a good pilot whom we trusted to fly our plane even though on occasions jokingly we had to remind him he was flying with a crew and was not a fighter pilot as he had been trained.

Take off time for this raid was 1345 in K2 "Killer" on 11 August, 1944. We were among the leaders coming up on the target and had a perfect view. It was such a pleasant afternoon that it was hard to believe there was a war raging.

Approaching the target there was always a certain amount of the fear and trepidation that we experienced when on a raid. As we got closer it was always a question did intelligence get it right? Did they have the latest on the number of guns or of searchlights? Have we been routed clear of flak positions? Are we away from the fighter packs?

On this particular raid there was not a great deal of flak over the target and our bombs were the fifth salvo to hit the target. Our second or third bomb hit an ammunition train standing in the middle of the yard.

It was a fantastic and exciting hit for me, as the explosion was the most tremendous eruption I had ever seen. It went like a flash of lightning, from my first bomb burst then raced right through the middle of the railway yard, erupting as it went into great explosions as the train was blown sky high.

What a measure of excitement to contemplate as we cleared the target area. We had blown up an ammunition train and we had succeeded in getting a bulls eye on the target. We claimed the blowing up of the ammunition train, but even though our photo was enlarged, and sent away to Commander in Chief Bomber Command, our claim was disallowed.

The disallowing of claims was so bad that the crews often were reluctant to lodge a claim. The resentment on the disallowing of claims always surfaced. If we were an RAF squadron there would be no doubt and we would be decorated instead of having our claim disallowed, or perhaps it was the reluctance of station officers to push a claim on behalf of the colonials.

Later from the plotting of the photographs taken on this raid, the Intelligence Officer stated there was no doubt in his mind; our bombs had definitely hit the ammunition train and started the tremendous explosion of the train. In his opinion our claim should have been recognised.

Our bomb load was 13 X 1,000 lbs. and 4 X 500 lbs.

CHAPTER SEVEN
EXPERIMENTS AND PROBLEMS

The crews lived from day to day and on most raids when planes failed to return it was accepted as matter of fact "Poor old so and so, he got the chop last night, bad luck for them" Poor old so and so may have only been 21 or 22 years old.

The ground crew, particularly of the plane that had gone missing, sometimes took the loss of the plane and crew a little more personally. The camaraderie between air crew and the ground crew was rather special, especially when a crew was assigned to a plane. The ground crew seemed to assume responsibility for the aircrew and in fact I suppose they owned us, we were their crew.

The air crew were tightly knit together as a working crew, eating together, sharing the living quarters, sharing their stand down times together and, as their lives depended on each other, they became very close and developed a bond that has lasted a lifetime.

On the squadron, life revolved around raids and we lived from day to day. In the morning, the first thought would be are we flying today? What are the orders? If we are on ops what is our fuel load? What is our bomb load? I suppose it could be said we were living in constant fear.

Once the flying orders were out, it was go and get the plane ready, attend the briefing, then waiting to see if the weather would hold, or whether for some reason the raid would be scrubbed. If it was on, then off to our planes, with the excitement and trepidation until we lined up on the runway and had clapped on the power and were on our way.

Once in the air the professionalism took charge and all minds were on the job, eyes peeled for fighter attacks, or for identification of points to assist in the navigation.

And then, as we approached the target, the tension usually mounted for the bombing run and in getting clear of the target. Once clear we could breathe a little easier as the tension had diminished a little, but we dare not relax until we were back on our home ground.

Headquarters decided to trial a raid on an experimental **"Y" cin (sin) fire bombing on Brunswick on 12 August. There were no Pathfinder aircraft marking of the target. We were flying Lancaster "B" take off time was 2130.

As the 2nd front had now moved inland, instead of climbing to a height over England we were able to climb on track converging in the bomber stream, saving at least half an hour and a great deal of fuel, before we crossed occupied territory.

We used our H2S, a machine transmitting a signal which when it hit an outline image of the topography it was reflected, enabling the viewer at the screen to map read through cloud. If we couldn't identify the target we were told to bomb something, but don't waste the bomb load.

On the way in after crossing the coast, any flak guns that opened up on the bomber stream collected a 2,000lb bomb from one of the Lancasters.

We passed close to Bremen where some of our planes strayed off course and were caught in searchlights and two were shot down in flames very quickly. Hanover had plenty of searchlights and flak, chasing others who strayed too far off course. South of Hanover we had a fright when, without warning, we were coned in a blue searchlight, and other searchlights quickly locked on to us.

** Footnote: *The cin (sin) was purely an incendiary fire bombing of the city of Brunswick using "Y" experimentally*

This was a most chilling and frightening experience when all of a sudden the glare of the searchlight have you completely blinded and your survival depends on the instinctive reaction of the pilot.

Ted flung the aircraft into a terrifying angle with everyone being thrown about inside the aircraft. We were just in time as the shells were exploding right where we had been.

As the searchlight made to follow us I waited until they almost had us again. Bomb Aimer to Pilot "Searchlight starboard - closing prepare dive starboard—steady, steady—go - dive starboard. We kept diving starboard and miraculously the searchlight moved away looking for other planes.

Twice a fighter closed in to about 400 yards, but for no apparent reason, excepting perhaps he was only a beginner, chose not to fire at us and broke off the attack. We were still miles from the target and fully alert to keep track of our course.

As we flew closer to our aiming point and I gave the order for "Bomb doors open" our Cookie (4,000lb. bomb) dropped away just before our aiming point for the release of our bomb load.

Our "Y" which had been working well suddenly packed up giving us no visual image of the ground below so we bombed the fire concentration. Later we found that the early bombs were several miles short and by the time we bombed well into the centre of the fires we were also many miles short.

The squadron operated three times in twelve hours, and our Brunswick raid had been the second raid.

It also gave us an idea of the value of "Y" and its aid to navigation. In conditions where we experienced heavy cloud on the flight over the enemy territory at least "Y" or

H2S as it became commonly known would give us a much better chance of identifying our position.

Our wireless operator who liked a drink or two or three often felt the urge to relieve himself on our trips and had taken to carrying an empty milk bottle. It saved the long trip to the elsen at the rear, and having to plug in and out of oxygen points.

After he had relieved himself into the bottle, he would drop it out of the photo flare chute after our target photo had been taken. It had been reported that the falling bottle howled like a banshee as it fell. He reckoned "Piss on them, then frighten hell out of them". Unfortunately, on this occasion his mind must have been on other things resulting in an erection in the bottle, and much yelling for assistance to get the bottle off with some help from the navigator.

With much merriment the navigator, assisted by the engineer, and using the back of the navigator's calculator managed to break the bottle. Our recommendation was in future use a beer bottle, a smaller opening maybe requires a straighter aim but with no fear of getting stuck.

At our usual interrogation on return we reported our 4,000lb Cookie had dropped early when the bomb doors opened, even though no bomb release had been activated.

After extensive interrogation by the intelligence officer, and the bombing leader, and several visits to the plane, I found myself in serious trouble and was ordered to remain on the station until this matter was thoroughly investigated.

An odd crew or two had dropped their Cookie in the North Sea on some raids thinking it was safer not to carry the big bomb to the target, as they were aware that if hit by flak the cookie would most likely blow them into eternity.

They also realised that without the weight of the big bomb they could fly higher and perhaps dodge some of the lighter flak. Most crews were concerned till the cookie had gone, but we had a job to do, and that cookie would do a lot more damage to the target than the rest of our bomb load and so that is where we intended always to drop it.

Despite insisting that I had never released any bombs early on any raid, after several investigations of the aircraft I was given a final chance of proving my innocence, before a possible court martial.

In company with the Engineering Officer Bert Newton and the Bombing Leader, F/Lt Les Tait we went to the aircraft. I was instructed to climb into the bomb aimer's position and fire the bomb switches, as I normally fired them.

When I was ready I yelled out, "Are you ready?", and they answered, "OK!" As the firing mechanism was electrically activated, it was sending a live current to fire the Cookie station, causing the firing mechanism to release allowing the bomb to fall.

The engineering officer had placed his hand on the aircraft near the cookie firing mechanism, while he leaned over to get a better view of what was happening. When I turned on the power to activate the bombing mechanism I heard a loud yelp and I immediately turned off the power and put my head down into the inspection opening to see what had happened.

The Engineering Officer had received a pretty hefty electric shock resulting in a thorough check of the wiring to see why he had received such a shock at the same time the cookie release mechanism had fired.

On further investigation they found where the wire passed through the floor it had become frayed and was shorting on to the firing mechanism, causing it to fire when the power was switched on for the release of our bomb load. I didn't even get an apology for the accusations, which had been levelled at me. Several other planes, on being checked also had bare wires.

On this raid on Brunswick F/O G.J. Garratt's gunners Compton and Poulson shot down an Me110 giving rise to a lot of celebrating and a lot of congratulations all round

From 242 Lancasters and 137 Halifaxes raiding the target 17 Lancasters and 10 Halifaxes were lost.

There was a loss of a massive 10% of the attacking force in one raid, with no appreciable damage to the enemy as our bombs had dropped into the forest about fifteen miles short of the intended target.

OF THIS AND THAT

On 14 August, flying Lancaster "B2", we flew to Church Broughton, dropping off our Squadron Leader Flight Commander. On the way back we flew a short cross country visual navigating by the H2S map reader through cloud and finally homing in to our base with the aid of Gee. The whole exercise was without reference to any ground assistance identification.

In the evening the Bomber Command band played a very entertaining station concert. As I had been playing a baritone in the Binbrook station band, we were invited to meet with some of the fellows in a mess party. The party did not go for very long.

Our flying and training was a very heavy schedule and there was no accommodation for casual visitors spare at Binbrook. The air crews considered that all accommodation at Binbrook was casual, because with losses and crews being lucky enough to get through their tour of operations, few stayed very long.

Training flights and short navigation exercises using our special equipment kept us busy on 15-18- 21- 23- 24 On the 25 we landed at Horsham, an American 8th Air Force Liberator drome, to drop off one of our Flight Commanders.

Our Lancaster was quite a novelty and although we were not allowed cameras (unfortunately) the Americans were lining the taxiways with their cameras as we were taxying to our take off point. Many photos were taken of our plane with its distinctive hand held dagger piercing the heart of a swastika with blood dripping down and the word "Killer" also with blood dripping down from beneath the name.

We were very interested in looking over the Liberators and the decorative motifs they had painted on the nose area of their planes.

One Liberator had been painted to resemble a fish complete with blue spots on the fuselage.

On 26-27-29 we carried out local navigational exercise training in Lancaster "B2". G/Capt Edwards led us on a very low level sweep round the countryside on one of these exercises. It was an exciting exercise flying behind our station commander who had won his Victoria Cross on a daring low level attack on Bremen.

Although it seemed dangerously low it was also exhilarating to go hedge hopping across the countryside. We flew so low a few horses and cattle reared up in fright, as we dodged past them.

Our satellite drome at Waltham was our target on the way home and as we came up over the rise we were so low that had we put our wheels down we would have landed. When we got back to our drome we climbed to height in order to make a regulation landing.

The Waltham station commander rang through as mad as hell about the 460 Squadron Lancasters flying so dangerously low across Waltham drome. He wanted to report to G/Capt Edwards. When told that Edwards had led the flight he hung up.

A standing joke on the squadron was that Hughie Edwards must have drunk kangaroo juice regularly, as he usually bounced quite a bit when landing.

It was about this time that I was singled out by the WAAF Sergeant in charge of the mess, I don't know whether she had just arrived, or whether she had been at Binbrook for a while. She, as the saying goes, had taken a shine to me, for what reason I never found out. She was a very attractive woman 25/35 years of age, and, much to my embarrassment, started selecting choice portions of food especially for me. The other fellows, quick to notice, started poking fun at me;

"Look out mate, she wants to rob the cradle!" and "What have you got, that we haven't got, when you can snare the more mature ones` "What do we have to do to get prime treatment, just give her some prime treatment, what's she like, etc"., and to her "Why does he get the best food, how can we earn that preferential treatment? And why don't you come and sit with us occasionally instead of with him"

Then she collected my mail, which didn't please me at all. I gave instructions at the mail centre that my mail was only to be delivered to me personally.

She suggested that I was looking tired and I should think about getting away to a nice place by the beach where I could live life to the full and do just whatever I liked even to stay in bed all day but I looked as though I needed somewhere quiet for a holiday. I couldn't think of a way to stop the attention without hurting her feelings. This worried me, as I didn't want any attachment.

Next she took to having her lunch with me at the table, and the excuse was she wanted someone other than the mess staff to talk to. I was due for leave and she suggested I should go somewhere to a nice quiet place, where I could relax and have a good rest. She would be quite happy to come along too and prepare my meals and look after me. She owned a house at Scunthorpe near the water, and I would be able to relax there, and we could have such fun together all on our own.

NOT SO LUCKY OVER STETTIN

On our 15th raid we were designated to fly Lancaster "J2" to Stettin. On 29 August we lifted off at 2110 with a full load of 1 X 1,000 lbs. 1 X 500 lbs. 7 X 150 X 4 incendiaries, & 7 X 12 X 30 incendiaries.

It was a long uneventful flight over the North Sea with some heavy cloud, which lifted a little as we approached Denmark. As we crossed the coast we encountered some spasmodic ack ack. There was also some fighter activity, aimed at stragglers who had wandered off track.

Suddenly about a half a mile to port there was a bright pink glow in the clouds, and then we saw the reason, a couple of planes going down in flames. Whether it was a collision which seemed most likely or fighters or ack ack we didn't know, but we were happy we had not been any closer to where they went down

Our scheduled bombing height was at 17,000ft. The briefing was to fly over Sweden at 17,000ft, as the Swedish gunners would fire their ack ack guns at us, but the shells would be fused to explode at 15,000ft. Approaching Sweden, where the lights were shining was a reminder of the days before blackouts, and the blackness that War had spread over most of the World.

As briefed, the gunners put on an impressive show with their guns. It was wonderful to enjoy the spectacle of ack ack guns blazing away, and the shells bursting just below us, and to know they wouldn't hurt us.

Passing over Sweden, we were routed almost due south, to approach the city of Stettin and the dock area, from the sea. This was wise planning, as we could make full use of our H2S to pick up the coastline and the river with the city off to starboard of our track.

After turning on to our new heading toward Germany, the searchlights, which had remained vertical stationary, were lowered to a horizontal position pointing on our track toward Germany. They waved up and down a few times, in a real heart warming gesture, as though they were wishing us God speed.

At 17,000 feet the cloud was closing in a little, and the Master Bomber nearer the target up ahead, ordered us to reduce height, with a minimum of 12,000ft for our bombing run. The message wasn't really concise and almost left the crews to choose their own heights

Whether or not some of the crews did not get the message, or whether they ignored the instruction, to reduce height believing themselves safer at 17,000ft no one knows.

Often these late messages were ignored as some crews thought they were moves by an English speaking German to disrupt the raid in some way. For those crews who reduced height it was a recipe for disaster, flying in the lower layer when the bombs began to fall. So many in fact it seemed like a rainstorm showering down from above. We in "K2" did get the message, and immediately reduced height.

In the pale moonlight it was a magnificent sight to see the massive harbour with the docks on the western shore. Further to our starboard were the main city blocks. Many ships were lined up at the wharves, whilst several were either anchored or lining up for docking. It seemed as though the enemy was not really expecting a raid so far north. No attempt appeared to have been made to keep the shipping scattered in case of an air raid.

Approaching Stettin the fighters became very active, and a couple of Ju88s flew across from the port side several hundred feet below us. I watched them closely as they lined up on a pair of Lancasters. I was helpless, I wished I had some way of alerting the crews but watched helplessly as the fighters shot down both Lancasters, one blew up as the fusillade of tracers hit into him whilst the other burst into flames as he fell arcing to starboard. I reported to the skipper as a precautionary measure for all to keep a watchout. The fighters seemed to be hunting in pairs at a lower height than at the height at which we were flying.

Despite the long flight over the water, it was a gratifying sight to be approaching the target, with our plane nicely lined up on course to the target. The markers had gone down, and the bombs were commencing to explode. When flying into the target zone with the ack - ack bursting in our path, it always seemed to take an eternity before we were able to release our bombs on target.

What a picture. The searchlight beams the fusillade of red, green and yellows ack ack tracers slicing up into the sky, the coloured markers being reflected from the water. Then just up ahead three more of our planes all within half a minute blown up by ack ack. How many more of our mates were getting the chop on this raid? They were being knocked out of the sky like flies.

It was apparent to the crews judging by our bomb load that this raid was designed to create as much fire damage as possible as we followed the first wave of the more heavily loaded explosive planes. Our load was mainly incendiary bombs.1/1000lb. high explosive, 1/500lb. high explosive. 7 racks of 4lb. x 150incendiary and 7 racks of 12lb. X 30 a much heavier incendiary load, than we usually carried.

The markers had gone down very accurately and I had guided Ted into a good position for our bombing run. I delayed the order to open the bomb doors, mainly because of the heavy ack - ack and also with fighters active in the vicinity. When I judged we were within 30 seconds of our bombing point I gave the order:

"Bomb doors open"..
"Steady.........Steady.........Steady.........Bombs gone ...., bomb doors closed" "Steady for photo".

Suddenly there was a terrific crash, one wing dropped badly, then we came up straight. There was a loud rushing noise coming from the cockpit. I moved back quickly to see if the skipper was all right and when he appeared OK I resumed my duties giving the "photo taken!". Although the noise was still going on, and it had become quite draughty, everything seemed to be operating correctly.

I soon learned an incendiary had come through the roof hitting the armour plating shield behind the skipper, giving him a good thump on the head, and making him dizzy for a moment (hence the wing drop). The bomb then deflected through the blackout curtain hitting the navigator, Don Hudspeth, on the arm, driving his watch down through the arm and breaking his wrist. The arm was torn badly and later required twelve stitches. The bomb ended up on the floor behind the navigator, and fortunately it hadn't exploded.

The wireless/operator quickly wrapped it in his bag, and shot it out the photo flare chute. He afterwards said he got rid of it as quickly as he could before it had time to explode, and before he had time to get scared about what could happen if it did explode. He also stressed that he handled it, as gently as he could, and when he shot it down through the photo flare chute, he made sure it didn't touch the sides. At that moment two more planes exploded and went down on fire.

I suggested to Don Hudspeth our navigator I would take over the navigation home once we were clear of the target. He assured us he would be all right, if not he would call on me. The perspex canopy over the cockpit had been badly smashed, making it extremely cold and uncomfortable on the return journey, otherwise we were fortunate no other damage had occurred.

Safely on our course on the homeward route, we had a couple of close calls with fighters flying across our path, about two hundred feet below our height, but no actual attack as we left the target area. Approaching Sweden, the massive fires of Stettin could be clearly seen behind us. We were again waved over Sweden, this time the searchlights waving westward on our track toward England.

Over Denmark, the fighters were very savage for a short time. To get clear of the area more quickly the skipper clapped on speed. Suddenly the rear gunner reported a pair of Me 109s climbing to attack from below us. A quick corkscrew at full speed, a manoeuvre that delighted our skipper (ex-fighter pilot stuff) and the fighters disappeared.

A few minutes later we had another attacker firing as he climbed toward us from the port side. Again the skipper dived port, into the attacking angle at full speed, and the fighter's tracers passed harmlessly above and behind us.

The skipper carried on corkscrewing a couple of times then ordering everyone to keep watch for any more fighters levelled off on our final leg for the run home flying at 20,000ft. We had just passed over Denmark and settled down for the long haul home.

The cloud was banking up ahead and we were encountering heavy turbulence when suddenly we were flying in a severe electrical storm. It was one of our roughest weather encounters, and Ted climbed as high as "J2" would go, 27,800 ft. where we were bouncing along, right on top of the cloudbank, and the storm partly underneath us.

The windows were being continually lit up by lightning flashes, with balls of blue fire playing round them. The propellers were also caught by flashes, which gave a real ghostly blue glow.

After a couple of hours flying in very rough conditions, and still above heavy cloud, Ted decided to let down fairly quickly as we were getting close to base.

We had always been advised not to fly if we had a cold. On this occasion I had a slight cold and suffered badly as I felt my eardrums were going to burst. After my complaint Ted held a much more shallow descent. Finally on the ground, it took me a couple of weeks to recover my hearing.

Our navigator, Don Hudspeth, was grounded until his arm recovered. We had been flying together for eight months, and it was a bad blow to lose one of our crew. It was also a blow to lose Don, as he was a terrific crewman, very obliging, a very good navigator, as well as being a hell of a nice bloke.

We had decided to volunteer for Pathfinders after the required 15 raids, but now with one crewman short on our 15th raid we did not qualify. Don did not fly with us again, and we had to finish our tour carrying a spare navigator each time.

As we could only operate when a spare navigator was available, this extended our time on the squadron. The raid on Stettin was very successful with 3 ships sunk and 34,000 people homeless.

Coming back from the target P/O D.C.Balfour claimed the destruction of a Ju88 without the Lancaster having fired its guns. Five minutes after leaving the target the mid-upper gunner reported a Ju88 immediately below, intent on tailing a Lancaster ahead.

Balfour pulled the nose up to avoid a collision, but the wings touched and the fighter dived straight down. The rear gunner observed it burning on the ground. Back at the station, the port wing was examined and the top surface was holed and the wing itself dented.

F/O Neil Hudson, when 25 miles short of the target, collided with another plane, possibly a German nightfighter, which knocked out his port inner motor, bent the propellers on his starboard inner motor, and caused damage to the underbelly and bomb doors. Fortunately he was able to get the bomb doors open to drop his bombs, and then struggled home on two motors.

P/O Peter Aldred was not so lucky. His plane was attacked by an Me 109 on the way to the target when crossing the coast of Denmark. His gunner's managed to fight off the German.

About 20 miles on, they were approaching the target at 17,000ft, when once again the gunners managed to fight off an attacking fighter.

Descending to 12,500ft on the Master Bomber's orders, they were hit by three incendiaries from the planes above, badly damaging Peter's right hand and the plane controls.

After bombing they were again attacked over the target by a fighter, but managed to evade him. With a great deal of difficulty the pilot managed to reach Sweden where they made a crash landing.

Some time later Peter Aldred was flown back to England in the bomb bay of a Mosquito which he thought was a bit of a come down from pilot, to just a load in the bomb bay. On his return to the squadron he described the Mosquito ride as the coldest, draughtiest and most uncomfortable air trip that he had ever had.

23 Lancasters were lost to fighters on this raid.

F/O Don Hudspeth remained on 460 Squadron flying as a spare navigator and ended up flying his last 11 raids with Sq/Ldr John Holmes. They were killed on a raid on Chemnitz on 6 March, 1945

WITHOUT A REGULAR NAVIGATOR

Our next flight on the 3 of September was a low level, climb to drop some practice bombs, some fighter affiliation with diving and climbing, do some corkscrewing and attempt to break off fighter attacks. As the stand in navigator on these exercises I missed the enjoyment of seeing what was going on outside. The navigation section was really only a narrow table with room for "Gee" & "H2S" with the navigator sitting on a seat, almost blocking the passage through to the rear of the fuselage. We were sent on this training exercise while "K2" was being repaired. When we landed from this training we were stood down for a few days leave.

Frank had asked me a few times if I would go home to Burnley, in Lancashire, on leave with him, as his mother would like to meet me. Checking on whether it was OK for me to come, Frank and I journeyed by train on the 4th September through to Burnley, Lancashire. Arriving at the city station, we walked up a hill to Frank's home, a small brick house in a row of tenement houses. Farther up the hill on the same street was a parachute factory and most of the employees walked up and down this busy little street.

Frank's mother was a lovely motherly type, who made me feel at home. She was a very jolly lady, and a very good cook. She rather spoiled us with the food over the three days I spent with them.

Frank's father insisted on taking me down to the pub for his mates to buy me a beer. I was the first Australian that they had ever met, and I was made very welcome. His mates wanted to buy me so many beers, I would never have survived had I not told them I was a rechabite and had taken the pledge. We had quite a bit of fun, although I hardly understood their broad Lancashire accents.

The next day I had an invitation to the parachute factory to see the girls packing our parachutes. It rather turned out the other way, with the girls having a look at a real live Australian airman. I was wolfwhistled, asked what I was doing tonight, and generally felt I was lucky to get out in one piece.

The manager felt it was a wonderful boost for the employee's morale, to meet someone who might have a use for the parachute they had packed. Perhaps my visit gave them a more personal interest in the war work they were doing.

I had returned from Burnley after three days, and Frank was fed up at home, as he didn't see eye to eye with his father, and had come back to the squadron a couple of days early. The squadron really was our home and the crew our family and we were more comfortable there even though we got wearied beyond belief. After a few days leave we wanted to be back flying with our mates. Flying dangerously was like an exhilarating drug.

With no raid pending on the evening of 9 September Frank and I went into Grimsby, where we sometimes attended a dance, in the hall at Cleethorpes. We enjoyed the orchestra of a couple of trumpets, a couple of trombones, saxophones, clarinets, and piano, playing the stirring waltz music of Vienna, the dreamy love songs of the 1930s and 40s and the Military Twostep and Pride of Erin, the Barn Dance, the Fox Trot and other dances.

Frank, who was a very quiet and shy Lancashire lad, later in the evening, said, "See that lovely young lady over there, dressed in a sky blue dress?" It took me a few guesses and queries to get the correct one. Then he said, "I bet you are not game to have a dance with her, and bring her back, and introduce her to me".

"Well Frank, if you are that scared, I'll do that just for you, but you will owe me. She sure is a humdinger isn't she".

As soon as the music started, I headed for the girl in the sky blue dress. She was about five feet five inches tall, with a very nicely proportioned slim figure.

Short dark brown, very wavy hair, lovely fair complexion, brown eyes, lovely natural slightly pouting lips, fine features, and a very bright personality. In my opinion a very attractive young lady.

When I asked her if I might have this dance, I got a lovely smile and: "Yes I would love to very much, thank you".

I was only an average dancer, and apologised telling her I hoped I would not tread on her toes or something like that, trying not to make a fool of myself. I felt her melt into my arms, and as we danced I thought what a lovely person, and what a pleasure to be dancing with her, as she made the dancing so easy for me. She told me her name was Emily, and she was only visiting her cousin in Grimsby for a few days.

I told her: "I was a bit down, when Frank, our mid upper gunner, suggested we come to the dance. He thought it might be something to cheer us up and let our hair down a bit. But dancing with you, has made me feel quite uplifted. I hope you didn't mind me asking for the next dance".

She said that would be a wonderful idea, she would love that, as she was a stranger, and apart from her cousin, didn't know anyone.

She came from Lancashire, where she was living with her mother, and worked in Lancaster. She said she liked the Lake Windermere area, which was close by where she lived. She felt sure, if I hadn't seen that area I also would enjoy it and should visit there on one of my leaves.

One dance led to another, and then another and I didn't even meet up with the cousin. During the next dance, I told her that Frank had bet me, I wasn't game to ask her for a dance, and wanted me to take her back and introduce her. She said "That's OK by me, but I don't want to dance with him. I would rather dance with you".

After the introduction to Frank we stood talking together for a while and then Emily and I waltzed off, and danced for the rest of the evening.

Frank and I had to leave before midnight to catch our bus back to Binbrook, and Emily asked me for a phone number as she might give me a ring.

Back on the squadron we did a couple of training flights with a spare navigator. Taking off on the 15th September at 1545 we headed for Wainfleet where we dropped six practice bombs separately. We then climbed away to a height of 20,000 feet, heading due west.

Our instructions were to remain on this heading to allow American fighter planes to intercept and then carry out a fighter affiliation with them. Three U.S. Thunderbolts came peeling out of the sun and made their attack in line astern.. The mid-upper gunner reported "mid-upper to pilot, Fighters attacking from starboard rear 1,000 yards" "pilot to rear gunner, do you see enemy" "rear gunner to pilot, yes enemy 800 yards, prepare to dive port". "Three planes line astern 600 yards, --------- 500 yards, they are a bit slow in their attack, ---------400 yards, corkscrew port! Go!" and we really corkscrewed. Ted was back to his fighter pilot flying and our corkscrews were quite violent.

The Thunderbolts overshot. They came round again and attacked from starboard in a wing tip to wing tip or line abreast attack. "mid-upper to pilot prepare to dive starboard 600 yards----500 yards-----400 yards, dive starboard!, go!" The Lancaster was much too manoeuvrable for the fighter pilots as the American Thunderbolts were not nearly as manoeuvrable, nor as good as Spitfires in our experience in the fighter affiliation training exercises.

"Bomb aimer to pilot, fighters 300feet below 10 degree starboard, dive and we attack the bastards, show them what it is all about!'" Ted didn't need any more urging, down went the nose, up went the engine revolutions to full power, and we swooped down over the three fighters, crossing them from right to left.

Had it been in earnest they would have been sitting ducks for our front and mid upper guns. To add insult to injury Ted banked round in front of the Thunderbolts gave a very good tail wag and we headed for home

Returning to base, we landed and taxied to our dispersal. When the motors had stopped we collected our gear and as we were leaving the plane at dispersal, Bill Young, our Sergeant in charge of our ground crew, said "What the devil have you fellows been doing, have you sprung a leak?"

He reached over to where the fluid was dripping from the plane just behind the exit door, held his hand under the leak, and looking at it, said, "Its not oil!" Sniffing it he said "Its not petrol, it looks like water!" and tasting it said "I'm blowed if I know what it is?"

"That's OK Bill" said Steve our W/Op
"Someone used the Elsen, (toilet) and our bloody Pilot in his fighter affiliation, diving and twisting, dodging those bloody Yankee Thunderbolts, has spilt it all! Did it taste good?" There were peals of laughter from everyone.

It was boring with no flying on 16 September, and I hadn't been thinking of going anywhere when Frank said, "Aren't we going into the dance tonight to see my girl, or are you too lazy?"

"Well if you would like, we could go, but we would have to catch the early bus back" I replied.

"Come on then, shake a leg, let's get cracking!"

We arrived among the first at the dance hall, and had a few dances, when during a break Frank said: "Hey, wake up Australia, over there near the door, look who has just arrived!"

I looked where Frank had indicated, and there was Emily giving me a wave. I made a beeline across to her

"What are you doing here, you told me you were headed home, but I didn't expect to see you again so soon?"

"Well" she said: "I rang through and got a couple of days extra leave, and I was hoping you may be here". "That's terrific, gee I'm pleased to see you! I really wasn't thinking of coming, but Frank talked me into coming, and I'm glad I did, and now I'm so glad you are here!"

"Would you like to dance with me?" I said as I held out my arms, inviting her to dance with me. With a lovely smile, she cuddled into my arms and said, "I'd love to, that is what I came for!"

She sure felt good, and she was great company, as we danced and talked. I found Emily's company was almost as good as a tonic. Flying was getting to me, and on our last couple of raids I had been violently sick, not airsick I didn't think just my nerves getting a bit raw. Despite the sick bouts I was not going to report to the Doc as I might lose out on flying with my crew.

Too soon, it was time to go back to base, as we were rostered for flying, so saying a fond farewell to Emily, we parted. She was going home the next day, and said she would love to call me now and again, if I didn't mind. She had enjoyed so much our meeting and the talks we had together. It made her feel as though we were old friends.

I agreed with her and promised to ring as soon as I had finished my tour of flying duties.

No questions were asked. "The Enemy Listens" proclaimed all the posters, and everyone seemed to understand. Then wishing her a pleasant journey home Frank and I went back to war.

The mess Sergeant WAAF was still anxious to set up a weekend away at her house, and at last I had the answer. I told her I had met this wonderful girl and had promised her I would keep in touch with her. I was over enthusiastic about this other girl and made a point of keeping the WAAF very well informed how lovely this girl was, and gradually I was left in peace to collect my own meals.

On 17 September we flew a short air test with Bill Young and Jack Hill aboard our newly mended "K2". Checking instruments, and engines, we found everything in order for our next flight coming up at midnight.

Flying K2 "Killer" and taking off at 0100 on the 18. We had been briefed to catch the fighters on the ground in a low level raid on a fighter aerodrome at Rheine.

This was real fighter bomber stuff, a real reversal; where the bomber was strafing with bombs the fighters on the ground. A low level raid in a Lancaster heavy bomber on a fighter drome seemed unbelievable but we were excited. We flew at less than 200 feet across the North Sea climbing to our 2,500 ft bombing level after crossing the coast.

With a bomb load, 20 X 500lbs the raid was intended to do as much runway damage as possible and to destroy the hangars and workshops. Needless to say we were anxious to catch the fighter planes on the ground. With only a couple of gun emplacements, light flak and the fighters caught on the ground it was good fun to make our run across the drome aiming at the runway, planes or buildings.

What a mess. Several fighters went boom, disintegrating as they blew into little pieces, others were blown over. Many buildings were destroyed and badly damaged. As we cleared from the area, the clouds of dust obscured the aerodrome, but we felt sure the drome would be unusable for a few days at least.

The gun sites at Sandgatte were becoming troublesome and on 20 September at 1505 in K2 "Killer" we were detailed on a raid to damage them and, hopefully, put them out of order.

Visibility was good over the target and as the bombs hit the emplacements it was very satisfying to see the guns and debris being flung right left and centre, and the earth churned and thrown aside leaving a multitude of great craters. The bombing resulted in a good concentration of explosions and much damage to the gun emplacements. Our bomb load 13 X 1,000 lbs. and 2 X 500 lbs.

On the return flight to base, fog had closed in, and we were diverted to Spilsbury, where we were bedded down for the night. We were impressed with their food in the mess and promised to drop in again for a meal if we were passing. Our home base was closed by the fog until almost mid-day and so we had time to get to know our navigator (W/Cdr Tony Willis"s had returned to 460 squadron for his second tour and Barrie Beaumont who had stated and done three trips with Ken Godwin, then became Tony Willis navigator. He had been crewed with us for this trip and did a further four operations with our crew. We had time to quiz him on his operations as follows:

"On the 2 December, 1943 taking off at 1650 hours they headed for Berlin in "G" George, and due to inaccurate wind forecasts the bombers became scattered, they were ½ an hour late over the target. The Germans had identified Berlin as the target 19 minutes before Zero Hour and many fighters were waiting.

Out of 450 aircraft a total of 40 were shot down, 37 Lancasters, 2 Halifaxes and 1 Mosquito. 460 (Australian) Squadron lost 5 of its 25 Lancasters on this raid including the aircraft in which two newspaper reporters were flying. These were Captain Creig of the Daily Mail and Norman Stockton of the Sydney Sun. The body of Mr Stockton is buried in the Berlin War Cemetery.

On 16th December 1943, Ken Godwin in "D" Donald on return to base found the fog had reduced ceiling visibility to approximately 200ft. and flying too low in keeping under the fog base, he crashed the aircraft with several injuries to the crewmen.

Barrie Beaumont was gashed about the face. In hospital when smoking he could blow the smoke out of three holes in his nose. He didn't fly with Ken Godwin again but was navigator to Tony Willis who had returned to 460 squadron to do his 2nd tour".

After our navigator, Don Hudspeth, was grounded with a smashed arm from our raid on Stettin, Barrie did five trips as our navigator to complete his tour. The engineer in Godwin's crew, after the crash on the 16 December, 1943, was unable to carry on because of his nervous condition and was transferred to Transport command, where he was engaged in ferrying aircraft across the Atlantic.

Ken Godwin was shot down on the Leipzig raid. His bomb aimer Vern Dellitt later had this to say:
"On 19 February, 1944 in "H" Harry they were detailed to raid on Leipzig. Taking off at 2330 with a 4,000lb cookie bomb and 8,000lbs of incendiaries, we climbed out and back over Lincolnshire, to reach 12,000ft before setting course and still climbing on track to reach the operating height when crossing the German Coast just South of Bremen. The course was then set to eventually, with a couple of corrections, bring our plane to a point 35Ks North of Hanover, where we were to change course for the run into the target.

The German fighter controller had only sent a small force of fighters to the mine laying off Kiel that night and recalled the remainder of his fighter pack to attack the main Bomber Force as it crossed the Dutch Coast.

The bomber stream was under attack all the way from the coast to the target and back".

From a force of 561 Lancasters, 255 Halifaxes, 7 Mosquitoes, 44 Lancasters and 34 Halifaxes whose loss rate was 13.3% of those dispatched and 14.9% of those which reached the enemy coast had turned back.
The Halifax 11s and Vs after this raid were permanently withdrawn from operations to Germany.

"It was a moonless night, with scattered light cloud, as we flew closer to Hanover. Suddenly the bright cleaving shaft of searchlights and bursting flak lit up the sky indicating we were close to Hanover. Ahead and over to starboard, a bomber blew up, and a second later another bomber received a direct hit and burst into flames as it arced over into a death dive toward the ground.

Mike Wiggins our stand in RAF navigator ordered a change course to 135° in one and a half minutes time. Our pilot Ken Godwin had only just repeated the course change to the navigator when a long stream of tracer bullets came pouring through the fuselage surrounding me in a ball of fire as they flew all round me on their way out into the blackness of the night in front of the plane.

A German fighter had riddled our plane from tail to nose, and setting us on fire, in a couple of short bursts of canon and machine gun fire. It was so dark it would have been impossible for the fighter pilot to see us without some form of radar aid. From the bomb aimers position where it was normal to see the searchlights and ack ack out in front of me it was a weird and frightening sensation to have these streams of tracer pouring out of the nose of our Lancaster on each side of me. They were so close the guns seemed to be shooting right over each of my shoulders.

The skipper immediately started checking on each member of the crew. As the bomb aimer I immediately reported OK and the engineer likewise, but the navigator was busily fighting a fire in his compartment and his black out curtain was engulfed in flames. There were no further replies from either of the two gunners nor the wireless operator. The engineer immediately went to the navigator's aid fighting the fire.

The skipper became very concerned at the glare around the back of the plane. The plane appeared to be well and truly on fire and starting to go into a dive and with the incendiaries loaded in the bomb bay starting to burn he gave the order to bail out.

I released the escape hatch a 23inches wide x 26 inches long, often called the parachute hatch, but it stuck and I had to give it a good thump with my boot to release it. I had got rid of my oxygen mask and headphones so that I had nothing round my head which could get caught and possibly choke me, and was almost ready to jump, when suddenly someone behind jumped into my back.

I was forcibly thrown through the escape hatch, my legs caught on the rear edge of the hatch and I was swinging pendulum like from the plane in the slip stream. Thankfully someone grabbed my legs and freed them shoving me plunging down into the blackness.

I had left the plane somewhere around 20,000feet and I was a little fearful lest my parachute didn't open. Being somewhat dazed, from my pummelling exit from the plane, I let myself fall for some distance before pulling the rip cord and had a moment of panic, which seemed like hours, fearful lest my chute didn't open.

It seemed ages as I floated down then in a break in the clouds I saw our plane a mass of flames heading earthward. I watched fascinated as it hit and exploded splattering the remains all over the ground. Blue Hennessy, (w/op), Jack Morris, (mid/upper gunner), both of Sydney, Hake Clarkeson, (tail/gunner) Wiggin, and Sgt Wood, (engineer) RAF all perished in the plane. Ken Godwin, pilot, escaped by parachute but was murdered on the ground. Mike Wiggins, navigator, and myself, Vern Dellitt, bomb aimer were the only survivors.

Descending through the layer of cloud in the descent was a grim experience, very bumpy and swirling air currents had me swinging almost horizontally under my parachute canopy.

The ground came up very quickly and I was lucky to land on my feet. My chute, collapsing in a heap, pulled me onto my back. I gathered them all up and hid them under the snow near a hedge. Wearing only one flying boot and two pair of socks on the other foot I made my way in the dark across the fields. It was so dark I was almost into farm houses before I saw them. The barking of a couple of dogs had me worried that they would raise an alarm. The rough frozen ground made progress very difficult especially with only one boot. To help preserve my mobility, as my unbooted foot was suffering and I was frightened of frostbite on my feet, I kept swapping the boot from foot to foot,

Using the small escape compass I traveled in a Northerly direction. After what seemed hours I heard the thundering noise as the bomber fleet, heading West, passed overhead. It was a most depressing moment to think that I should be up there heading back to a crackerjack breakfast and the comparative comfort of a warm bed, instead of in enemy country, where I was feeling my plight badly. The cold, and already feeling hungry, was giving me a fit of the miseries. I was extremely tired and although I lay on the cold hard snow I could not sleep. Deciding to keep moving I carried on and came to a single track railway line which I followed for some miles, hiding to one side as each train came by.

At daybreak I spotted an old shed on a disused target range pit where I hid during the day. I slept fitfully on a piece of old Hessian spread over a rough seat, but it was too cold, even the water in my little bottle had frozen. From my silken escape maps I planned to head for Rostok where I hoped to get a ship headed to Sweden.

As soon as it was dark I headed out and later in the night I crossed over a marshy section which was covered in ice. Several times the ice broke and I got my feet wet but I carried on and finally reached high firm ground. I kept moving all night to keep warm and was lucky at it got lighter to spot an old horse stall out in the open, seemingly miles from anywhere. I entered and was soon asleep.

About three hours later I was awakened by a couple of farm hands, who thought I was an American. They walked me about a mile to the neighboring village, leaving me at the Burger masters office. I was guarded by a soldier, until later in the day, a covered truck in the charge of an officer came to collect me. Despite the fact that I was ravenously hunger and pleaded for food I did not receive any.

I was taken to the local fighter dome. A number of American airmen had also been brought there and we were being interrogated. Apart from my name, number, and rank I would not answer any more questions and I was left alone while the interrogating officer concentrated on the Yanks. Information that a couple of them gave was in my opinion more than what they should have given. The interrogation was interrupted when they brought in our navigator, who was visibly the worse for wear showing cuts and bruising about the face and head suffered when escaping from our burning plane.

We were talking with a Yank when a high ranking fighter pilot strolled in his chest covered by several decoration ribbons, signifying his large tally of allied planes shot down. He had been educated for several years at an English public school and spoke perfect English with no trace of an accent. He had spent two years in several parts of America and after chatting socially for a while the yanks suddenly decided he had shot them down?

They discussed the method of the attack and their defence. This good natured sporting discussion on planes, equipment, ammunition used was an example of efficient, deceptive interrogation socially disguised. After a few moments the officer fighter pilot left and we were taken to another compound and locked in a room. Here we were given some rough food which had been cooked by French prisoners, who did their best to make the food as appetizing as possible. We had an impromptu party with one of the Yanks acting interpreter and some song singing.

About mid-day, next day the air raid sirens started wailing and the Luftwaffe went into action. Motors started coughing into life, as the ground crews warmed up the fighter plane motors. In a matter of minutes, the pilots were gunning their motors, and taking off straight from the dispersal area, in all directions, regardless of wind direction. As they reached a third of their take off run another lot were starting their take off in a direction 90° from the earlier planes, and when airborne another flight was taking off in the opposite direction underneath them. Me 109s, 110s and Fw 190s approximately 100 had taken off in a keen, wild control in about 15 minutes. Once airborne they flew around the drome formatting at various heights and set off climbing fast in the direction of Hanover.

An American raid was in progress with Fortresses escorted by fighters, and we could hear the bombs exploding and the guns firing continually. The sound of the screaming engines of the diving, dog fighting planes was music to the ears even though it was in deadly earnest. It was a grim reminder of the hell fire we had experienced such a short time before. The German fighters, short on fuel, were landing, refuelling, and taking off again, while the raid was still progressing.

The following morning we were loaded into a train which took us into Hanover, where we changed trains for Frankfurt. At the camp in Frankfurt I was placed in a tiny cell only slightly bigger than the sleeping bunk, no windows for ventilation. Across the end of the cell there were two large pipes which were used for heating and these heating pipes the guard regularly turned on absolutely roasting me over a period of eleven days. Ever since I have not been able to take heat as medical diagnosis has been that this heat torture had ruined my thermo regulatory centre of the brain".

After two years as a prisoner Vern was returned to England where he recovered his health enough o enable him to be retuned to Australia.

Knowing of Barrie's record we were happy to have him along as an experienced navigator. After our lunch at 1435 we returned to base in 35 minutes flying.

With 549 aircraft attacking, we raided Neuss on 23 September. Visibility was not particularly good with much of the target obscured by fog and low cloud but, thanks to our H2S, once again we were able to clearly identify the area. The fires were silhouetted on the clouds after the first wave of bombers had dropped their loads in the dock area and the surrounding factory buildings. A local German report said there were 617 houses and 14 public buildings destroyed or seriously damaged, 289 people killed and 150 injured. There was little flak. Our bomb load 13 X 1,000 lbs. 4 X 500 lbs.

Timed to take off at 0720 on 25 September flying in "G2" we attacked gun sites in the Calais area. Bomb load was 13 X 1,000 lbs. and 4 X 500 lbs. Due to the uncertainty of the front line and the heavy cloud cover we were ordered to orbit, not a particularly pleasant way of flying in a bomber stream, as there was always an extreme danger of collisions. We were recalled, after flying over the target for some fifteen minutes, and no bombs were dropped.

With 188 aircraft on the raid and due to the low height we were flying, and accurate flak, 8 aircraft were shot down but this raid was declared a non counting raid. This was not fair and above board when, even though many of our fellow aircrew had got the chop, and we had risked our lives in flying the raid, it could not be counted in our tour of duty.

The next raid was on guns and troop concentrations on Cape Griz Nez The clear weather on 26th September, made the sighting of the target much easier resulting in extremely accurate bombing. There was much damage. The trip was uneventful. Our bomb load was, 13 X 1,000 lbs. and 4 X 500 lbs.

A break in the weather created an opportunity for a raid on Calais, with 341 aircraft on the target. Take off time on 27 September was at 0740. Arriving over the target we found it covered in cloud.

The Master Bomber called us down below cloud to bomb, at a very low level. It was extremely rough from turbulence as we passed over the exploding bombs. The raid had a good result. Our bomb load was, 13 X 1,000 lbs. and 4 X 500 lbs. Perhaps we were a little battle hardened but this raid was not really very interesting as we felt we were only being used to help out the army, and on some of these types of raids, our capacity was not being used to its full effectiveness.

With the weather next day still reasonable, the briefing was for a raid on Calais taking off at 0815 on 28 September. There would be an attacking force of 494 aircraft, with fifty aircraft per target bombing several positions. Some planes were able to bomb, but as the cloud conditions worsened the Master Bomber called off the raid.

Because the raid was cancelled after zero hour, even though many of us had been unable to bomb against the master bomber's instruction, we were allowed to count this as a trip, but only after the crews had demanded a fair deal on these short trips. Afterwards they were counted as half a trip. How funny, how can anyone fly half a trip?

Flying Officer Ritchens flew on this raid with us to gain experience before taking his own crew on a raid. Our bomb load 13 X 1,000 lbs. and 4 X 500 lbs

Soon after this raid the Germans in the Calais area surrendered to the Canadians.

The use of radar was being seriously considered in the bombing of targets as bad weather was creating difficulties in sighting the target. Many times the aircraft had been unable to bomb because the target had not been correctly identified. Back in "K2" flying in a group formation on the 2 October, we flew over the City of York, using radar as a means of identifying the target.

I had been promoted Warrant Officer from 4 October and received my new peaked officer cap, and badges.

American Third Army forces were headed toward the Saarbrucken area and requested a raid to cut the supply route in that area on the 5 October intending at the same time to cut the Saarbrucken railway. Take off time was 1830 flying in K2 "Killer". This was the first raid on this area for some time, and was set up to cause as much fire damage as possible. Our bomb load, 1 X 4,000 lbs. and 14 X 450 lbs. incendiaries (clusters)

We were bombing in the third wave of bombers and as we approached the target, the city was blazing from end to end. There was not a great deal of flak over the city. However on the way out of the target area fighters were very active, and we had several close shaves, with them passing very close. Because the fighters were so close, and the closing speed usually too fast as the fighters were angling in from the side and front, our gunners found it impossible to get a shot at them.

A Fw 190 made a belly attack firing about 200 rounds, before Ted our pilot, put K2 into a dive toward the attacking plane's line of fire. This manoeuvre immediately decreased the angle between the planes, resulting in the fighter plane's bullets passing out wide. It was too quick for the rear or upper gunners to return the fire.

An Fw 190 pilot aimed for us and broke off the attack at 400 yards. We had no further attacks. It seemed that in this target area the German pilots did not have the same level of experience as the pilots we had usually met up with on the bigger more defensive targets. A German report revealed heavy damage resulting in 5,882 houses destroyed 1141 seriously damaged, 344 people killed.

We returned to base without further incident. However the weather had closed in at base, and we were diverted to Shipham. Number one priority was to get the Lancasters back to base so as soon as the weather had cleared at base. We took off and returned at 1120.

There was always work to be done on the planes after a raid, and first priority was to have them on standby, for bombing up immediately flying orders were received for the next raid.

Following the parachuting of the British Parachute Regiment known as the "red devils" into the Arnhem Gap

Bomber Command was detailed on 7 October to attack five nearby targets where the supplies were getting through to the German forces.

On a Saturday afternoon Flying in K2 "Killer" in a force of 340 Lancasters and 10 Mosquitos of 1, 3, & 8 Groups we carried out a very successful raid, on Emmerich an important road and rail centre, on the Rhine River.

Emmerich was almost entirely destroyed, with 2,424 buildings demolished and 689 damaged. Surprisingly, a very high smokestack was left standing at one of the factories on the Western outskirts of the city. There were casualties on the ground with 96 soldiers and 641 civilians killed.

From a maximum effort on this raid 460 Squadron out of the 31 Lancasters sent, lost only one commanded by Flight/Lieutenant Eric. R. Greenacre, DFC. who was on the fourth trip of his second tour, having completed his first tour on 460 Squadron in 1943. He was quite a long way south of the target when they were hit.

We saw only five parachutes blossom, just before the plane nose dived to the ground. The Germans took the crew members prisoner. When released Eric Greenacre and a few others had difficulty in getting back to England. They stole a small keg of rum and used it to bribe truck drivers to give them a lift to the coast. The trucks were ferrying supplies from the French coast for the Allies. The English engineer in this crew became a Group Captain in the post war RAF.

Flying /Officer D.K.Gratton in PB254 AR-K was hit by incendiaries over the target causing a serious fire in the Wireless/Operator's compartment. Gratton gave the order to bale out, and three baled out.

The Wireless/Operator grabbed the incendiary in his jacket and threw it out down the photo flash tube, and managed to put the fire out. On their return to England Gratton made a crash landing at Hawkinge in Kent.

From reports on the squadron after the raid some of the crew members who baled out were shot by ground fire as they came down on their parachutes. The navigator W/O K.G.Potter, from Hobart, died in the descent.

We were well aware of Dr Goebbels and his propaganda about the *"Terrorfliegers"* the term he used in his broadcasts in describing the bomber command aircrews and of the damage they were doing to his beloved *"Fatherland"*. Of course it was easy to forget the damage the German aircrews had done to English cities, London, Coventry, York, Hull, Bournemouth, Brighton, etc.

This propaganda broadcast to the German people stirred up such hatred of the Bomber Command aircrews that should they be shot down and parachute to save their life their safety was in jeopardy, as the German people were known to have attacked and beaten them up before the authorities rescued them. On occasions this mob attack had also developed into a lynching.

This type of treatment we knew happened as many aircrew had been shot to pieces either by the fighter pilots, or shot from the ground as they parachuted down, whilst others were killed after capture. Not a great deal could be done about this type of, for the want of a better word "murder" but we recognised the possibility of being shot when parachuting as one of the many hazards of our profession

Our target photo showed another Lancaster going down in flames, after being hit by an ack ack shell. His port inner motor was set on fire, and the plane nosedived. As it went down the wing tore off and the plane curved away to the right, blowing up on impact on the South bank of the Rhine River. No one escaped from the plane.

I always thought had he not been hit, then that shell had our "K2"s number on it. There were five planes shot down just round us, in less than a half a minute.

Our photo was enlarged and forwarded to Commander in Chief Bomber Command.

Our bomb load, 1 X 4,000 lbs. 2 SBC 60 X 4, 6 X 750 cluster incendiaries, 6 X 500 cluster incendiaries.   On this raid we were escorted by 21 squadrons of Spitfires and 7 squadrons of Mustangs.

One of our ground crew had pestered the skipper to take him on a nice easy raid to see what it was all about. The intelligence report on Emmerich indicated it was an easy target, so Ted told Artie Shaw, it was O.K. for him to come along with us on this raid.

In a Lancaster there was not much room for any extras and the best place for Artie to get a good eyeful on the way out, was for him to stand right behind the engineer's seat.

After we skirted the barrage from Antwerp, he became quite talkative, and had to be told to keep it quiet, as we needed our intercom clear.

In running through the target, with five planes shot down just round us, Artie was getting quite nervous. As he said afterwards he just didn't like the little black puffs all around us. When he knew it was heavy ack ack bursting round us, it frightened hell out of him.

Our route back to base took us over Amsterdam, which had been liberated, but to have some fun with Artie, I reported we were definitely on track, and we were coming up on Antwerp. (Actually we were approaching Amsterdam).

Artie immediately started pleading with Ted not to fly over Antwerp, as we might get shot down. Once again Ted told him to keep quiet, until we were safely past Antwerp.

Artie got very worried, and was anxiously waiting staring goggle eyed out the window watching and waiting for the shells to start flying. We were enjoying his agitation.

When he found out there was no ack ack, he guessed we had been pulling his leg. He was so relieved we were safely over the English Channel we couldn't stop his nervous chatter.

When we landed he was first out, kneeled down and kissed the ground and turned on us "Never again, you bastards, you could have got me killed. Fancy telling me that was an easy trip, I'll never fly with you again!" I bet in the years ahead that he would have been very happy, as he would at least have done one trip.

This raid brought to mind a comment passed by an earlier pilot on 460 Squadron. Flying Officer Joe Munsch, who said he and his crew were just lucky to have survived. He often saw Lancasters falling from the sky over Germany "like peas from a pod". Some were in mid air collisions. German night fighters and flak shot down some, and some hit by bombs dropped by other Lancasters.

In the evening Frank and I decided to go to the dance at Cleethorpes. It was a soothing place to relax with some good music and a break away from Binbrook. I was having a dance with a lovely lady who said "You Aussies have a wonderful life, always at this dance enjoying yourself, you don't seem to have a lot to do".

I was feeling a little raw after our raid in the afternoon and seeing many of our mates get the chop (shot down).

I said to her: "What were you doing this afternoon at three o'clock?" She thought for a minute, and then she said: "Well, let me see, I did the washing after lunch, then I hung it out. Oh and then, I was talking to the next door neighbour over the side fence. Why, what were you doing?"

"You know how the English paratroopers the "red devils" were caught and trapped in the Arnhem Gap.

We raided Emmerich completely destroying the city at 3 o'clock this afternoon. It is one of the supply routes for the Germans who have the paratroopers trapped and the idea was to cut the German supply line.

Unfortunately we had five planes shot down just round us, as a result 35 of our mates got the chop in a couple of minutes. The reason we are here tonight is to try and forget about it", She was most apologetic, realising that appearances can be misleading.

Training was always on and even though we were nearing the end of our tour we still had to keep up our training and also help train the new crews. On 10 October with F/O Finemore as 2nd pilot for experience, fighter affiliation, and bomb dropping, we flew a cross country exercise.

We were rostered for a cross country on 12 October, with landing at Middle Wallop to drop off one of our flight commanders. When we were approaching the drome, the Squadron/Leader asked Ted to fly over Little Middle Wallop, an unsealed grassed Spitfire fighter drome.

He had landed a Lancaster on the field and if Ted thought it would be OK to land, then that is where he would like to be dropped off.

Our approach was full flap, just above stalling speed and with braking hard, we managed to stop on the drome, even though the surface was very rough.

After dropping off the S/Ldr and wishing him a pleasant leave, we taxied downwind to the perimeter fence for our takeoff. Ted taxied as close to the fence as possible and then turning half into wind, with the brakes full on, he called for full take off power.

With the revs full on, he released the brakes, and the old girl fairly leapt into life, racing across the rough surface.

Not able to lift off before the end of the grassed runway, we ran a few yards over a ploughed section of field before lifting off.

Climbing to 1,500ft Ted put the nose down at the centre of the landing field. He then proceeded to beat up the drome in a breathtaking exhibition, from 1500 ft to ground level, then a steep climb, so steep we could look back down over our tail, and see the dust swirling, where we had just passed over.

So steep was our climb, that Ted rolled out at the top of the climb, and after a steep turn, came down again in a steep side slip straightening up at the last minute, as though to land. We were so low, if our wheels had been lowered, they would have been running on the ground: "O.K. Ted you're not flying in a bloody Spitfire, that's enough, let's go!" was our order.

No heavy bomber operations were flown for 48 hours in preparation for this raid, 14 October, on Duisburg Steelworks.

We flew "K2" ND 615 on the old girl's 72nd and last operation before the old plane went back to training command (1656 CU) where she served out the war. She copped a parting shot as we returned with a pretty good sized hole in the side from the moderately heavy ack ack barrage over the target.

With 1,013 heavy bombers taking off at 0647, our orders were to fly under 200 feet over France, climb to bombing height at the German frontier, in order not to alert the fighters where the raid was heading. We had an escort of several squadrons of RAF Spitfires and Mustangs.

Over the target 3,574 tons of high explosive and 820 tons of incendiaries were dropped. 14 bombers, mainly Lancasters, were shot down before the ack ack positions were damaged by the bombing and put partially out of action.

Our bomb load was 13 X 1,000 lbs. and 4 X 500 lbs.

On the same night, at only twenty minutes after midnight, we lifted off in Lancaster "T", the spare aircraft. Duisburg was again the target with 1,005 heavy bombers dropping 4,040 tons of high explosive & 500 tons of incendiaries.

This time we climbed to 12,000 feet for our rendezvous with the bomber stream over Beachey Head. The night sky was cloudless with excellent visibility. From 100 miles short of Duisburg we could clearly see the fires from the morning raid. As we approached the city we could see the fires were widespread and were burning fiercely.

Over these cities in the Ruhr Valley we had lost so many aircrew mates that I doubt whether any of the crewmembers on this raid felt any remorse at the destruction we were inflicting on the city.

We were certainly dropping bombs but they in turn were doing their utmost to shoot us down either by ack ack or by the hundreds of fighter planes constantly flying in the German skies looking to destroy the intruders.

But then such is war, someone starts, and then it becomes a free for all and the side, which can wield the most power, usually comes out on top. The participants are the ones who die or if they are lucky they survive.

Over the target, the German defences seemed to have lost their cohesion, and the ack ack was only spasmodic. It gave the appearance of the defenders being punch drunk, with their firing not nearly as effective as on the morning raid. On the return we could see fires for 200 miles. Bomb load, 13 X 1,000 lbs. and 4 X 500 lbs

Once again that look of extreme fatigue was showing on the young faces, worn out and hardly able to sit at the table to eat. I stood in front of a mirror and thought, who the hell is that old fellow, before I suddenly realised it was myself at 21 years of age.

At this stage I felt absolutely punch drunk and as to any thoughts of the future I don't think I had any. We were trapped on the merry-go-round as our trips slowly crawled toward the finish of our tour.

On 16 October we were listed for a quick flight airtesting of turrets, guns, engines, bomb doors and equipment, in the new plane which was our replacement Lancaster ND 971 "K2". We certainly hoped this plane would be as lucky for all the crews who were to fly this plane as the old "Killer".

Taking off at 1645 on 19 October we climbed on full power to our rendezvous point for a raid on Stuttgart. Ever since being last over the target twice, and lucky enough to escape being shot down, we had always made it a policy to be early in our time slot over the target.

We had enjoyed a reasonably quiet run to the target, although the weather was shocking and very rough. We had to climb to 24,000feet to get above the weather front.

The old "K2" could not reach that height so we felt our new plane had a little more "oomph" in getting us up higher. Suddenly, our stand-in-navigator started giving instructions on the bombing: "We must bomb on the red! We can't bomb on the green! We have to wait two and a half minutes to zero hour before we bomb!"

"Bomb Aimer to Navigator: keep quiet please this is unnecessary chatter interfering with our bombing run!" Bomb Aimer to Skipper: "Right 10 degrees, Steady ---------Steady ----------Left-Left ---------Steady Bomb doors open, Steady ---Left---Left a little----- Steady bombs gone, bomb doors closed", suddenly:

"Navigator to bomb aimer, we have to wait for a photo"
"Bomb aimer to Navigator, Ok---Ok—don't get excited!
We've done this before. We always get our photograph".

We were lucky over the target with not very much flak, or perhaps because of our new plane flying so much higher perhaps we were over the top of the light flak. Fighters were also lacking in numbers as we passed through the target area. As we neared the coast of France the weather cleared considerably and the return to base was uneventful.

When we stepped from the plane, our rear gunner Dick Bates, said to the navigator: "How many trips have you had matey?" and the navigator said; "That was my first !". Dick replied "Well you certainly learned a few things tonight, especially when to speak, and when not to speak on the intercom!" Our bomb load was, 1 X 4,000 lbs. and 12/150 X 4lbs. incendiaries

On 23 October, taking off at 1637 we were to join in the biggest RAF air raid of the war on Essen. There were 1,055 heavy bombers taking part. The tonnage to be dropped was 4,538 tons (incl. 509 X 4,000 lb cookies)

As we approached the target many thoughts came to mind. Here we were on our crews twenty seventh raid. A new "K2" would we be as lucky as we had been. We had seen many crews shot down but we were not going to get the chop. It would always have to be someone else. Can we last with only three more to go??

Suddenly, just underneath us I spotted a Lancaster weaving madly (weaving had been an earlier tactic aimed at dodging fighters or flak but had generally been discontinued on account of the danger of collisions in a heavy bomber stream).

What was he doing below the main stream over the target, he watch his height rather than he concentrate on weaving? Flying just under other planes was a dangerous habit when the bombs were being dropped.

Our crew believed that straight and level and perhaps a build up of speed was the quicker way through a target and had saved our skins a time or two. But for the moment we keep an eye on this weaver as we don't want him to get too close as he is dangerous and could be involved in a collision.

Down go the markers as the ack ack opens up. The sweeping beams of the searchlights are trying to pick up the raiders. Down below the bombs were exploding and the shock waves from the cookies were creating a shimmering mass of shock rings. With 500 plus cookie blockbusters going down, it wasn't hard to imagine the chaos below.

The ack ack was still pretty deadly but although the air was alive with flak it wasn't being nearly as frightening as we had experienced; perhaps we were becoming a little too confident, and had better watch what we were doing. Our raid went very smoothly with not much of a problem with the flak over the target. Otherwise it was uneventful.

Reports from Essen indicated a very damaging raid. There were 607 buildings destroyed and 812 seriously damaged. There were 612 people killed and 569 injured. Our bomb load was, 1 X 4,000 lbs. 14 X 14 clusters incendiaries and 2 X 60 X 4lbs.

F/O Richen's Lancaster was hit over the target, and his mid upper gunner, F/Sgt Jack Cannon, of Melbourne, was wounded and rendered unconscious. On the way back to base the plane crashed into a hill, blowing up on impact. F/Sgt Cannon, the only survivor, was blown clear still strapped in his turret.

The turret landed in a tree, approximately a half of a mile away. In the dark Cannon recovering consciousness, climbed from his turret, not knowing he was up a tree, and in doing so fell to the ground injuring both ankles. To hide any evidence of someone landing by parachute, he buried his parachute and harness.

He then took the knife from the hidden pocket in the top of his flying boot, and cut the tops from his flying boots, giving them the appearance of local work boots. He wandered round for two days, and then seeing a large stately building and believing himself to be in Germany was being extra careful.

He sighted an old man working in the field and half crawling, half-walking crept up behind him. Placing his arm round the farmer's neck, and holding the knife to his throat, he asked in German (from a small multiple language card we carried): "Where am I?" receiving no answer, Cannon asked in French: "Where am I?" still receiving no answer, in exasperation he said:

"I wish you bastards could speak English!" to which the elderly farmer answered,

"Thee be in Norfolk lad, over yon is Kings Lynn!"

From the time that F/O Richens had flown on his experience raid with our crew, his bomb aimer Wren Stobo had befriended me and looked to me for guidance in settling in on the squadron, and learning the ropes.

He was a very striking fellow in colouring very fair, his hair a flaxen colour and could easily be taken for albino except his eyes were blue. For some reason he was very popular with the girls.

A couple of days before this raid Wren confided in me, that he had received a white feather from Australia, accusing him of being a Jap dodger and I could see it had visibly upset him. I said to him don't let it worry you, the person who sent the feather should be the one receiving it. I think we should let our hair down and head to the dance in Grimsby tomorrow night if we are not flying. We agreed this would be a good outing.

Before going out on any raid Wren maintained that for his luck it depended on firstly, a kiss and a cuddle with a WAAF (of course not so politely stated) and secondly to piss on the Lancaster's tailwheel before the takeoff.

In this crash Wren Stobo was among those killed. I often wondered whether or not he was shooting a line, as a bit of bravado, and whether it was the kiss and a cuddle or the piss on the tail wheel he missed out on that last fatal raid to Essen.

With our tour almost over we were becoming very conscious of our luck to survive and it was doubly upsetting losing Wren as a friend. It was a reminder not to make any close friends among bomber aircrews, because the friendship had a horrible tendency to be short lived. Secondly, never make appointments you may not be able to keep.

I was rather conservative in my good luck charm. In my luggage I carried a German Iron Cross, given to me by my uncle. He took it from a dead German in the first World War, and presented it to me for luck, hoping I would bring it back home.

I also carried in my top left hand battledress pocket, a sprig of Scottish heather, given to me by a Scotch family I had met in Girvan whilst flying from West Freugh. As soon as the debriefing was finished on the 24 October Ted was told we were stood down for ten days leave. Why can't we carry on and finish our tour instead of this waiting? Tension was mounting in the crew and we were all of a mind to get the operational flying finished as we were so close to the end of our tour.

Only three more trips to finish our tour and here we are off on leave to sweat it out for a few more days.

Dress Uniform (Menzies Blue Orchids)

Laurie Woods on the RAAF Reserve Nov. 1941 training in Hobart.

Aircraftman Class 11 (AC2) Summer uniform (Cutin's Cowboys)

RAAF Station Band Ascot Vale ready for the welcome home to the 9th Division from the middle east. This band led the parade in April 1943. Included 4 aircrew (myself extreme left front row) awaiting overseas posting.

Australian Aircrew at Camp Myles Standish, Taunton, Massachusetts. USA June. 1943

Litchfield Cathedral and crewmembers:

Steve Turner (NSW), Don Hudspeth (Tasmania), Laurie Woods (Tasmania), Ted Owen (Victoria).

Flight Sergeants: Laurie Woods, Steve Turner, Ted Owen, fooling in the snow.
Lichfield No. 27 Operational Training Unit earlyJanuary 1944.

Below: Aircrews preparing for a three day shovelling snow from runways.

A game of tennis on the squadron court
Cpl. Jack Hill, Melbourne, F/Sgt Laurie Woods, Hobart, Sgt. Bill Young, Newcastle, NSW

K2 crew l to r: Dick Bates (rear gunner) Roma, Qld,
Don Hudspeth (navigator) Hobart, Tasmania,
Frank Mayor, (mid upper gunner) Burnley, Lancs
Peter Odell (Engineer) Sandy, Bedfordshire Front:
Steve Turner, (wireless/op. air gunner) Red Hill, NSW,
Ted Owen (pilot) Warrnambool, Vic.
Laurie Woods, (bomb aimer) Hobart, Tasmania.

Crews who flew raids in Lancaster "K2" 460 squadron.1944

P/O Neal 23 P/O Owen 18 P/O Tardent 7
P/O Daley 5 F/O Grimmett 3 W/Cdr Doudlas 1

Vic Neal and his crew who flew 23 raids in K2 "Killer" speaking with Binbrook CO Group Captain Hughie Edwards VC DSO DFC and CO 460 Squadron 22 yr Wing Commander RK Douglas DFC AFC. The crew left to right: Bill Young, Sgt in charge of the ground crew, GR Beard, bomb aimer, CW Erbage, (obsc) rear gunner, Vic Neal pilot, Bill Gourlay navigator, P Robinson (obsc) W/OP A/G.

Another 460 squadron crew who flew seven trips in Lancaster K2 Killer

Tom Dally S.Aus	Geoff Tallents Vic	Norm Healy W.Aus	Roy Brough, Qld
Rear Gunner	B/Aimer	Mid Upper Gunner	W/Op. A/Gunner

Frank Williams	Ron Tardent, DFC.,	Len Child UK
Navigator	Pilot	Engineer

Inspecting "G for George"

Right Hon. John Curtin Australian Prime Minister official visit Binbrook May 1944
Speaking with Station Commander 460 Squadron
Group Captain Hugh Edwards, VC., DSO., DFC.,

During this visit Group Captain Edwards very forcibly pointed out that the number of white feathers being received by the Australians on 460 squadron was a matter of concern. It was bad for the morale of aircrew, not only for those airmen who received them but also for other airmen who knew of the white feathers arriving. It was not confined only to aircrew but many groundstaff airmen had also received them.

The Prime Minister promised to do his best to stop the feathers being sent. Dr Evatt, Minister of Defence who also visited promised to do his best to have the practise stopped.

226

Waiting for the word to go

460 SQUADRON CREWS AT DISPERSAL WAITING FOR THE WORD TO GO
Squadron Leader Tony Willis on completion of 2nd tour advises crewmember

Flight Commander, Squadron Leader Tony Willis was a very popular member of 460 squadron and displayed true leader qualities during his time at Binbrook. He always mixed freely with the crews as one of the boys and was very encouraging to new crews, assisting them wherever he could .

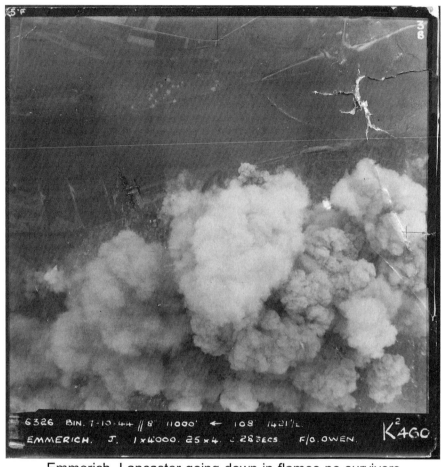

Emmerich. Lancaster going down in flames no survivors. This photo enlarged and sent to Commander in Chief, Bomber Command.

Douai. This photo enlarged and sent to Commander in Chief, Bomber Command. Our bombs scored a direct hit on ammunition train in centre of station yard. Subsequent photo showed terrific explosion running right through the middle of station area.

6/1/1944 Gelsenkirchen 4,000 lb. bomb & incendiaries.
Black puffs in centre are oil storage blown up.
(Photo: RAAF Intelligence Binbrook)

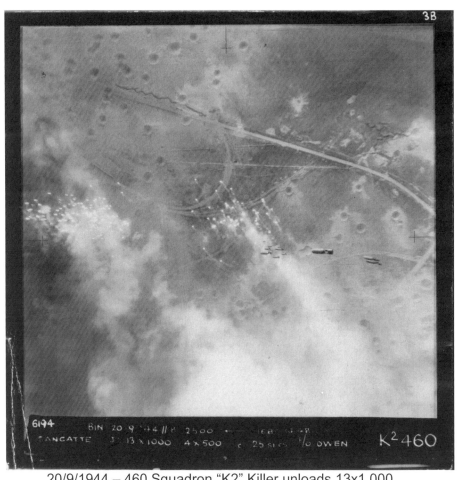

20/9/1944 – 460 Squadron "K2" Killer unloads 13x1,000 lb & 4x500 lb bombs
2nd frontline German troop & gun concentration.

29/8/1944 Stettin incendiary through the roof, hit pilot on head, he dropped one wing, while photo taken then recovered and flew level again.

Photo taken mid Sept 1944 with mid upper gunner Frank Mayor. The author W/O Laurie Woods, early Nov 1944 on completion of his tour showing a marked appearance of fatigue.

CONFIDENTIAL RECOMMENDATIONS FOR HONOURS & AWARDS
IMMEDIATE

AUSTRALIAN

Christian Names: Lawrence William Surname: WOODS
Rank: Warrant Officer (now P/O) Official No.: Aus.408463
Command or Group: No.1 Group Unit: No.460 Squadron, R.A.A.F.

Total hours flown on operations............149.20
Total number of sorties......................30
Total hours flown on operations
since receipt of previous award..............N/A
Number of sorties since receipt of
previous award...............................N/A
Recognition for which recommended............D.F.C.
Appointment held.............................Air Bomber

Particulars of meritorious service for which the recommendation is made:

On the morning of November 9th, 1944, W/O. Woods, an Australian, was the Air Bomber of a Lancaster aircraft detailed to attack the synthetic oil plant at WANNE-EICKEL.

On the run up to the target at a height of 20,000 feet, the aircraft was hit by heavy flak and fragments entered the cockpit and one splinter caused a severe wound on the Captain's face.

W/O Woods assumed control of the aircraft after the target had been bombed and flew it back throughout the entire arduous journey to this Country, where the Captain was assisted back into the pilot's seat to execute a fine landing at MANSTON.

This W/O Bomb-Aimer had no previous practical flying experience, his only assistance in the art had been gained from a few hours spent in the Link Trainer.

During the journey to this Country high cloud and icing were encountered and this caused a temporary unserviceability of the Air Speed Indicator and artificial horizon. At no time was the Bomb-Aimer flustered and he displayed skill, initiative and determination of a high order. His course flying and ability to maintain height were extremely accurate and in consideration of his inexperience the whole performance was remarkable.

It is considered that this incident is an outstanding example of coolness, initiative, resource and purpose and was undoubtedly the means of a valuable crew and aircraft being returned to this Country to further the Nation's war effort.

This was W/O Wood's thirtieth sortie and a fitting conclusion to an excellent tour. In view of this sterling display I strongly recommend the immediate award of the Distinguished Flying Cross.

Group Captain Commanding,
No.460 Squadron, R.A.A.F.

Date:- 23rd November, 1944

REMARKS BY STATION COMMANDER:
I agree with the remarks of the Squadron Commander. This is a fine example of initiative, skill and purpose at the right moment. In addition this Warrant Officer has completed a very successful tour of operations and I strongly recommend him for the immediate award of the Distinguished Flying Cross.

Group Captain Commanding,
R.A.F. Base Station Binbrook

Date:- 23rd November, 1944.

REMARKS BY BASE COMMANDER:
I agree with the Squadron and Station Commander's remarks, and strongly endorse their recommendations. This Warrant Officer has previously done splendid work.

Air Commodore Commanding,
No.12 Base, R.A.F.

Date:- 23rd November, 1944

REMARKS BY AIR OFFICER COMMANDING:
Strongly recommended for the Immediate Award of the Distinguished Flying Cross.

Air Vice Marshal,
Air Officer Commanding,
No.1 Group, R.A.F.

Date:- 25th November, 1944.

CHAPTER EIGHT

STOLEN HAPPY MOMENTS

When I returned to the barracks after this raid, I had a message to ring Emily urgently. After getting cleaned up I rang through, and, when I heard her voice on the phone, I said: "I got your message, what is this about a problem?"

She replied: "Its nothing too bad, but I can't tell you over the phone, it's really nothing very serious." After a little more talk I said: "We have just been stood down for ten days and we're not happy as we would rather keep flying, What can we do with ten days, just waiting around to finish our tour?"

"Why don't you come up to the Lakes District and spend a little time there then perhaps do a day trip to Lake Windemere, or something similar. That will be a change and help keep your mind off the flying?" On the spur of the moment I said "OK, then I'll be on the train tomorrow should be there about lunchtime. I'll give you a call!"

This worked out fine for me, I needed to get away from the squadron for a break as things seemed to have been closing in a little. When you lose a mate a change of place, or a change in the routine seemed to help most.

Early next morning I was up and away to Doncaster on the bus. I never tired of waiting for a train at Doncaster, as there was always a lot of train activity, which I loved. Some people sit and watch fish in a tank but for me it has always been trains. I found this extremely relaxing sitting on the platform and watching the trains go by.

Doncaster was a junction, so whichever way you were travelling, there was never too long a wait. Having checked the train's arrival time, I rang through to Emily and told her my 1315 arrival time.

She told me to wait at the station and she would meet me there. She could be a little late, but not to worry, she would be there as soon as she was able.

The train journey across from Doncaster was most enjoyable, sitting back listening to the staccato bark of the engine's exhaust and the accompanying clickety clack of the wheels on the rails.

The country was looking nice and green and reminded me of parts of Tasmania. The passenger train was not heavily loaded and I had the compartment to myself. This suited me fine as I could sit and just let my mind drift, in a relaxing sort of way.

I had learned from my work on the railway that the activity of a station or area could be gauged by the layout of the yard, the wagons being loaded or unloaded, and any trains waiting to be cleared. This had always grabbed my attention and I was very interested in the wagons and coaches on the other sidings as we arrived at the platform.

When I looked out to check that this was the correct station, I saw Emily. She was dancing almost on tip toe straining to see better, then suddenly she spotted me, and before the train had stopped, she was by the door.

"Hello Laurie, Let me look at you! Why are you wearing a peak cap, what does that mean?"

"Hi Emily, wait a minute. Hullo! I'm very pleased to be here, it's wonderful to see you looking so good and getting so excited, I have been promoted I'm now a Warrant Officer and wear a peaked cap."

"You look tired, have you had a nice trip, did you enjoy the scenery?"

"No! Emily, I'm not tired, only worn out. Yes, I had a nice trip and I enjoyed the journey.

And now tell me what are your problems? And where are we headed?" I took her arm and headed to the station exit.

"Well, now you are here in person, there doesn't seem to be a problem. If we head over to the other side of the square we can catch a bus."

"I have booked us some accommodation at a lovely hotel in Kendall, which is not more than half an hour away." "Tell me Emily, did you book single rooms or a double?" she looked at me, and with her lovely smile said, "Double of course, do you mind?" "Of course I don't mind with someone as lovely as you, but ever since I met you I haven't even kissed you. You are taking a chance."

"Well the kissing part, I'm looking forward to making up a little bit of lost time."

Very soon we arrived in Kendall, only a small village, and the main street had a real twist right in the middle. It was easy to visualise the old horses and coaches rattling through to the coach stop, with the wheels grinding on the cobblestones. Being a country village, the war hadn't really come near it. The hotel was a charming old coaching house type, and I imagined it a very homely and very cosy hotel.

The room booked by Emily was in the back of the hotel, and overlooked the surrounding houses, giving a lovely view across the rolling hills in the background.

After booking in, and being shown the room Emily closed the door and taking me by both hands, asked me if I liked the room and the thought of ten days together.

In answer I put my arms round her and drew her tightly to me, gently kissing those pouting, lovely soft lips. "This is what I like, this to me is so wonderful, to have you here all to myself, it's so wonderful to have you in my arms and nothing to do other than give you nine days of pleasure."

She smiled, and wrapping her arms round my neck and squeezing into me ever so hard, she raised those lovely eager lips, seeking to be kissed.

Her lips were made for kissing, and I could feel her pressing need for plenty of loving. Still kissing passionately, I cupped her lovely face in my hands and softly massaged her neck and her ears, stopping only to give her an extra big hug. Soon I was exploring her clothing, feeling what needed to be undone, and gently started undoing the fastenings.

As I completed each part of her clothing, I lifted it over her head, and dropped it to one side. As each piece was shed it was a delight to run my hands over her lovely soft skin, velvety and desirable.

With no more clothes to remove, I took her in my arms and laid her on the bed.

She felt wonderful, and I fondled her all over, as I gradually shed my clothes. I kissed her all over exploring her intimately. By this time she was enraptured, and it was such a pleasure to satisfy her, again and again as the shadows lengthened outside the windows.

There was no attempt from either of us to stop these caresses. It was such a relief and pleasure to be in the arms of such a gorgeous and responding lover, amazed at the pent up passion, but absolutely enjoying it to the full.

For the first time I was able to study her intimately

She had a wonderful personality, a gorgeous body and an absolutely captivating smile to go with it. Her breasts were delightfully soft, but what I liked about them, was the way they firmed up under a little fondling, seemingly ultra sensitive. I could not get enough of her.

It was my guess, she had both been starved of love and affection, and I was strung up with tension and needed a complete change from flying and the associated tension. Here we were together for nine days with not a thought of the war, and the time was ripe to enjoy each other and not worry about what tomorrow might bring. The pent up hunger released by the touch of a passionate being, assuaged all the tensions and anxieties of the past few months.

For the next nine days we occasionally went for a walk, one day to the lovely old church. We went inside and sat for a long time together in silence just soaking up the peace and quietness.

Another day we took the bus to Windermere and hired a row boat and rowed out to the spot where Major Seagrave had crashed in his speed boat. But our main interest was in enjoying each other, determined to make the most of what time we had and not think of how soon the time would pass and bring us back down to Earth.

It was also away from planes and the thoughts of war, and also obliterated the awful nagging thought of only three more trips. Would we make it and survive?

CHAPTER NINE
BACK ON FLYING OPERATIONS

All too soon the time had flown and it was time to return to Binbrook and back to work. I had one raid to make up on the other members of my crew and I was rostered to fly with F/O Maxton on 4 November in Lancaster "Y" in his crew. It was a raid on Bochum. The take off time was 1720 and our bomb load, 1 X 4,000 lbs. 6 X 1,000 lbs. and 6 X 500 lbs.

The Hague was now in Allied hands and made an ideal rendezvous point for the outgoing bomber stream. Instead of using up fuel in climbing to our formation height over England, now with the rendezvous over The Hague we climbed on track arriving at our bombing height of 18,500 feet, thus saving approx forty five minutes of fuel. Turning on to our new heading we flew direct for the target.

Although the act of weaving had been discouraged because of the danger of collision, particularly in the target area, some pilots still weaved in the belief that they were safer either from fighter attack or they might dodge any ack ack.

F/O Maxton was a weaver, and was continually doing so as we flew toward the target. The weaving seemed strange as I knew this pilot had done a familiarisation raid with Group Captain Hughie Edwards our VC, DSO, DFC, station commander and there was never any indication that the Group Captain weaved. In fact his press on regardless instructions indicated get in quick get the job done, and get to hell out of the target area.

The gunners reported jet fighters to port about 3 miles. They didn't make any move to attack, but rather turned off in the opposite direction. As we approached the target I suggested to the skipper that he cease weaving until the bombs had gone and our target photo taken.

He came back instantly declaring: "I'm the captain of this aircraft, and I will fly it as I see fit, not as you think. Remember matey you are only the bomb aimer. If I choose to weave that's it, I'll weave."

I thought for a moment then: "Bomb aimer to skipper, when we reach the target, you need to fly straight and level for the bombing run." Again over the intercom:

"I'm the captain of this aircraft, and I will fly it as I see fit, "

"OK skipper this is the bomb aimer! prepare to orbit! and we will keep orbiting till you wake up to yourself. Cease this stupid idea you have of weaving. Now orbit!"

After some thought process: "Pilot to bomb aimer. We fly straight and level, prepare to bomb."
"Bomb aimer to pilot OK, skipper, bomb doors open."

We completed our bombing run without further incident, and as we flew out of the target area searchlights were very active and the flak was pretty heavy. The thought flashed through my mind if a pilot insists on weaving what is the best evasive tactical action. It was a hypothetical problem so I decided I would wait and see and if a searchlight should come close then would be the time to act. We had a reasonably clear safe run even though the flak was heavy. We had left the searchlights behind and our run out of the target area was reasonably event free and we enjoyed a safe return to base. One of the most relieved moments of my life was when I stepped from that plane I vowed if I had to fly with another pilot similar to this one I would refuse. He ignored me completely, but his navigator and one of the gunners thanked me. As they said: "We have almost collided with other aircraft a couple of times, but he still carried on with his stupid weaving, we hope you may have stopped him. Anyway thanks for getting stuck into him over it!" I sincerely hoped they would finish their tour safely.

I told them I was happy to get back, and hoped my effort may have helped in some way to cure him of his weaving. It was not only his weaving, but his attitude he was the superior being and his crew were only along for the ride.

From German reports on this raid there was a great deal of damage done to the city, with more than 4,000 buildings destroyed or badly damaged.

Back with my own crew we lifted off at 1155 for a daylight raid on Gelsenkirchen, on the 6 November. What could we expect? Would it still be such a shocking target? The thought had us all on tenterhooks. Our previous raid to Gelsenkirchen had been our yardstick as the most dangerous target we had attacked, but on this occasion the raid was in daylight and we were being escorted by a team of fighter aircraft. It seemed like 500 Spitfires and Mustangs.

It was with much trepidation that we approached the target on our bombing run. Now, whether because of daylight, with not so many of the tracers visible, or whether we were so much more toughened up since our last visit, we seemed to have an easier run through the target. It was not the same harsh and frightening target this time. We were flying higher than on our previous visit and only the heavy flak was bursting round us The flak bursts were fairly concentrated over our bomb release point and it was a fairly heavy barrage
As we dropped our bomb load of 1 X 4,000 and 14 X 150 X 4lbs. incendiaries (clusters) there was still some amount of flak to worry us.

On return to base at interrogation some of the newer crews stated this target was one of the toughest so far. We were probably getting used to the rough targets as we approached the end of our tour. Only one more raid to go. Can we make it?

CHAPTER TEN

THE LUCKY LAST TRIP

On our excellent record our crew was considered a top crew on the squadron as well as being one of the senior crews so we were chosen on 9 November 1944, as the right flank leader. "A" flight commander the centre leader, and "B" flight commander the left flank leader of an arrowhead formation, leading Bomber Command on this raid.

Our navigator for this trip was the squadron navigation leader as our stand-in navigator, Flight Lieutenant Phil Coffey DFM., and we joked with him that we were happy because he wouldn't let us get lost, this being his fifth trip with our crew.

We were to attack the Fischer-Tropsch plant and synthetic oil installations at Wanne Eikel, in the middle of the Ruhr Valley, Germany.

Avro Lancaster aircraft K2 "Killer" was the most photographed Lancaster of 460 Squadron on account of the striking emblem of the swastika being pierced in the heart by a dagger, then with the drips of blood leaking down from the wound. It was a unique emblem. We were to take off at 0805. After climbing to our operating height we were flying just above a heavy cloud layer at 18,500 feet. Looking back over the bomber stream once we had reached our operating height was a terrific sight. The leader to our left, and the whole bomber stream of approximately 1,000 heavy Lancaster and Halifax bombers, strung out keeping station behind us.

Even though there was about nine-tenth cloud cover just below the height of the bomber stream we had a good run to the target. I had just released our bombs on the target when I heard the first crash of a barrage followed by: "Laurie, Laurie, Quick!" from the pilot. I dropped everything, and headed for the skipper.

He was slumped over the control column, and the plane was starting to nose down into a dive. I grabbed hold of the control column and heaved back on the stick, to hold the Lancaster from going steeper into a dive. I signalled the navigation leader (our stand in navigator) to plug in my oxygen, as I had left my oxygen point and needed to be quickly plugged in to the emergency point beside the pilot's position. Lack of oxygen at this height impaired the ability to move quickly and slowed down persons reactions. The engineer had plugged in to this point, well knowing this was an emergency point, it adding to my problems while I desperately tried to hold the plane steady.

The skipper had been severely wounded in the face. He was bleeding profusely from the face wound and was only semi-conscious I directed the navigation leader and the engineer to lift him from his seat, while I climbed into the pilot seat and took complete control of the plane, all in about 15 seconds.

Being a navigator, and familiar with the course, I pulled K2 up and flew above and over the leading Lancasters clear of the rest of the stream on a due West course. I estimated this course would bring us close to Manston, a special emergency landing aerodrome on the heel of England.

In this violent movement up and over the leaders to get onto a westerly course the gyro compass had toppled, but I set course by the sun, whilst opening the four motors up to 2,850 revs, plus 9 pounds of boost (I think), a maximum power setting from Rolls Royce for up to two hours. I estimated we would either be home, or not, in under two hours, even though our trip to the target had taken two and a half hours.

Once clear of the bomber stream I put the nose down, to get us below oxygen height as quickly as possible, in order that the other crew members could take the skipper's oxygen mask off, and treat the wound, under his left eye, which looked really bad. At the time I had grave doubts whether he would remain alive very long.

I requested the navigation leader to give Ted a shot of morphine. He said he had never ever done anything like that and he couldn't. I said he must do it, as I couldn't do the injection and try to fly the plane as well.

Finally he administered a shot of morphine, as Ted seemed to have lost consciousness.

We were later reported, back at 460 squadron, as last seen by Flying Officer Henry Baskerville in a power dive to port, of the main bomber stream He had followed us a short way but couldn't keep up, and he presumed we had crashed near the target.

There was very heavy cloud cover from 18,000 down to 1,500 feet. I levelled at 18,000 feet and despite very rough flying conditions, waited for a break in the clouds.

When a break in the clouds showed I put the nose down steeply, (power remained on all the way). We descended in the break about 4,000 ft. and then went into the cloud again. I was determined not to waste valuable time nor to try circling because we were still in Germany and very vulnerable if we were attacked by fighters

The midupper gunner became very concerned and reported the icing was extremely bad over the wings. Icing over the wings a very dangerous flying condition as icing destroys the ability of the wings to lift the plane, and keep it flying.

With no alternative, I pulled back on the control column bringing the nose of the aircraft up and we climbed out of the clouds. The plane was frightening, listing right over to starboard, with all the instruments had iced up, and the airspeed indicator and artificial horizon was not working.

It was rough weather and flying the plane in such rough conditions I found it extremely difficult. I did wonder a couple of times whether we would get back safely, and whether I would see my family at home again. I didn't dwell on these thoughts as I was determined to save Ted if at all possible. Surprisingly, I had not much thought for myself, it was a matter of a job to save Ted and the crew.

I levelled the plane and had to wait about a half an hour for another break in the clouds during which time the skipper stirred became restless seemingly only semi-conscious and wanted to know where we were and if things were O.K.

I ordered the navigator and the wireless/operator to disconnect him from the intercom, as I didn't want him to become more agitated than he appeared to be. His heavy breathing on the inter communication was a little disturbing. I ordered the navigation leader to give him a part shot of morphine to settle him down.

The next break in the cloud was showing ahead, so I put the nose down, angling into the cloud before the break and despite heavy icing, even though the midupper gunner was getting quite agitated about the heavy icing spreading over the wings, almost pleading in his extremely broad Lancashire accent to get out of it. I held the descent and came into clear air, about halfway down to the cloud base, even though the going was very rough.

The ice cleared a little from the wings, and I estimated at our height, we shouldn't experience much more icing, before coming below the cloud base.

I wasn't going to turn or circle, so I kept the descent going and went into cloud again at about 3,000 feet, with another bout of not such heavy icing on the wings. We flew into reasonably clear but very rough air at 1,500 ft, as we crossed the French coast.

I had been fighting the plane all the way, not game to strap myself in. My left hand was pressed to the canopy to keep me firmly in the seat. It was extremely rough flying weather, and the plane had a definite list to starboard.

We crossed the English Channel the plane being severely buffeted flying in the very rough conditions. About half way across the English Channel, flying at a height of 1,500ft. just under the cloud base and estimating we didn't have much longer flying to reach Manston aerodrome, I requested my first check on our course and requested a position fix from the navigator, which resulted in a 5°starboard correction to our heading.

As we approached the drome, I had formulated a contingency and addressed our problem to the crew, on what would happen on arrival at Manston. I told them it was my intention to climb to 3000 ft. over Manston (the minimum safety height for baling out) where they could bale out if they wished, and I would then attempt to land the plane with our skipper. However if the skipper felt able to land the plane himself, then I would help him.

The rear gunner immediately volunteered to stay, quickly followed by everyone else. I immediately ordered the Wireless/Operator to send a

Mayday call; "Pilot severely wounded in face, bomb aimer flying, headed for straight-in landing Manston".

The Mayday call was answered and the requested landing immediately "Okayed".

The midupper/gunner requested if he could shoot off a few bursts of his guns, while we were still out over the sea, as he hadn't fired them during his tour. I gave permission for a few bursts, but advised him we were still in enemy territory and not to fire too much, but keep plenty of rounds in reserve in case there were enemy fighters around.

We were still all on our own and probably a sitting duck, if we were attacked. I ordered both gunners to keep their eyes especially alert for enemy planes, and not to relax, just because we were almost home.

Shortly after, the runway showed dead ahead, and so I set up for landing, reduced speed, flaps 15 degrees and miraculously the plane levelled up, straight and true.

I guessed we had slight damage to the flap control mechanism, or the hydraulics. Just a fleeting thought, I sure hope the wheels were not damaged and that they go down and lock.

At this time, the skipper was plugged back in, and was indicating he wanted to get back to his seat. After dropping the undercarriage, and with relief seeing the indicators showing the wheels were down, and locked in position, I climbed out of the seat and held the control column steady as we lifted him to his seat. With everyone in their designated crash position, I kept a close check on him as we came in for our landing.

In order that his full concentration was on landing, we signalled him not to worry about controlling flaps, engine speed etc. the engineer Peter Odell did all this. He only had one eye for the runway, and made his best landing ever. A great sigh of relief went up from everyone.

As we ran to a standstill, the skipper collapsed over the controls, and I ordered the engineer to cut the motors and turn off the fuel. We were met by fire tenders, ambulance etc. who came screaming along close by, putting on quite a spectacular display, in case we didn't stop or something happened, like a fire, or explosion, or undercart collapse.

The medics carried the skipper from the plane, and he was operated on later by 2 eye specialists and a nose specialist. They removed a shell splinter approximately two inches long by a quarter of an inch square, which had gone, end on, just under his left eye.

He still had the splinter, as a souvenir, with part of his cheek bone fused into it until he died. The specialists' report was "had it penetrated any further he would probably have been killed instantly". He recovered, and apart from sleeping with one eye open for many years due to nerve damage, he was quite all right, with no damage to the eye itself.

What luck! We had made it! We had finished our tour!

When I returned to my home my mother told me that she had been dozing and had a premonition that I was in deadly danger. She woke very startled and headed straight for the kitchen to make herself a cup of tea. She was joined there by a visiting minister of religion who was staying overnight with my parents, and he inquired if she was all right, as she seemed very disturbed. My mother explained her premonition and the minister suggested that a good prayer from them both would be the best way to help, if I was in danger.

In discussing this with my mother we found that her premonition had occurred at exactly the same time as I took over the controls of the Lancaster from my seriously wounded skipper.

HONOURS AND AWARDS

The pilot Flying Officer Edward Charles Owen, and Warrant Officer Lawrence William Woods, received an Immediate Award Distinguished Flying Cross,

I was immediately commissioned from Warrant/Officer to Pilot Officer, (having been a warrant officer for only one month and four days).

The navigation leader, spare crewmember on the trip, Flight/Lieutenant Phil Coffey, received a Distinguished Flying Cross to add to his Distinguished Flying Medal,

The wireless/operator Flight/Sergeant Steve Turner, a Distinguished Flying Medal.

My personal opinion was that Sgt. Peter Odell, the flight engineer, should have also received a decoration before the wireless operator. He had been of great assistance to me in setting the motors on the power settings I had ordered and generally had supported me in the cockpit, allowing me to concentrate fully on flying the plane. But my opinion was not asked for at the time.

And so ended a very wild ride, the last trip of our tour of operations, and grounding for at least six months. This was obligatory as laid down by Bomber Command, to let the nervous system recover from the battering of six weeks on duty, followed by six days leave.

In our case we were flying this routine of six weeks on six days off on operations for five months.

Flight/Lieutenant Phil Coffey, Navigation leader, and Pilot/Officer Dick Bates, reargunner, were both scrubbed pilots, and were both of the opinion, after we landed that there was no way that they could have possibly flown home under such conditions.

We were reported at base (Binbrook) as having been shot down over the target and last seen in a power dive to the port of the mainstream.

We had landed at 12 noon and the first plane down after us was at 1240 p.m.

We took off at 0805 a.m. bombed the target Wanne Eikel Lat. 51 31 N 7 09 E at 1036 am and crash landed at Manston, Lat 51 20N 1 20 E at 1200 hours, the bearing was 272 Magnetic We had a 35 knot (41m.p.h.) headwind. The outward trip had taken 2 hours thirty minutes and our much faster homeward trip one hour twenty five minutes
Our bomb load was 1 X 4,000 lbs. and 16 X 500lbs

Next day we were flown to Binbrook in Lancaster K2 by a 460 Squadron pilot Pilot/Officer Woods (no relation).

Two days later I was sent to London to be measured for my officer's uniform. On the squadron I kept on getting a greeting "Good show, Gong!" "Gong" was the slang for a decoration, and going to London was good. I would get away from this gong business.

I had travelled to Doncaster to catch the London train, and was waiting on the platform when one of the squadron people came along the platform with the greeting "Good show the other day, Gong, don't you think?" I mumbled something about don't know and excused myself slipping into the toilet to get away. I got on the other end on the train, away from this 460 squadron fellow and the gong greetings.

I was very wary that he might come and join me and I kept a close watch to make sure he was not in sight when we arrived in London. All I wanted to do was to try and forget the last flight and to thank my lucky stars that I was able to do the job and save our plane, and myself.

Arriving in London I went into a hairdresser, where I had been a previous customer, to have my hair cut. It was just on 1300 hours and the barber said to take a seat he would only be a moment.

The next thing I remembered the barber was shaking me: "Would you like me to cut your hair now or come back tomorrow, I've just closed the shop it's 6.30pm. You have been asleep so soundly I didn't like to wake you". I replied: "If you would cut it now please, I have a lot to do tomorrow" he was very sympathetic about my sleeping telling me when I came in I looked dead beat and as soon as I sat down I had gone out like a light.

Next day I was measured for my uniform, filling out the forms etc. I then went to the Boomerang Club for lunch. It was a popular meeting place for Australians and was fairly crowded.

After collecting my food I asked a couple of Australian Navy fellows if I could sit with them, as there was a spare seat at their table.

I asked them where they were from, how they enjoyed the navy life and what ship they were on. When they said submarines I immediately said I wouldn't have that on for all the tea in China. No way would I go in a submarine.

They countered by telling me anyone must be mad flying with everyone shooting at you, at least under the water they only had to worry about depth charges, if the enemy could find them in all that water.

Just a matter of opinion I suppose, but it was interesting talking with them as fellow travellers in another country, and of their experiences.

I stayed in London only briefly as I wanted some sort of action and I wanted to get back to the security of my crew. I returned to Binbrook only to find all my crew gone, either on leave or posted to another station.

Don Hudspeth, was also on leave. For the first time in just under a year I was lost, I didn't have a crew.

I reported to Flight Lieutenant Les Tait our 460 Squadron, bombing leader. He told me I had been selected to go to Blackpool on an air sea rescue officers course. It was intended to appoint an air sea rescue officer to each squadron with rank of Flight Lieutenant.

Leaving in two days time on 28 November the course sounded interesting and could lead to promotion and probably an appointment on the staff on 460 Squadron at Binbrook. I hadn't been to Blackpool, the famous pre-war pleasure resort and I looked forward to the course, and a chance to see Blackpool

I was to accompany a navigator who had just completed a tour on 463 Squadron and had been chosen to do the air-sea rescue officers' course. I believe his name was Colin. With travel documents, we set off for Doncaster, where we caught the train to Blackpool.

This was a change. I was now an officer, and travelled first class. We hadn't gone far when Colin pulled out his cigarettes offering me to sample one of his "Senior Service" cigarettes, which he had acquired when visiting an American Squadron, where they had been diverted recently.

We were sharing a compartment with an Englishman who had a rather high opinion of himself, sitting stiff backed and hadn't even acknowledged our presence.

I was very amused at the difference between the second class passengers who were usually very friendly, and this particular gentleman who, except for a frosty stare when we first entered the compartment hadn't spoken a word. He immediately spoke up, saying this was a non-smoking compartment, and we were not allowed to smoke.

Colin asked who would stop us from smoking, and he replied that he would call the conducter, who would soon stop us! We could step out into the passage and smoke there! I suggested that we leave the smoking for a while.

We sat in silence for a while and I was thinking this fellow sure thinks he is so correct, with his bowler hat, umbrella standing upright between his knees, both hands gloved, one on top of the other resting on the top of his umbrella handle. To complete the picture, his boots were polished, as a gentleman should polish his boots, and he was wearing light grey spats.

Colin turned to me, and said: "Did you hear about Flying Officer so and so, and his navigator in London on leave, and how they invited this very attractive young lady to have a drink with them on the last night of their leave.

They were having a wonderful time, and suggested it was time one of them took her home. The young lady, said: "I have a confession, I'm a prostitute, and you could both come with me, but it will cost you 20/- each". They counted up, and they only had 19/6 left between them.

She said she would give one of them bed and breakfast for the amount. They tossed a coin and the pilot won, and went off with the young lady.

Next morning she fed him bacon and eggs gave him back his money together with a parcel of goodies. She took him in her car to the railway station, and made him promise on his next leave to come to London and spend it with her. She had enjoyed his company so much, she would take a holiday from her occupation, if he came to spend his leave.

Each time now he goes to London and spends his leave with her, and she treats him marvellously. He wanted to marry her and take her back to Australia, but she said no, if they had a difference of opinion, then he might accuse her of being a prostitute.

She refused his proposal, very much to his sorrow, but he is hoping she will change her mind."

As he finished the story Colin said: "Now what about that cigarette?" The old gentleman then piped up: "Excuse me gentlemen, I don't mind if you smoke, I became very interested in your story. It reminded me of an occasion a group of us had to go to London. After the meetings we were taken to the Oxford Circus area, to a couple of young French ladies, in their early twenties."

"They proceeded to show us how sex should be performed, and what an amazing exhibition it was, a real education for us. We were then invited to choose which one we would prefer to engage for a session. Of course only a few were chosen, but not me." This was rather amusing for me, his aloof attitude had disappeared on the mention of the story concerning sex, and he became quite friendly.

By this time, we were arriving in Blackpool and he asked where we were staying. When we told him, he said he knew the area where Mrs Meade's Guest House was along the waterfront, and he very kindly walked down to the road and pointed out the way we should go.

There were twelve of us on the course, all RAF excepting for one American from the USAAF, and myself the only Australian. Needless to say in the room sharing, I was left over with the American.

Mike, I believe his name was. He had been a bombardier in a Flying Fortress and had been severely wounded across the middle of his back and all down his right leg. He told me the most amusing thing about his wounding was the terrific explosion and the same time the plane lurching, and then the navigator who was just in front of him, stood up, and felt himself all down the back even looked at his hands to see if he had any blood on them. Mike casually rubbed his back and was horrified to see his hand covered in blood. After a few moments the pain really hit him. He had completed fifteen missions and after his wounding had immediately been grounded. He was most likeable person. Unfortunately we never recorded each others name and address.

The course was straight forward, all about air/sea rescues, vectoring searches, use of dinghy & equipment, radios, sailing, organising searches, even an experience one afternoon when we were taken to Fleetwood where we drifted for an hour on the freezing water just off shore.

As the chief instructor said "Unless you know what it feels like, you can`t relate to the urgency of their rescue" We could all assure him, "Cold enough to freeze the etc's off a brass monkey".

The next day we went sailing in the large "Q" type dinghy, and also in the airborne lifeboat at Fleetwood. It was good fun but terribly cold on the water.

On 5 December the class and instructors were all assembled for a special announcement by the school's Commanding Officer;

"I am pleased and proud to announce the following;

"The Air Officer Commanding No 1 Group

His Majesty the King on recommendation from Bomber Command HQ has granted the Immediate Award of a Distinguished Flying Cross to

Flying Officer Edward Charles Owen
Aus 409435 and

Warrant Officer Lawrence William Woods,
Aus 408463

For outstanding service in the face of the enemy.

Congratulations on your outstanding effort.

In case you cannot obtain the ribbon locally for this award I have enclosed one ribbon

Signed Air Vice Marshal Wrigley".

A second letter of congratulation and well done was the read from

"Commander in Chief, Bomber Command."

The congratulations had me in a real panic. I was a reluctant hero. I had only done my job.

With all the excitement, and as the CO was a navy Lt/Cdr he ordered "a splicing of the main brace" and miraculously glasses and a bottle of rum appeared. We then got back to our studies.

Next day I turned up and the CO said: "Where is your decoration ribbon. Why aren't you wearing it? It is now part of your uniform."
"Sorry Sir I have no excuses, and I'm sort of still getting used to the idea." Well, tomorrow report to me with the ribbon on!" he replied.

When Mrs Meade heard this, she was so excited, kissed and hugged me, and demanded my jacket, so she could sew the ribbon on for me. Everyone made so much fuss. I was pleased to get away on my own.

After six weeks of solid study on all the factors we might experience in the air sea rescue of flyers who were unfortunate enough to end up in the sea and in need of rescue, or a search and rescue of them, we were set a written test. If we didn't qualify we would have had to repeat the course

My results of the test were top class and I returned to Binbrook, a fully qualified Air/Sea Rescue Officer

GROUNDED! NO FLYING

I rang Emily to tell her of my movements, and of my decoration, which she was very happy and excited about. She told me she was tied up with working a lot of overtime through the Christmas and New Year period and wouldn't be able to have any time off.

With leave for Christmas, I spent a couple of days at Epworth with the Johnson family. They were terrifically happy about my decoration insisting in parading me up and down the street on any little excuse. Then off to church on Sunday, where they showed me the spot where John Wesley had reputedly stood on the cover stone of a crypt, and had even worn footprints. This was the spot where he started his Methodist ministering.

Being at a loose end I returned to Binbrook for New Year. As there were no orders for an immediate appointment as Air Sea Rescue Officer on 460 Squadron, on the 20th January I was posted to the Aircrew Allocation Centre at Brackla. The idea of the centre, or rather school, was to ascertain the best possible way, by aptitude testing and examination, that the Air Force could utilise each persons, aptitude and individual experience.

Catching the northbound train at York I was thrilled to board "The Flying Scotsman" to Edinburgh although she wasn't flying faster than 40mph. I stayed overnight at the "Old Waverley Hotel" and then on to Nairn, on the train line south of Inverness, and then by bus to Brackla. The countryside was covered in snow! And it was cold?

I wrote a letter home to say: "A farmer had paused on the bridge to light his pipe. It was so cold the flame froze on the match. In disgust he threw the match down on the bridge where he was standing. When the warmer weather came the flame thawed out and burned down the bridge."

Mid winter was definitely not the time to be in the north of Scotland, but the classrooms were heated. At night in our Nissen hut we built up the fire in the pot belly stoves (two stoves to each hut), and stoked them as much as we could before going to bed. With all our clothing or paper between the blankets we managed to keep warm overnight.

Our only break whilst on this allocation course was a weekend in Inverness. We had caught a bus to the railway station at Nairn, where the station master told us our train was 27 hours late: "How do we get to Inverness then?" We asked him. "Well, if you wait about 45 minutes, yesterday's train should be here, and you can travel on that one!"

Although snow was forecast we didn't care, as it really didn't matter if we were stranded in Inverness. The city didn't really have a great deal of attraction. We stayed at McDougall's Hotel, and on the Sunday afternoon headed back to Nairn.

It had commenced snowing, and when we arrived there was no bus to take us back to camp. The snow had caused the road to be closed. No question, we had to walk. As we left the rail station, the locals with snowballs and insults attacked us: "You stinking Air Force, bloody Australians, we'll teach you to steal our chickens, take that, and that!"

We didn't know what this was about, but the snow fight that developed warmed us up. We wondered why the locals were so mad at us, just because we were Australian. We forgot about it as we headed through the snow trudging single file toward the RAF station. The first person had to break a track and after leading so far, he would allow everyone to pass and he would take up the rear. In this way everyone shared equally breaking track.

The evening meal had finished when we arrived, but the cooks very kindly got us some food when they heard we had to walk all the way from Nairn. It wasn't until 50 years later I found out why we were attacked by the locals with their snowballs.

The previous course, including ring leaders Geoff Tallents, and Roy Brough, earlier crew members in K2 "Killer" thought when they got back to camp they would be late and miss out on their food. They nicked the farmers' eggs, and cooked them in the mess on their return to camp, but we suffered the revenge from the locals.

In the tests at the end of this school, I gained top marks in the school and was offered a four year navigation school at Cranwell, or repatriation to Australia. As the war in the Pacific was still very much a war, and with prospects of flying Lincolns or Liberator bombers against the Japanese, I chose repatriation. I couldn't see myself remaining in England for another four years.

On the way back to Binbrook I stayed in Edinburgh for three days, and apart from sight seeing, and spending one evening at a circus, I was having a let down, a fit of the miseries. I wanted some sort of action. I returned to Binbrook and found my uniform was ready in London for a fitting.

Being virtually on extended leave, as there was nothing for me to do, I could remain in London for a few days. On the spur of the moment I rang Emily and told her. She was delighted as she had some days off due to her, would I like her to come down to London with me, as she was very much looking forward to being with me.

On the spur of the moment I said, "What a wonderful idea, it would be just like having all my Christmases at once. When and where can we meet, give me a call as soon as you can organise it".

She said, "Oh, wonderful, maybe in a couple of weeks. I need a lot of cheering up, and some of that love as well". My reply to this was, "It's making me feel very anxious already, give me a call as soon as you can get it organised."

I had made all arrangements about my fitting and would be able to get my new officer's uniform within two or three days. This activity lifted me no end. At least I would be occupied. I was missing the flying and I suppose more than anything the separation from my crew which was the hardest to bear as we had been together, a very close group, sharing our lives for the last year.

Being at Binbrook among all the new faces was a little disconcerting. New crews were constantly arriving, and old crews, completing their tours or going missing. In such a short time there were no longer many familiar faces on the squadron.

I was finding that after two months of stepping off the fast lane I was a complete stranger. I only existed in the squadron record book. It was therefore very pleasing to have an activity taking me away for a few days.

Having had a call from Emily I was able to make arrangements about my uniform and was on the train headed for London, looking forward eagerly to the meeting with Emily. All the doubts were behind me. London, by now a reasonably familiar city, was ahead, and it was always an exciting city, with plenty of all types of entertainment.

On arrival I visited the tailor in Oxford Street, for the fitting of my uniform. I really was more comfortable in my battle dress, which most aircrew wore constantly.

After the tailor I headed for the Lancaster Hotel, (or Lancaster Gate Hotel) opposite Hyde Park, which Emily had suggested as a very reasonable and fairly central Hotel to spend our time together.

Early next morning I set out for St Pancras Railway Station, reasonably early, as I always enjoyed exploring the surrounding areas and I certainly wanted to be in plenty of time for the arrival of the train.

English trains were usually very punctual, and right on time the engine driver was drawing the train to a stop at the platform. I felt a little apprehensive, being a rather shy person, but when I spotted Emily, my shyness and apprehension were blown to the winds, as I hurried over and took her in my arms, for such a big hug and long welcoming kiss.

She leaned back and looked me in the eye and giving me her very charming and provocative smile, said: "Gee that was terrific! What about a repeat?" After the repeat I took her arm and we headed for the taxi rank.

Once settled in the bedroom, after a fierce kissing and hugging session, I asked: "Well, what is there in London you would like to see, or what would you like to do, while you are here?" "That's easy," she replied: "I came to London to see you, and what I am going to do right now is make love to you!"

"If we have the time, or the wish, to see something later, well, we will decide after, and now you stop wasting time with your talking!" she said, as she shed her dress. Lying on the bed half undressed, holding out her arms in an enticing way, I could not resist the invitation and had soon joined her.

Even though the urge was mighty strong, it was difficult not to make love immediately, but we had plenty of time. It was much more pleasurable to hurry slowly. Bit by bit we shed our clothes, in between the kissing, and the stroking, until we were completely ready for lovemaking.

She was ever so precious, and whilst I felt I could devour her, I also wished to handle her like a beautiful precious doll.

I don't know which emotion won, but after not having the pleasure of her for a while, and remembering how wonderful she had felt before, I couldn't restrain myself and almost devoured her, savouring to the full her efforts in this wonderful welcome for me.

Time stood still, and for a long long time it was just the two of us, engrossed in giving pleasure to each other. Finally, Emily stirred and suggested that perhaps we should look for a little nourishment to keep our strength up. I was amazed. Time had flown and it was almost normal bedtime. We showered each other slowly, and then dressed, and went out looking for somewhere to satisfy our hunger.

We found a lovely coffee lounge, where we could sit in a secluded corner. We took our time in eating and talking about nothing in particular, mainly of our time together.

The utter relaxation of this meeting was already having a very soothing and satisfying effect on me. No longer did I feel strung up, wanting to do something but not knowing what I needed to be doing. I felt completely at ease with life, and I thanked Emily so much for having come to London to join me if only for a little while.

We spent a lot of time in Hyde Park. It was a wonderful relaxing time. At times we felt like going for a rowboat ride on the Serpentine, as it was so relaxing just drifting, and watching the waterbirds, and enjoying each other's company.

Whenever we desired each other, we took the opportunity, for time was passing. Soon would come the parting, something we didn't look forward to, putting it out of our minds and enjoying the present.

Finally the day came when I saw Emily off on her train. It was rather sad not knowing if we would ever meet again.

HEADING HOME

Next day I returned to Binbrook to find I was posted to Brighton to await repatriation to Australia. I found Don Hudspeth, the last time I saw him and over lunch we caught up with each other's news. The rest of the crew had been posted out to other units. Don described to me the miraculous escape of fellow Tasmanian, Group Captain, Keith Parsons, C.O. of 460 squadron. His Lancaster had been badly hit in a collision – two engines were on fire – the aircraft was in an uncontrollable spin and he had ordered the crew to bale out. He fought in vain to control the aircraft. The engineer couldn't open the jammed escape hatch. The altimeter was gyrating madly and with little height left, the pilot thought "I'm going to get out of this". Above his head the broken perspex seemed the only way out. Standing on his seat he managed to force his way through the jagged hole. His pants were ripped and his leg caught, but as a last desperate effort he pulled his rip cord releasing his parachute, which pulled him clear of the aircraft. Seconds later he was flat on his back in the snow, his burning Lancaster only 50 yards away. He had just made it and the snow had cushioned his fall, enabling him to be back at his squadron desk three days later.

Before leaving the area I called on the Johnson family for a couple of days before bidding them goodbye and after picking up my luggage from Binbrook I headed to Brighton on the second day of March.

I rang Emily to tell her of my leaving for home. My heart was heavy but my ties to Tasmania and family were too strong.

Time in Brighton passed slowly. There was nothing to do as we waited for word on when we would be leaving for Australia. I spent a couple of short periods in London but generally had nothing to keep me occupied.

Finally orders were posted, we must be packed ready to leave next day. For those listed on the draft it was all excitement, whilst those who missed out were not so happy. Leaving Brighton at 2100 by train, headed for our ship, travelling through Doncaster and Newcastle, We stopped at Edinburgh for a cup of tea and biscuit at 1330. Arriving in Greenock at 1600 another cup of tea and biscuit and then on to the magnificent Dutch liner "Nieu Amsterdam" 35,000 tons.

Loading of food and troops was carried on all day and at 1930 we had our first meal in 36 hours. Next day the ship was being loaded all day and at 1930 there was dancing on the promenade deck. The following day 22 April more loading and again dancing in the evening.

At 2140 the anchor was weighed, and, escorted by two "R" class destroyers we set set off down the Clyde River heading for Australia and home.

April 23 The destroyers suddenly opened fire blazing away to port astern at something just over the horizon. The ship was ploughing into a heavy rough sea, and the large waves were causing the ship to rise and fall but the motion was not unpleasant.

The destroyers occasionally steamed in close by our ship and we could see the bow of each destroyer dipping into the waves and as it rose out of the water, the ship crested the wave water flowed back over the foredeck. Whilst it was fascinating to watch the destroyer "shipping the water" we were pleased our ship was not being affected so much by the rough sea. Apart from playing cards or sitting round talking quietly, everybody seemed to be down in the dumps, and deep in their own thoughts.

It was a big break to be leaving England, where many of us had very quickly grown into manhood. We were leaving behind many comrades who would never return and also some comrades who might still not make it home. Many had friends and family who were being left behind, not knowing when they would meet again.

We had counted through all our original course mates from Somers and from 134, we could only count 23 still alive. The next day being Anzac Day, we had a service in the usual format.

On 26 April we had altered course, and steamed almost due east until at 1230 we were picked up by a Catalina flying boat escort. Later at 1500 a Halifax relieved the Catalina, and shortly after, an escorting American destroyer joined us.

At 1700 we caught and passed a convoy of 31 ships, all shapes and sizes, mostly coal burners with a couple of cruisers escorting. They were barely doing 10 knots, and the smaller ones were making heavy weather of it. We were also pitching a little in the following swell.

At 1900 the Catalina suddenly dropped a smoke float astern of us, and one cruiser and the destroyer dashed across to investigate, but there was no further action.

On deck next morning, the ship was sailing so smoothly, we thought we had stopped but for the beat of the propellers. We could see land away to starboard, and guessed we had passed through the Straits of Gibraltar sometime during the night. We had also lost our escorts.

On 30 April at 1800 we sighted land and as we sailed closer we could see the lights red, white, and green as we approached the entrance to the Suez Canal. The canal was the most interesting part of the journey.

On 1 May, the ship hauled on board two boats and their Egyptian owners, selling all sorts of wares, mainly camel and goat skin bags etc. They were dropped off in the evening. We sailed past three burnt out hospital ships, and also a shipload of German prisoners, just arrived from Italy.

At Ismalia, two British destroyers headed for England passed us by, signalling "Bon Voyage". At 1445 we watched a flight of Ansons, dropping 100lb bombs over the sand. A short while later, we passed two Italian battleships, captured in Alexandria in 1942, and still steamed up, and ready to go with Italian crews on board. At 1600 we passed by the remains of a ship which had been blown up and pieces spread for 100 yards along the side of the canal. At 1800 we dropped anchor at Suez for refuelling.

Next morning 2 May at 0800, two American Thunderbolt fighters spent half an hour in a mock shoot up of the ship. Most of us reckoned a pair of Lancasters, would have done ever so much better.

At noon we weighed anchor and steamed our way down and out of the canal at 1500. A submarine surfaced about 3 miles to port and signalled: "Good Luck headed home" It was so hot that many of us slept on deck on the night of 6 May, awakening in the morning to see the African shoreline over to starboard.

What a momentous day V.E. Day 8 May. At 1000 hours the gunners had a practice anti-aircraft gun testing. None of us would have wished to fly through that barrage. In the evening we listened to Churchill's broadcast of the German capitulation, and at 2100 as a celebration, the splice of the main brace took place, with a portion of whisky for everyone.

Being a Tasmanian I had found fellow Tasmanians with whom I cobbered up with

Bill Gourlay, DFC., from Launceston who completed his tour on 460 squadron as navigator in Vic Neale's crew. Bill had designed the swastika emblem on K2 "Killer"

F/Lt Dave Whishaw, DFC, a Beaufighter pilot, from Carrick in Tasmania,

We whiled away many hours together on the way home

AUSTRALIA

On 16 May at 0825 a Beaufort began escorting us and we sighted our beloved Australia at 1240. We were ordered below decks approaching Fremantle, docking at 1430 and had been instructed, no shore leave. We would not abide by this, and threatened we would go over the side, unless we were allowed on shore.

The Officer Commanding Western Approaches, carried out an inspection on the wharf in the morning of 17 May. We were then released with a twelve hour pass. The West Australians had to report back and would be released on arrival in Sydney. We kicked up hell, and the West Aussies were allowed to disembark and finish their journey in Perth.

Many of us hitched a ride to Perth on top of a truckload of timber, having a wonderful view of Perth approaches, as we entered the city. It was so exciting to be back in Australia, the whole scene had that special homecoming beauty, clean, colourful and the sight of Australian type homes, was a sight for sore eyes after the grime and destruction of war torn England.

Our first action was to have a feed of good Australian steak and eggs, which we had only dreamed about since leaving Australia. The joy of the food was dimmed by having candles on the table for illumination, brought about by a coal strike which resulted in no electricity hence candles for illumination.

What was worse was there were no trams running restricting our scenic tour of Perth. It was unbelievable that in the middle of a war some Australians should strike and in doing so disrupt a city, creating a chaotic situation.

From our point of view, many of our aircrew mates had received white feathers, as cowards and Jap dodgers, and died in the battleground in the skies of Europe to save the freedom and our Australian way of life, as well as those who fought the Japanese in the Pacific area. Their sacrifice was not made to give these strikers the luxury of sabotaging the home front. Our comments on these strickers were not suitable for publication.

Having enjoyed being loose in an Australian city for a few hours it was back to Fremantle, where I bought some grapes, the first grapes in two years. After consuming too many, I ended up with a severe tummy ache.

After two nights in port, tugs came alongside and with some shouting of orders, tow ropes were attached. Slowly the 35,000 ton liner was turned in midstream and when ready the tow ropes were cast off, and waving to the crews of the six submarines tethered at the wharf, we steamed out at 1510 on 18 May to resume our voyage.

Crossing the Bight the ship was untroubled by the swell whilst some merchant ships we passed and a couple of destroyers going the other way were making heavy weather of the swells, diving into the troughs then rising toward the crest of the next wave, with water cascading back toward the bridge and the cascading overboard.

There was a great deal of speculation. Would we turn South, and steam up the Derwent River, to the wonderful Harbour at Hobart, or maybe berth in Melbourne. We didn't favour that, then perhaps Sydney. Our guessing was over when in the early morning darkness we turned North East and then later North, it had got to be Sydney.

Arriving off Sydney Heads at 0700 on 23 May we were fogbound. Picking up a pilot at 0845 as the fog was clearing we moved in through the Heads at 1000, passing by the outbound H.MS. carrier "Indomitable" accompanied by two destroyers and two submarines.

The wonderful harbour was bathed in the clear morning sunshine and, as the fog dispersed, came our first sight of the bridge and gradually as we steamed up the harbour the whole scene and the surrounding shores became an unforgettable sight.

It was amazing the hundreds of people on board, thronged the rails, just spellbound, whilst the Australians were exultant and could be heard moving among the others saying again and again – "There you are, isn't that a beautiful harbour, Take a look at our bridge, isn't it a terrific sight. I told you it was a beautiful country". Everyone was in agreement and after the long voyage everyone was happy to be going ashore on dry land.

At 1030 we passed by H.M.A.S "Australia" in dry dock and, 1100 berthed beside the H.M.S. "Illustrious". At 1400 a band played us off the ship.

On disembarking a rookie Pilot Officer immediately started yelling, "Line up here, you airmen". A couple of the fellows looked him over, and he yelled at them "Come on, I mean you airmen".

One of our group, dressed in a light weight Macintosh similar to those worn by naval officers, which was RAF issue, walked up to this rookie officer, and undoing his belt and buttons, he removed his mac. He stood there - a Squadron Leader, wearing DSO and DFC ribbons.

The rookie officer just stood still at attention, and we could see he wished the wharf would open up and let him drop out of sight. When he had been "told" and it was all sorted out, we climbed aboard the buses, and headed to Bradfield Park, where travel was to be arranged to our home towns.

F/Lt Dave Whishaw, DFC, a Beaufighter pilot, from Carrick in Tasmania, through a Mr Houson and Mr Oxborough in Melbourne, had arranged passage for himself and very generously had me included on the Holyman's plane through to Launceston.

We were greeted off the train in Melbourne, by another band, staying overnight in Scott's Hotel, accommodation arranged by Dave's friends.

Next morning we were at Essendon in plenty of time for the plane. Landing at Flinders Island, the 24 year old pilot Frank Griggs, (ex RAAF Flight Lieutenant DFC., DFM.) invited Dave and myself to have a cup of tea with him. He had returned from England and as pilots were in demand for the civil airlines he had taken this job. After the loading and unloading of mail etc., we were airborne at 9.35am and one hour later we were landing at Western Jnc. Dave Whishaw had done his initial flying at Western Jnc. and was quite emotional arriving there to meet up with his family, who, after sorting out the luggage and receiving all the welcome embraces, kindly gave me a lift to the railway station.

Greeting my wife I became fascinated by this lovely little extremely fair curly headed daughter of mine. She was two and a half years old, and seeing her father for the first time she was a little bit shy. For the first few days she would race to me and then suddenly shy away, but gradually, as my wife Marion had introduced me by way of photographs she came to accept me. After a few days in Hobart we travelled by train to Deloraine where my Mother and Father were so happy to have me home. I reciprocated their feelings. It was a hectic couple of weeks with the welcome home parties and my Father and Mother enjoying my home coming in the same manner as many Australian parents welcomed home their family members on their return.

Leave was never long enough and after six weeks disembarkation leave we returned to Melbourne in time for the Japanese surrender, and the VP victory parade through Melbourne. We received a glowing tribute, over the loudspeakers, and much applause from the crowds.

Less than three months later I was released from service to take up a position in the Head Office staff of the Commissioner of Transport

And my war was over.

Reminiscing in the post-war era

The many years have rolled by since the end of the war, and all the arm chair warriors and arm chair historians are busily having their say.

We have been branded Terrorfliegers, Jap dodgers, war criminals who indulged in indiscriminate bombings etc.,

As I sat in my armchair I would say "How the hell would they know, all they have done is read through a lot of the reports and the records and then they pop up their heads, put pen to paper above their names, more probably than not hoping to have a best seller and make their fortune".

But they weren't there. They are only regurgitating what others have written. They are parasites on the memory of those gallant airmen who lost their lives defending freedom and hoping in doing so to make a better world for all of us.

Read the reports and sit and think what a wonderful job was done by Air Chief Marshal Sir Arthur Harris and others. Air Chief Marshal Harris received little credit while he was doing the job, and suffered a lot of criticism for the job he had done.

Just imagine that you have to sit and organise what he did, and make it co-ordinate with what everyone wants, and to satisfy the demands of the other services.
He also had to try and conserve his planes and the manpower at his disposal, whilst each night he consigned the cream of the nation to an almost certain death and in many cases, no known grave.

At the same time he had to marshal his forces to strike at what he considered would yield the ultimate benefit for the Allied effort. Having in mind the indiscriminate bombing of London, Hull, Coventry, York and many other

English cities. The civilian population who were on the receiving end was also demanding its pound of flesh in the damage, which Bomber Command was causing to Germany and the German war effort.

And now we who still remain alive do not get very much credit for the sacrifices in five years of taking the war to Germany and serving in the forefront of the fighting. In doing so we considerably lessened the impact of the war on England and on the devastation of English cities.

I suppose it has been the reluctance of the airmen in not being able to talk of their war service and I found it was a very long time before I could discuss very much about my war experiences without almost breaking down. Therefore I had nothing to say.

Looking back over the years I feel that the best counselling I have ever had is at the squadron reunions and also on Anzac Day when meeting up with those people who have undergone the same experience and who understand our type of war.

It was difficult when nightmares dragged us back into wartime memories, and in seeking medical assistance we had to endure comments from unsympathetic medical people purely because they had not experienced such a battering of the mind and the nervous system.

Comments like, "You are only young, you will get over this" or "It is only in the mind, why don't you knuckle down and get back to work" did not help the peace of mind in any way.

We were not counselled, as counselling was unheard of, and so we resumed our lives determined to do our best. Civilian life was extremely difficult after service life. Many of our service mates went through a period of years where they just drifted before finally picking up their lives

In uniform we were gratefully accepted if we were fighting in the immediate areas. However the homefront people were not so kind to those who fought as we did in the far distant theatre.

Many of us volunteered before Japan entered the war. It was not our choice but we served where we were sent, realising that in the Australian theatre it would have been a terrible waste to keep highly trained aircrew to fly in the antiquated warplanes in the Australian theatre.

When we finished our courses in utilising our training to the best advantage, Germany was the target; it was also the area where the equipment was and the area where many Australian airmen were sent.

Approximately 9,000 members of the RAAF served in Bomber Command and although they were about 2% of all Australian enlistments for all services, yet they accounted for 21% of all Australian combat deaths during the war.

Not only did they suffer these casualties but also a great number of them went to their deaths and their bodies do not rest in a known grave. Many carried with them the memory of having received from Australia white feathers as a sign of cowardice because they were in the European theatre fighting the Germans even though the Japanese forces were threatening their homeland.
Why we ask did we risk our lives for people who sent white feathers to war heroes. I suppose we will still be asking these questions until we too pass away.

I personally feel we were young and idealistic and we were looking for a better world in which to raise future generations. Whether we succeeded by any small measure only the future will reveal.

What we gained personally was an everlasting bond with our mates, and the belief that we are part of a wonderful country which is worth fighting for. A country when all the fighting is over is a wonderful place to come home to.

The offhanded treatment served up to the returning aircrew from the European theatre by RAAF members was surprising. It seemed there was a lot of jealousy and hostility but human nature being what it is it was not surprising to us.

At the war's end there was a mad scramble in the RAF and in the RAAF to get into a theatre of war where they could qualify for some ribbon, whilst at the same time deny ribbons if possible to those who earned them the hard way.

The reunions of my 460 Lancaster squadron, with its brilliant record of achievement is now a highlight of my fading years as once again I sit with my fellow airmen from all parts of the world and reminisce our days of danger and of glory those many long years ago.

Always our reminiscing includes those who served and the 1,018 of our 460 squadron comrades who failed to return

> "For your tomorrow
> They gave their today"

Letter home from Flight Sergeant Geoff Tallents, bomb aimer, of Flying Officer L.V.Tardents' crew, completing a tour of operations in April 1944.

"I heard some bad news the other day. A pal of mine who had completed a tour of ops. was killed while instructing a sprog crew on a training trip. It seems hard that he should have been over enemy territory 30 odd times and then be killed over England while instructing. Gee! There is only about half of our original course left. I believe Bill Walker is just starting his ops. I haven't heard from him or Don Strong either for ages.

Last night a doodle bug cut out right over the top of the house and landed in a gully not ¼ mile away. It must have been very low. The engine noise woke us all. This will be a rather unique letter, as it will be posted in Australia. That's if I'm up in time to catch a pal.

"G". George, an aircraft from our squadron is to be flown home in a few days and the two ground staff lads who will go home in it have been at 460 squadron for years. That is how I know them. The chap who will be posting this is Cookie Ower. Keep your eyes open and you will probably see his photo in the paper. Greg is sitting at the same table as I am writing to his mother so she will get a letter carried by George.

At the moment I am organizing an Aussie rules football team, and am collecting some good recruits, but I am to be posted to Scotland on the 31st of this month. I'll be near Inverness.

My squadron, which is 460 squadron, the senior Australian bomber squadron and which incidentally has the best results in Great Britain, greatest weight of bombs carried, most number of aircraft serviceable etc. is situated at-----. The ground crews are mostly Aussies and we are like one big happy family. Our CO is Group Captain Edwards VC, DSO, DFC. Not a bad cove.

In the morning when operations are called on, we are all tensed up from the word 'Go', and immediately set about our various duties to prepare for the op.

The navigator to prepare his charts and every one is a hive of industry. The ground crews give the craft a good do over and the pilot goes out to see things are correct. You see tractors dragging dozens of trolleys all laden with bombs for the armourers to haul up into the bomb bays. If it is a cookie (4000lber) and incendiaries on the trolleys, everyone says 'Ah, a Town'. If 1000 lbers it is 'Whacko, a railway siding' or something similar. Then the rumours get around about the petrol load. If it's 2,150 gallons the rumours are Stuttgart, Munich, or Frankfurt. If it's 1,400 gallons the cry is 'Happy Valley' meaning the Ruhr. The saying is that you can put your wheels down and taxi along the flak of Happy Valley.

My job is to clean the two front guns, collect all my gear, parachutes, harness, Mae West etc. Then take them out to the kite, put in the guns, check my bomb sight, check all my switches, inspection lamps and fuses, plus a lot of other little gadgets that I have to use. I then help the ground crew clean my perspex. but they generally kick me out as they consider it their job. Everyone is flat out to help each other. The ground crew are proud of their aircraft and proud of the crew if they are a good type. They always give us the thumbs up sign on taxi-ng out.

With all this completed and everything stowed away in its correct place we go to our billets for a rest.

At 6.30 the navigators go to their briefing and prepare the charts. At 7.00 we (the bomb aimers) join them and rule in the maps. It is then that we learn the target. Stuttgart for instance. After we have everything completed we stroll down for the operational meal. An egg (generally cold) on toast and a piece of bacon. The rest of the crew look at us with inquiring eyes, but everyone knows that it is a sin to talk in the mess. Enough news leaks out as it is.

It is a common saying "If you want to know where you are going, go down to the village and ask the publican".

After the meal at 8.00 the crews troop up to the main briefing room and there on the board (the whole wall) is the route to and from the target marked out with a piece of red wool. "Gosh! Stuttgart, 9½ hours". But everyone takes it very calmly, confidently. They know they have the best bomber in the world and the confidence that the engines are in perfect running order. Thanks to the ground crews.

After a good look at the route the bomb aimers are more interested in the target map (a very large map of Stuttgart city) everyone takes their seats in crews. The skipper, the nav., and the bomb aimer discuss tactics.

The door opens, everyone stands. In come the Air Commodore, the Group Captain and the Wing Commander. The Winco orders sit down and reads out the crews and their aircraft. F/O Tardent **K2** etc.

The met. man gives the weather report etc., but the intelligence officer is the one with the real gen. After briefing the CO wishes the crews good luck and everyone leaves knowing exactly what to do.

The navigator goes to his section and finishes off his log and the rest of the crew catch the buses out to their kites. "So long Bill see you over the target". Or "See you at interrogation".

At the kites the skipper runs the engines up. The gunners test their turrets, the wireless op. his set, the engineer his temperatures etc. and the bomb aimer all the navigational instruments. Everything OK the crew climbs out and yarns with the ground crew while waiting for take off. The navs. arrive and everyone straps on the harness and Mae Wests. Shortly engines are heard starting up all over the drome. The new crews take off early and circle over the drome gaining height, but the older crews smile and wait. They know that circling over your own drome is wasting gas, helping to tire you out, and the risk of collision at night is very high. After perhaps ten minutes we climb into the kite, taxi round to the take off point, receive a green from the air drome control and turn onto the runaway.

A last glance at the floodlit control car to see the WAAFS and airmen waving us a farewell in the dim light. "All set?" says the skipper. "Rear gunner OK "Midupper OK" and so throughout the whole crew. Then a surge of power as 4 Merlin engines are opened up to full bore. Slowly first and then **K2** leaps into life, bowls along the runway, the engineer holding the throttles fully forward 90mph, 100/110, and 120mph. And skipper holds her on the runway till the 2,000 yards are almost used up (to get as much air speed as possible before lifting her off the deck), then he gradually trims her back till she flies herself off. "OK Undercarriage up" says Skip. "The course is 110 deg." says the Nav. and we're on our way to Stuttgart.

I generally help the navigator by taking fixes till we are crossing enemy territory. Then I go down the nose of the kite to keep a constant look out to front and underneath for enemy fighters. I have to drop out strips of tinfoil to fox Jerry's radar equipment. This prevents him from plotting our position.

When we pass through a search light belt and numerous flashes of flak are seen on our course, I direct the Skipper through by saying, "Alter course 5 deg. port". Then when we are clear, I'll say "OK Skipper resume course". We continue our way right up to the target.

Half an hour before reaching the target I switch on my sight, check that I have fused my bombs and that all my computations are correctly set on the bombsight.

Ten minutes before the target I notice some flares going down and report them to the Skipper. Then I see the markers going down. Specially trained Pathfinders drop these. Mostly second tour men. These I report to the Nav. who logs the time. Then I say "Right Oh Navigator I'll take over", and immediately sight up the target. I'll say, "Left, left 5 deg." and the Skipper alters course 5 deg. port. The Navigator will then tell me how long it is till 'time on target' and I will tell the Skipper to speed it up a bit, if I consider we are a bit behind time.

I continue to give corrections "Left, left, steady" or "Right, steady" till we have the target correctly coming into sight.

Then I'll order "Bomb doors open!" make a final correction and press the tit.

Away falls 17,000 lb. of death raining on the city of Stuttgart. Most people think that the danger is now over, but that is not correct. On coming out of a target, the night vision of each crew member is probably only 50 or 60% due to the flares over the target.

Coming out of Stuttgart we very nearly collided with a Jerry night fighter. It was coming head on. We didn't see it and it didn't see us thank goodness. We passed about 10 ft over the top of it. It looked 10 inches to me. On the run up to the target the two gunners estimated that they saw 15 aircraft shot down.

On leaving the target everyone takes a drink or eats a piece of chocolate to ward off sleep. It is very tiring sucking in oxygen for hours at 20,000 feet.

If **fighters attack K2**, the gunners warn the crew and everyone keeps off the intercommunication except the gunners and the Skipper. Then the battle of wits begins. I climb into the front turret in case of attack from the front, and the Skipper throws the mighty 4 engined bomber all over the sky at the orders from the

gunners. It is essential to do the correct evasive action at the right time. Not too early and certainly not too late. One good burst is enough to put an aircraft into a mass of flames.

If it is daylight when we cross the French coast, I generally take over from the Skipper and fly home to our base in order to let him have a spell. I love doing this, it is a real thrill. Of course he lands the old kite.

On landing we are taken to interrogation where we report all that is required (after a cup of tea and a biscuit. A smoke for those that do.)

From interrogation we go to the mess and have breakfast, then to our billets for a clean up and sleep.

I have just scribbled this in a terrible hurry to let you know what we've had to do 32 times. I think it may interest you. However it is all over now till I'm allowed to go back on a second tour, if ever, **Love, Geoff**".

The Anatomy of a Bombing Operation on 460 Squadron.

By Sgt. John Watson

I arrived at 460 Squadron, (RAAF) Bomber Command in September 1942, in charge of four Australian groundcrew airmen from 455 Squadron, (RAAF), Coastal Command.

I couldn't have been responsible for two greater villains than "Bluey" Russell, and "J J" Miller who disappeared every time we changed trains, and I was so relieved to get them to Breighton with the party intact.

On arrival I was re-united with Harry Tickle, Bernie Topley, Claude Turner, and quite a few others who arrived in Britain with me on the Blue Draft, in 1941.

Breighton being on the Yorkshire Moors, was flat and windswept, and if it had been any more dispersed it would have lapped over the edges of the County. Taking the Squadron Offices, the hospital, the Amenities and the Cookhouse as centre, the Nissen Huts where we slept were a mile away in one direction, while the dispersal points where we worked were a bike ride of two miles in the opposite direction. The drome was dispersed for one main reason, to avoid being bombed out by the Luftwaffe, and it wasn't bombed in our time as the Luftwaffe could get lost flying from one side to the other.

A bike was the key to all activities functional, physical and operational, and about as necessary to an airman, as a horse was to a cowboy. Bike "borrowing" was as widespread at Breighton as horse thieving in the Wild West. I never had my bike stolen, because I had the seat adjusted so high that even I found it was uncomfortable to ride, and I was 6' 3."

At one time so many bikes had been reported "borrowed" in the nearby village of Bubwith that the local policeman came into the camp to investigate the matter, and his bike was "borrowed".

Some aircrew who had to walk back to camp one night nicked a steamroller, and carelessly ran it off the road.

Our arrival at 460 Squadron coincided with the replacement of the two-engine Wellingtons with four-engine bombers, first by Handley Page Halifax aircraft. As the conversion training progressed the aircrew were convinced that the model we had was a lemon. The aircraft had poor flying characteristics resulting in unexpected crashes, causing the deaths of several groundcrew as well as aircrew. Another contemporary replacement, the Avro Manchester, was a dismal failure and caused more 460 Squadron crashes and casualties.

A V Roe Aircraft was so concerned when they found their Manchester was second grade, that they put their designers onto solving its chronic problem in advance of obtaining Air Ministry approval to do so. They stretched the wings of the Manchester with other wing sections already available, and installed four Rolls Royce Merlin engines instead of the two Rolls Royce Vulture engines.

They now had an aircraft called Lancaster that required only a redesigned tail section to change the Ugly Duckling into the Swan. Great concern was held for the squadron's future until it was ordained that we would convert to Lancasters.

By the time we were supplied with the Lancasters its reputation as a dream aircraft was being firmly established, and the glowing reports from the aircrews being converted to them buoyed up the whole squadron, and that reputation was never compromised.

When our first Lancaster was delivered to the Squadron, it proved to be a winner right from the start. It was proudly flown by air crews and serviced by ground crews for the rest of hostilities, and never let us down! 460 Squadron carried out 5709 Lancaster sorties over Europe, dropping 24,232 tonnes of bombs, the greatest aggregates in Bomber Command. The aircrew were awarded 363 decorations, while the groundcrew consistently maintained the highest level of serviceability in Bomber Command.

The Lancaster. the first off the rank when so desperately needed, gained the advantage over other splendid bombers that were produced later in the war, and it flew so superbly. It carried a greater bomb-load over such a long range, and more importantly for the crew, it returned to base even after sustaining devastating damage.

With every new plane, a set of canvas covers was supplied for the engines, landing wheels and the cockpit canopy. Whenever an aircraft went missing a new set of covers came with the replacement aircraft. These surplus covers were used to provide cubbies for the ground crew, who had to stand by at the plane, in usually shocking weather, until the planes took off on operations, or ops were scrubbed, or we were stood down.

While the planes were away, we could have a sleep, but someone had to be there at landing time to guide the planes back on their own dispersals in the dark, using only a torch in the blackout. We gave the crew a welcome home, a cigarette, and took reports of damage or malfunction of any equipment. A plane overdue meant an agonising wait until all hope was gone, or a report that they had landed at another drome.

After you lost a few close aircrew friends, you tried not to get over-friendly but this changed as crews approached the end of their tour and then the waiting became a most anxious time.

Each groundcrew consisted of six men with Sergeant engine, or airframe fitter in charge, with a Corporal engine or airframe fitter to assist him, and the rest being flight mechanics (riggers)
This team remained constant and was responsible for keeping "their" plane serviceable.

Other trades such as electricians, instrument makers, radio, radar, gun and bomb armourers operated on an itinerant basis. They came around, serviced and tested their components on each plane each day.

With this completed, the engine fitter "ran up" the engines to test their performance for maximum revolutions, optimum boost pressures, and operation of the propeller pitch controls.

At maximum revs, each of the engine's dual magneto systems was switched off in turn to check the drop in revolutions should one of the dual systems fail during take-off or night. While this went on the electricians, radio. radar, instrument technicians and the armourers checked the operation of their respective equipment.

This "run-up" ensured the engines were capable of lifting the total weight of the plane, the bomb load and fuel, and that all equipment was functioning correctly.

If the aircraft was on operations the night before, any faults reported by the retuning crews were attended to. The plane and engines were minutely examined in case pieces of flak (anti-aircraft shell) had entered the plane and caused damage not otherwise evident. The smallest fragment of flak could do great damage to some equipment.

When important pieces of equipment were replaced or adjusted, a test flight was done by the aircrew, and the ground crew Sergeant, to ensure the plane was performing correctly.

Then came the fuel and oil tankers to fill up the tanks, 1250 gallons (5,600 litres) of 100 octane petrol, and 35 gallons (180 litres) of oil for the tank of each engine. Glycol coolant levels for each engine were topped up. Oxygen cylinders were filled, hydraulic reservoirs checked.

All of these items were checked off and signed for by the Sergeant, who then certified on RAF Form 500 that the aircraft was fit to fly. It was then entered on the "may" list of serviceable aircraft on the Squadron. This Daily Inspection took place every day, hail, rain or shine, and was usually completed before midday.

The Station Meteorological Section made a local weather forecast every hour, and sent it by teleprinter to Group Headquarters who prepared a new composite weather map of Europe and Great Britain every hour. This was augmented by reports from weather flights and robot equipment dropped over Europe. These up-to-date forecasts were used as a guide during the planning of the operation, and used for the data given to crews at each squadron's briefing before the raid.

On the basis of our "may" fly list, the Group Headquarters advised each squadron their allocated number of aircraft. This detailed the target, take-off time, target area, the bomb-load, the route to and from the target, altitudes to fly, the timing, weather, navigation details, and expected enemy response.

The Squadron, detailing allocation of crews to each aircraft drew up the Battle Order. Finally specialists in each aspect of the crew's functions briefed the crews on all of the foregoing information.

In the meantime the ammunition and bomb-loads consisting of .303 gun rounds, and combinations of 4,000 lb "Blockbuster Cookies", 2,000lb and 1,000 lb hard case bombs and incendiaries were delivered to and loaded into the planes.

Everyone then dined and waited for take-off. It was a tradition that aircrew on operations were served bacon and egg on return from operations. Because these were very scarce commodities, someone suggested that they should have them before they went, because if they were shot down or killed they would miss out. This change was adopted.   -

Take-off was usually just before dusk, and a crowd of women and men from the groundcrew always assembled at the takeoff area to wave farewell and wish them luck.

It was an inspiring sight to see perhaps a hundred or more bomber aircraft from surrounding dromes circling around in the dusk for about half an hour, gaining the designated altitude before setting course for the target.

The Germans developed equipment early in the war, to record the number of signals given out when each wireless operator tested his radio equipment before takeoff. With this, they could work out the approximate strength of the attacking force.

Later, when the Allies discovered this, they counterfeited such signals to thoroughly confuse the enemy.
During the war, almost everything developed by either side as an offensive or defensive weapon was detected and counteracted by the other, so it was a war of the scientists as much as anyone else.

For instance the Allies developed a piece of equipment called "Village Inn" that warned our rear gunners of aircraft approaching from the rear. In total darkness, he could identify whether the plane was an enemy, or not: This equipment was designed to self destruct when the plane was shot down. The Germans were able to make up another model from the pieces, and develop the device that detected our H2S signals and located our planes.

When Germany developed a system that enabled their radar operators to "talk" the Luftwaffe fighters to "close in" on a bomber, our side sent up our German speaking radar men to confuse the issue by giving conflicting advice. When Germans put female radar operators on the job, we sent women to counter their move. Often our side just blotted out their signal with the amplified roar of a Rolls-Royce engine, or at other times used a loud recording of one of Hitler's speeches.

As the Bomber Offensive developed, and German counter measures also evolved, it became obvious that the number of bombers employed and the weight of bombs carried were immaterial unless they actually struck the intended target.

Many factors were involved, included the ability to navigate the aircraft to the target and then, more importantly, to place those bombs exactly where they were intended to strike.

First it was necessary to develop the means to enable the navigators to overcome unforeseen meteorological conditions, and reach the target area with the plane intact, on time.

Secondly, the target must be precisely identified and the plane manoeuvred to the precise position and altitude, and the bomb-load released at the right time. If these factors weren't achieved the whole exercise was a failure. Many difficulties were encountered when changes occurred in the forecast wind direction

Compass readings registered only the direction the aircraft was pointing, but not necessarily which way it was travelling. Allowance had to be made for "drift" if your "pocket of air "changed the direction it was travelling.

In daylight, drift can be observed, measured and allowed for by studying a point on the ground. On a clear night taking an astronomical fix on the stars enabled a change of course to be calculated. Cloudy, dark nights, the only recourse was either a Long-range Directional Radio Beam, or a reliable position indicator based on a gyroscope, but none of these latter aids were available at the time.

The Germans evolved equally effective measures to mislead the sometimes inexperienced crews. This was achieved by creating decoy fires and flares outside the critical target area. Once early arrivals were deceived and had bombed the decoy fires, the following crews were more easily led astray.

This problem was tackled by the development of the Pathfinder Force, specially trained in use of the latest target identification strategies. They dropped special predicted target flares for the guidance of the Bomber Force.

The Pathfinders remained in the target area to augment the flares, and correct any tendency to wander off target. If this "creep" was not corrected, the error was compounded. The Master Bomber directed the whole show, and gave a running commentary and necessary instructions whenever corrective action was required, by the crews,

Whenever an aircrew survived a tour of thirty operations, they threw a party for their groundcrew in gratitude and relief as the chances of an aircrew surviving a first tour were about 40%, and of surviving two tours about 11%.

In York, there was a place called Betty's Bar, where everyone at such a party recorded their names on the mirrors surrounding the walls with a diamond supplied by Betty, and those names were still there in 1975!

In Binbrook the place to celebrate was the Marquis of Granby, now unfortunately closed.

Out of every 100 Aircrew who served with Bomber Command, 51 were killed on operations, 9 were killed during training, 2 were seriously wounded in crashes, 12 were taken prisoners, one evaded capture, with only 24 surviving unharmed.

These were the highest casualty rates of any allied service and, according to Group Captain Parsons, who commanded 460 squadron in late 1944/45 the rate of aircrew KIA (Killed in Action) rose to 85% during 1943 and 1944 when casualties reached their highest peaks!

On 460 Squadron, 45% were lost in their first 5 operations, which proved that there was no training substitute for the grim experience learnt in actual battle over the target.

THE RAAF AND BOMBER COMMAND –
A RETROSPECTIVE   (Extracts only)

Presentation to the RAAF Europe Association - Friday October 6th, 2000

Dr Alan Stephens,
(Ph.D., ex RAAF Wg/Cdr, RAAF Historian)

Street names at Australia's premier military training establishment, the Australian Defence Force Academy in Canberra, honour notable wartime actions. While every one of those actions was a matter of life or death for the men involved, when measured against the broader sweep of history some scarcely merit the description 'battle'. It might seem remarkable, therefore, that three of the greatest battles in which Australians have fought aren't acknowledged.

Those three battles all took place in the skies over Germany during World War II, and were fought by the men of the RAF's Bomber Command, many of whom were members of the RAAF.

The first was the Battle of the Ruhr from March to July 1943, the second the Battle of Hamburg from 24 July to 3 August 1943, and the third the Battle of Berlin from November 1943 to March 1944.

Statistics can never tell a story by themselves, but the figures from those three epic clashes reveal a fearful truth. No Bomber Command aircrew who fought in all three could expect to survive.

An operational tour on heavy bombers consisted of thirty missions. Crews were then rested for about six months, usually instructing at a training unit. That 'rest' was, however, in name only, as more than 8000 men were killed in flying accidents at bomber conversion units.

They might then volunteer for or be assigned to a second operational tour of twenty missions.

Over the course of the war the odds of surviving a first tour were exactly one-in-two - the classic toss of a coin. When the second tour was added the odds slipped further, to one-in-three. And during the battles of the Ruhr, Hamburg and Berlin it was statistically impossible to survive thirty missions.

No other sustained campaign in which Australians have ever been involved can compare with the air war over Germany in terms of individual danger. The men of the RAAF who fought for Bomber command amounted to less than 2 per cent of all Australians who enlisted in World War II, yet the 3486 who died accounted for almost 20 per cent of all deaths in combat.

The RAAF's most distinguished heavy bomber unit, No.460 Squadron, alone lost 1018 aircrew, meaning that, in effect, the entire squadron was wiped out five times. It was far more dangerous to fight in Bomber Command than in the infantry.

Perhaps the loss rate would be less distressing if the sacrifice of the men who had to bear it had been properly acknowledged. Regrettably that hasn't been the case. The example of the Australian Defence Force Academy's ignorance is merely one of many.

Such was the prejudice of influential politicians and public figures that a Bomber command campaign medal was never awarded, despite the obvious importance and magnitude of the crusade; while the man who led the fight from 1942 onwards, Air Chief Marshal Sir Arthur Harris, was the only commander of his status to be ignored when post-War peerages were handed out.

According to the Nazis' minister of war production, Albert Speer, following the Hamburg raids he 'reported for the first time to the Fuehrer that if these serial attacks continued a rapid end of the war might be the consequence'.

An objective review of the statistics presents a powerful and grim picture of the physical and mental devastation the bombing caused.

It's important to appreciate that that devastation didn't really start' until mid-1944, with over 70 per cent of the bombs dropped on Germany falling in the last year of the war. The effect was profound.

I now want to talk about some of the specifically Australian aspects of the experience.

The bomber offensive may have been decisive in the allies' eventual victory but for the RAAF it brought mixed results. The problem was the RAAF's inability to control what happened to its aircrew, which in turn made it impossible to control its destiny.

Throughout the war it was the British Air Ministry's preference to post the first available, suitable person to the squadron most in need, an approach which was sensible and easy to administer.

As a consequence, Australian airmen found themselves dispersed across the length and breadth or the RAF. But at the institutional level the practice undermined the RAAF's ambition to form squadrons with an identifiable national character, and whose contribution would be clearly Australian. For the RAAF, the policy was an institutional disaster.

That disaster manifested itself most obviously by stifling opportunities for senior command. Because there were no genuine Australian squadrons, nor could there be Australian wings and groups, which meant that promising RAAF officers were denied the experience which would have come with those formations.

The effect was insidious. Concern about the quality of the RAAF' S senior echelons was to be a problem for the post-war Air Force for ten years. Perhaps a more resolute national stance on the employment of Australians in Bomber Command might have eased that problem.

No single group of Australians from any service did more to help win World War II than the men who fought in Bomber Command. But so intertwined were the RAAF crews with the RAF that it's almost impossible to identify' a distinctive Australian effort.

It is an Institutional tragedy for the RAAF that the story of its Bomber Command crews can't be fully reconstructed, and that their experiences weren't lived out within a wholly Australian context. RAAF history remains immeasurably the poorer for the loss.

The outstanding RAAF unit of the war was No.460 Squadron, which took its twin-engined Wellingtons to war for the first time in a strike against Emden on 12/13 March 1942. Only two months later, on May 30/31, the squadron contributed eighteen aircraft to the dramatic thousand-bomber attack on Cologne.

No.460 Squadron, which by then was flying the premier bomber of the war, the four~engined Avro Lancaster, and, together with other RAAF units, was in the vanguard of Bomber Command's operations.

During the autumn and winter of 1943-44, which culminated in the Battle of Berlin, the Australian squadrons typically provided about 10 per cent of the main bomber force.

Four RAAF squadrons fought in Bomber Command's worst night of the war, the notorious strike against Nuremberg on 30/31 March 1944 when ninety-five of 608 aircraft - almost 16 per cent - were lost. The 545 allied airmen who died in the space of about eight hours exceeded the 507 killed during the entire Battle of Britain. Five of the RAAF's sixty-seven aircraft were shot down.

The magnitude of the Australian bomber crews' contribution to victory in Europe can be gauged by a brief summary of some of their major actions.

The critical point is that, for 5¼ years, without a break, they fought in almost every notable operation. In addition to the fearful campaign against German cities, RAAF aircrew attacked the enemy's railways, roads and bridges; oil refineries and storage facilities; factories; submarine pens; secret weapon sites; army formations; warships; and canals.

Thirteen Australians serving with the RAF's No.617 Squadron took part in the famous darn busters raid on 16/17 May 1943, including two of the war's greatest bomber pilots, Flight Lieutenants Mickey Martin and David Shannon. Other RAAF crews dropped 5500 kilogram Tallboy bombs on viaducts and 10000kilogram Grand Slam bombs on bridges; while No.456 Squadron's achievement in laying 256 mines in August 1944 was a Command record.

Let me conclude.

Most Australians know the meaning of Gallipoli, and many have some understanding of what their countrymen achieved at places like Tobruk and the Kokoda Trail. It's unlikely, though, that more than a handful have any appreciation of either the sacrifice or the contribution to victory made by the 13 000 or so Australian airmen who served with Bomber Command during World War 11.

Whatever the morality of the combined bomber offensive may be, three indisputable facts stand out. First, the men of the RAAF who fought in that offensive did so at the lawful direction of their government. Second, in terms of casualties, theirs was the most savage and most dangerous sustained campaign fought by any Australians during World War II. And third, theirs was the major contribution of any Australians to the defeat of Germany and, therefore, to the allies' ultimate victory.

It was the men of Bomber Command who alone opened a second front in Germany, four years before D-.Day; and it was the men of Bomber Command who alone inflicted decisive damage on the German war economy. As Albert Speer lamented, Bomber Command's victory represented 'the greatest lost battle on the German side. The time is long overdue for the men of the RAAF who fought in the great air battles over Germany and Italy during World War II to receive far more generous recognition of their extraordinary achievements and courage.

Reference to Bomber Command in Churchill's speech to House of Commons 20 Aug. 1940 received from Air Marshal J. W. Newham AC (Retd)

"The Few"
August 20, 1940
House of Commons

On August 15, the crisis of the battle of Britain was reached. All the resources of Fighter Command in the South were used. The most difficult and dangerous period of the Battle of Britain was between August 24 and September 6, when the German attack was directed against the R.A.F. airfields in the South of England with considerable success. In his speech Churchill coined the phrase "The Few" to describe the R.A.F. fighter-pilots. The phrase stuck.

" The gratitude of every home in our Island, in our Empire, and indeed throughout the world, except in the abodes of the guilty, goes out to the British airmen who undaunted by odds, unwearied in their constant challenge and mortal danger, are turning the tide of the World War by their prowess and by their devotion. **Never in the field of human conflict was so much owed by so many to so few.** All hearts go out to the fighter pilots, whose brilliant actions we see with our open eyes, day after day, **but we must never forget that all the time, night after night, month after month, our bomber squadrons travel far into Germany, find their targets in the dark by the highest navigational skill, aim their attacks, often under the heaviest fire, often with serious loss, with deliberate careful discrimination, and inflict shattering blows upon the whole of the technical and war-making structure of the Nazi power.**

On no part of the Royal Air Force does the weight of the war fall more heavily than on the daylight bombers, who will play an invaluable part in the case of invasion and whose unflinching zeal it has been necessary in the meanwhile on numerous occasions to restrain.

We are able to verify the results of bombing military targets in Germany, not only by reports which reach us through many sources, but also, of course, by photography.

I have no hesitation in saying that this process of bombing the military industry and communications of Germany and the air bases and storage depots from which we are attacked, which process will continue on an ever-increasing scale until the end of the war, and may in another year attain dimensions hitherto undreamed of, affords one at least of the most certain, if not the shortest, of all the roads to victory.

Even if the Nazi legions stood triumphant on the Black Sea, or indeed upon the Caspian, even if Hitler was at the gates of India, it would profit him nothing if at the same time the economic and scientific apparatus of German war power lay shattered and pulverised at home.

Copy of Speech by
Marshal of the
Royal Air Force.
Sir Arthur T. Harris, Bart
(RAF Bomber Command
Reunion Dinner
London, 30 April, 1977)

.

Marshal of the Royal Air Force, Sir Arthur T. Harris, Baronet, Knight Grand Cross, The Most Honourable Award of the Bath and Office of the Most Excellent Order of the British Empire, Airforce Cross, Doctor of Laws, Commander-in-Chief, Bomber Command from 1942 to 1945.

Mr. Chairman, Members of the Committee, Ladies and Gentlemen, not forgetting our two "M'Lords". I want to thank you all for the marvellous reception you have given me tonight and if I went much further on that theme, I do not think I would be able to control my feelings. All I can say is, I thank you all from the bottom of my heart.

Now I go from there to tell you that, as you probably know, I am an old ga-ga and garrulous. <u>I have a lot to say which I think you ought to hear</u> unless you've heard it before. I realize that a lot of you came a long way and have a long way to go, therefore if any of you have to get up and leave, I can assure you that I won't be either put-off or put-out. So please take that as to what I really mean. I won't be a bit worried if you have to go because I know why, for one reason or another.

You know the work our crews did in Bomber Command and whenever I speak of the Bomber Strategic Offensive, I couple with it 50-50 our gallant

American friends of the Eighth United States Airforce.

Whenever I think of what they achieved, I realize that you have never really been given adequate recognition of what you all did. As a matter of fact, you have on many occasions been the object of the type of author or the type of journalist who knows perfectly well that where he could not find a market for the ordinary tripe he is capable of, he could always sell a good sneer or a good smear. But I get my facts straight from the horses mouth. I do not go digging around the other end of the animal like those people I referred to. And we have some very fine horses running for us, ranging from the most senior American Commanders and, oddly enough, to the most senior German Commanders in the last war.

You will, no doubt. most of you heard of Albert Speer who was not a dyed in the wool Nazi - anyhow, to start with he was a brilliant architect and he got tied up with Hitler because Hitler liked drawing pictures, with his assistance, of the magnificent buildings they were going to erect at the end of the victorious war, in order to usher in the beginning of the 1000-year Reich which, thanks largely due to you fellows, never materialized.

Now Albert Speer, as you know, was in prison for 20 years. As a matter of opinion, I think unjustly, for doing his damnedest to defend his own country. When he came out of prison, he wrote two books and he was kind enough to send me copies of both of them and he inscribed them - as one of the inscriptions he has repeated in the letter preface, what he said in those inscriptions and in his own words he has said that of all the war books that he has ever read and he has read a lot of them, the effect of the strategic bombing of Germany is always under-estimated. He goes on to say and these are his own words written in his own hand, as well as repeated in the book, that the strategic bombing of Germany was the greatest lost battle for Germany of the whole of the war, greater than all their losses in all their retreats from Russia and in the surrender of their armies at Stalingrad.

He then goes on to develop the reasons why he makes those statements, starting right back in June 1942. There was a meeting amongst the "high-ups" in Germany as to whether or not they would do this, that and the other thing. When it came to the question of whether they would develop the atom bomb and don't forget that before the war the Germans were ahead of everybody in that particular nefarious pursuit, when it came to the question, luckily for us and the world at large, Hitler dismissed it, he said he would have nothing to do with it because it was all "Jews" science. That was a very luckydecision.

Albert Speer comments in his book, apropos of that decision, at that very date he was glad, because he could not possibly have spared the enormous amount of skilled, semi-skilled and unskilled labour for such am ambitious project as the manufacture of the atomic bomb from the necessity of using these people to repair the bomb damage to the German armament industry. That was in June 1942 and of course that damage went crescendo afterthat.

His next statement that might be of interest to you was that he reckoned, as Minister of Armament, which he had then become, that by the end of 1943, when we were really getting going with about a quarter of the force we asked for and the Americans had hardly got going with their Mustang Escort Fighters, that we had already deprived the German armies on the Russian front by bomb damage to industry of 10,000 of their bigger calibre guns and 6000 of their heaviest and medium heavy tanks. Well that was quite a subscription towards the war - all done by the strategic bombers. But he goes much further than that. He made that remark about the Bomber Strategic Offensive being the greatest lost battle of all for Germany and he goes on to explain why. The 8.8 cm dual purpose anti-aircraft mobile gun, was capable of competing with the very heavy frontal armament of the Russian tank. No less than 20,000 of those guns had to be taken away from the German armies, all their fronts, kept away from them and scattered all over Germany because of the unpredictability of where the Strategic Bombers were going to strike next.

Speer said that that reduced the anti-tank ability of the German forces on all fronts by half. When you realize that no army of either side ever advanced a yard without their armoured spearhead first busting a way through the defence, you can realize what is meant when the strategic bombers cut their anti-tank defences by half. He goes on to say that the requirement of being prepared to defend every German city and every German vital factory against the possibility of bombing any one of those particular places, meant the stationing all over Germany of hundreds of thousands of men, who should have been in the forces.

Field Marshall Erhard Milch, who commanded the German anti-aircraft defences said he had 900,000 fit, he stressed the word fit, men in his anti-aircraft command alone. When he says fit, he means that they were fit to have been up in the front line of the German armies on the various fronts and not clicking their heels around Germany waiting for the strategic bombers and wondering where they were going to strike next. Well, if you know of any individual army on the allied side which, throughout the war, <u>deprived the German armies of well over a million men and half their anti-tank ability,</u> I would personally be very obliged for the information.

Now when Erhard Milch said that he had 900,000 men, <u>you can certainly add that another two or three hundred thousand fit men</u> who, because they were skilled tradesmen, had to be retained in Germany and not called up for army service because their skills were required to keep the Nazi machine ticking over and the repair of bomb damage. I mean men like electricians, plumbers, railway workers, people who ran the oil manufacturing plants and so on and so forth. So there you get that enormous subtraction from the German strength, both in artillery and manpower, which was <u>caused by the Strategic Bombers and nobody else.</u>

Now as I said, you don't seem to have got adequate credit for that, anyhow in this country but you certainly get it from the people who were immediately concerned, such as Eisenhower, "Monty" and the German leaders, as I mentioned, Albert Speer, General Sepp Dietrich, etc. etc.

What Eisenhower had to say about you was this: 25 years after the war, the Americans released a lot of stuff from their top secret archives, amongst them letters exchanged between General Marshall, the head of the American Army and General Eisenhower, and in this one particular letter, Marshall refers to the fact that the joint chiefs of staff in America had decided that our invasion of Europe was going so well that the time had arrived to take away the direct command of the British bombers and the American bombers from Eisenhower and return it to the heads of their respective services, Sir Frank Portal and General Arnold, because those two heads of services had other theatres of war to compete with as well as Europe.

In Eisenhowers reply and I have a copy of his reply, he said, although Marshall expressed his apprehension that that would result in Eisenhower getting less support from Bomber Command than he had been used to, Eisenhower said that he had no such fears and his actual words were that <u>he had come to regard the British Bomber Command as one of the most effective parts of his entire organization,</u> always seeking, finding and using new ways for their particular type of aircraft to be of assistance in forwarding the progress of the armies on the ground. That was a pretty good recommendation from that source but we have others.

You know Monty was not by any means given to praising idly but I have heard Monty say on two occasions, both vast public banquets given to him, once in the city and once in Cape Town, I heard him say that he regarded the <u>British Bombers as having been the greatest of all in the destruction of the German armies as a whole.</u> Now that was pretty good coming from a soldier not given to praising otherslightly.

On the other hand I have seen articles written, in particular by a man described as a very well-known military correspondent, in which he made two remarks. He said all the Bomber Command ever did was to raise better obstacles in front of the progress of our armies than the

Germans could have done themselves. That was one remark. The other remark he made was that they took no part whatsoever in the Battle of the Ardennes where the Germans, as you know, nearly broke through the Allied lines.

Well, whether you like to believe that or not is a matter for your personal tastes but I would say this, that although that fellow said that we raised these appalling obstacles in front of our own army, I would agree to this extent that our grade one prize boffin, dear old Barnes Wallace, who I am sorry is not able to be here tonight but I hope you will send him your best wishes - if he had come here I would have recommended that after this dinner you should have debagged him for grave dereliction of duty in not designing the one urgent requirement of the army, which I am sure he would have done with half an hours thought on the back of an old envelope and that was a bomb that made a self-filling crater that yawned deep and wide to embarrass and entrap the enemy but automatically filled it up as soon as it sensed the approaching footfall of an Alliedsoldier.

Now lets take the statement that you fellows took no part in the Battle of the Ardennes where, as you recall, in this last frantic effort by the Germans to break through our lines, was just held up on the verge of a breakthrough by what? By the Allied General on the spot (this is history as it is made) firing off at them an unheard of or unexpected secret weapon. Thinking that his position was hopeless, the Germans demanded his surrender and he fired off his weapon, which was a rather mild four letter word... and that is history "as she is wrote". But when you come down to brass tacks and find what really happened - to stop that offensive you will find that Hitler, as soon as the offensive began to be held up, told Albert Speer to get up at the front and tell the General on the spot, Sepp Dietrich, that he was to go on at all costs - at any cost and he was not to stop.

Speer relates in great detail, his tremendous difficulties in getting to the front at all. The Ardennes country is terribly difficult country, almost impossible even for tracked vehicles to cross country. There are only two comparatively poor and precipitous road routes through it and everybody especially the French, saying that the Germans will never come through there. So it was quite likely to offend you and the said that in spite of the fact that this was the third occasion that the Germans had come through since 1870.

Well Speer relates the tremendous difficulties in getting up there at all. He says that sometimes he only made good a mile in an hours struggle and you can bet as Hitler's representative he would have been pushed, pulled and carried, car and all, round, over and above any obstacles that existed.

Finally he arrives at the headquarters of the advanced armoured force on which the whole offence depended. Their job was to break through the join between the American and the British Canadian armies, turn sharp to the right northward, pushing them into the sea again for another Dunkirk and there they were, held up by that rude American General who made that remark which apparently forced those tough Germans who had fought through all that way regardless of shot and shell - to rock back on their heels, turn round, burst into tears and go home and complain to mother about that rude man - that is now history.

When Speer eventually got to Sepp Dietrich's

headquarters, he encountered that one German General who dared even mildly answer back Hitler. The reason being that he started his career as Hitler's private chauffeur in the early days of Nazidom and had once, very unfortunately for us and everybody, saved Hitler from assassination, so he could mildly answer back and Speer relates how he said to Sepp Dietrich that the Fuhrer's orders are to go on at once at all costs, you are not to stop. The answer he got was not a four-letter word even like the one the American General used but just a statement to the effect - "Go on? How can we go on, we have no ammunition left and <u>all our supply lines have been cut by air attack</u>". Well that of course is a fairly potent reason for not going on with an offensive. And who cut the supply lines? <u>You fellows cut it and nobody else</u> and the reason it was you and nobody else was that in the atrocious weather that existed over those critical day and nights, all our bases on the Continent were almost permanently shut down, the American bases in East Anglia to the extent where they couldn't use their ordinary formation escorted daylight tactics but you fellows, your crews, would get off in any muck and mire, even if they could not see. As one cockney gunner once remarked to me, "you couldn't see y' hand in front y' bloody face!" He said that they'd get off in those conditions provided there was somewhere to get down in the morning, and luckily where one base went out, one came in and so on and so forth. At the end of the day you fellows did the job and Speer gives a very informative account of what he called his "nocturnal discussion" with Sepp Dietrich that night. As they sat there listening to the unending roar of heavy engine bombers overhead in the fog and the crash of bombs behind them, Sepp Dietrich remarked to him, "You know, people don't understand that not <u>even the best troops (meaning his own troops and they were picked troops), could stand this mass bombing.</u> One experience of it and they lose all their fighting spirit". Speer's concluding remarks of that conversation was "what a scene of German impotence, we've no defences anywhere".

Well you know what happened after that. Monty attacking in the north with the 21st Army Group and some borrowed Americans, and George Patton, the famous Cavalry Leader with the American armoured force attacking in the south, sent those weeping "boche" back to where they came from and a lot further as well. Well now, that remark of Sepp Dietrich's was not patent to him by a long way. Shortly after our invasion got established in France, <u>Rommel remarked to his superiors, "if you can't stop the bombing we cannot win,</u> and it is no good going on because all we get by going on is to lose another city every night". <u>He said, "make peace, or drop the atomic bomb if you have got it".</u> But of course I told you why they hadn't got it. He was not the only fellow that made that remark by a long way.

As our armies advanced along the north coast of France, they urgently required the channel ports such as Le Havre, Boulogne and Calais, etc. Those ports were manned by 20,000 German soldiers, not only sworn to die but under a master who they knew very well would see that they died if they didn't do as they were supposed to. <u>They all surrendered - 20,000 troops, with a total loss of 150 casualties to our armies. Thanks entirely to mass bombing.</u>

In the pocket diary of a senior German Commander who surrendered at Boulogne, were written the words, "can anybody survive this carpet bombing? Sometimes <u>one is driven to despair when at the mercy of the Royal Air Force</u> without any protection. It seems that all fighting is in vain and all losses are in vain". Well, there you are, one after another, the German Generals said the same thing.

Now when it comes to our side and the American side, I told you what Eisenhower had thought of us but after the bombing that did so much in the battle of the Ardennes, he sent me a "Thank you" message and I replied thanking him for his message and I said that his message had been passed on to the crews responsible and I finished my signal by saying, "you know by now you can always depend on my lads for anything short of the impossible". Tedder relates how that signal of mine was circulating around Eisenhower's headquarters and scrawled across my signal in Eisenhower's handwriting were the words "<u>Goddammit</u> (you know in the American language that is all one word), <u>they have already achieved the impossible</u>". - now, there is a so-called famous military correspondent saying that Bomber Command did nothing but make an infernal nuisance of themselves where our armies were concerned on the Continent, and the Commanding Chief saying that you fellows achieved the impossible on behalf of the armies. Who would you like to believe?

Well, I have got very little more to say except that quite apart from the fact that those facts I have given you do indicate beyond doubt, agreement with Albert Speer's statement that <u>the Strategic Bombing of Germany was the greatest losses of all their losses in the war.</u> I would say that you also scored the biggest air victory of the war, because you did what Baume said was the one thing you had to do to defeat an enemy was to drive them on to the defensive and you certainly did that. Over the last year or two of the war, the Germans did nothing with their airforce, which had been the major cause of their easy sweep right across Europe, Poland and every else at the beginning of the war and their easy victories but <u>they did nothing over the last year or two of the war but make fighters and trained fighter pilots</u> in a despairing effort, which failed in it's object to protect the Fatherland from the Strategic Bombing and <u>that was a fact.</u>

The effect of that was firstly, that it put an entire stop to the bombing of this country. It is quite true they started off with these comic rockets and things. Well you know, the V2 rocket for instance, the thing that created quite a bit of alarm and despondency. The maximum possible production of these V2 rockets was a thousand a month and <u>it took 5000 of them to carry as much explosives as an attack by the Strategic American and British bombers.</u> So there are the comparative values.

Now and I told you I think, that you have won certainly one of the major ground battles. What I told you about Albert Speer certainly one of the major air battles in driving them entirely on the defensive but what you have never been given any credit for - you certainly won the major battle of the European war. Who said so? Speer again. I have read an account by a so-called expert naval correspondent, who said that in all the war, Bomber Command only sank one submarine.

What did Speer say - he was responsible for the production of submarines and everything else. This simple sentence in one of his books - "We would have kept our promised output of submarines for Admiral Doenitz' U-boat war <u>if the bombers had not</u>

destroyed a third of them in the ports. Well, who was right? The navy wanted to pinch all our Lancasters to go looking for haystacks all over the Atlantic - looking for needles in the haystacks, or we who set the pace, to get the submarines where they came from.

The German Admiral in charge of the training of U-boat crews in the Baltic wrote a letter in which he said, "Without trained U-boat crews you cannot have a U-boat offensive and I cannot train crews if you cannot keep these damned air-raid mines away from my training ground". Well, they could not keep them away, although the major expensive effort by the German navy during the war was trying to conquer the 30,000 tons of mines that you fellows laid in waters approaching every port that the Germans used from the Baltic, through the whole of the North Sea coast and down to the Bay of Biscay. You can be quite certain that apart from the other wreckage they caused, those mines certainly accounted for quite a number of other submarines who disappeared (if my German pronunciation is right, I'm not very good at it) "Speroz der sank" - 'disappeared, sank without trace.'

Those mines incidentally, coupled with the bombing, virtually annihilated the German Merchant Marine on which they depended for the import of vital ores from Scandinavia for their basic industries and the Swedes who were forced to participate in that trade, when they realized towards the concluding stages of the war that the German pistol in the back of their neck was no longer a serious threat, they withdrew what was left of their Merchant Marine from the same trade, sooner than put up with additional losses of men and ships. So that is what you achieved in the Naval war but that was by no means all. Few people realise that at the beginning of the war the German navy had a high seas fleet consisting of about 17 absolutely super battle wagons ranging all the way from the big fellows, the TIRPITZ (Willy Tait finished off the TIRPITZ with his merry boys), the BISMARK, all the way down to the heavy battle cruisers and the pocket battleships, etc. - 16 or 17 of them. What happened to them. Did you ever hear? No, well I'll tell you what happened to them. The Navy sank three of them, the Fleet Air Arm sank 1 - that's 4 (I have to add up on my fingers in my old age), the Norwegian shore defences sank one during the invasion of Norway - that's 5. The Russians navy did so much damage to one that it was out of action for nearly the whole of the war - that's 6, <u>Bomber Command kept two out of action by repeated damage,</u> so that during the war that they would never really have been available for anything in the nature of fleet action - that's two more gone - where have we got to - that's 9. <u>Bomber Command sank 6 and really hardly got a "Thank you"</u> for it - so there you are - two left - the Prince Eugen and Nuremberg and in the closing stages of the war, they were lying outside Copenhagen - cold meat to the big bomb that Willy Tait & Co were putting on their machines and I happened to be out of my office for five minutes - occasionally I had to leave my office for five minutes - my Deputy Commander had taken the half day off (one of the six half days he took of during the entire war) either to attend to his own business or have his business attend to him and my naval liaison officer was an absolutely first class fellow and of the most assistance to us with the mining.

When I got back to my office, there he was, all in a tremble and he said, I've had to counter-command the attack on the EUGEN and the NUREMBERG." I said, "Why?" He said, "Orders from the Admiralty." Well of course you could not blame the lad, to a naval officer an order from the Admiralty is one above a direct command by the Almighty, so he done it and there he was all of a tremble. It was too late to turn the bombers back again. But those two ships were cold meat and the fact that they escaped enabled them rather spitefully to expend most of their ammunition on bombarding around Copenhagen, doing quite a lot of damage and killing quite a lot of Danish friends and would be allies.

When the destruction in the ports became absolutely intolerable, the Germans had a bright idea to prefabricate their submarines inland, send the huge sections down to the ports so they'd only be a few days or weeks being buttoned together rather than months being built from the keel upwards and destroyed in the process by bombers but that didn't work either because the prefabricated sections were too big to go by rail or road. They could only go by canal which was exactly why the Strategic Bombers, the Americans and the British, kept on busting up the two canals concerned, the Middleland Canal and the Dortmund Ems, with the result that those prefabricated sections - the deliveries of them to the port - quickly sank from a maximum of 120 sections in one month to a few handfuls and to zero.

Well I hope I have told you enough about your share in the Air War, the Naval War and the Land War and nobody can take that away from you because I say it's all from the horses mouth.

From the leading Germans to the leading Americans and the leading British, even Lord

Alanbrook, the head of the army, who was no friend of the Airforce, always making inordinate demands on what we should do for them, he admitted in his private diaries which were published after the war by Sir Arthur Brown, <u>he referred to the brilliant skill of the bombers and the outstanding assistance they gave to the army during the invasion.</u>

  Well when you consider that our invasion of France consisted of 37 divisions with a large content of green and inexperienced troops and that joint experience in the First War - the soldiers always said that if you want any chance of success in the attack, you must be two-to-one advantage in numbers and material over the enemy - those <u>37 divisions chased 60 German divisions clean across Europe</u> from the Atlantic to the Elbe, totally destroyed the German army of half a million men - the 7th Army, captured tens of thousands of prisoners, all their equipment and beat them down to unconditional surrender at Lunberg Heath and that was largely due to two things - the Germans lack of anti-tank defences and <u>the complete, not air superiority, but absolute air supremacy of our fellows</u> over on the Continent - thanks to the fact that the bombers had forced the German airforce to spread nearly all its efforts on a failed attempt to defend their own country,

 Thank you for listening to me.

EPILOGUE

THE EXALTED FEW

Lucky to Survive

Aircrew who took over from a badly wounded skipper and flew the plane back to base.

An **American USAAF, Capt. John C. Morgan,**
    co-pilot on 407th Fortress Squadron
    raid on Hanover on 26th July 1944 Award;
    Congressional Medal of Honour.

Englishman, **Fl/Lt, George Martin**,
    navigator on 405 Canadian Squadron,
    raid on Dusseldorf on 2/3 November 1944. Award;
    Distinguished Service Order.

Australian, **Warrant Officer, Alec Hurse,** bomb aimer,
    on 75 New Zealand Squadron, raid on Nantes, on
    11/12 June 1944. Award;
    Conspicuous Gallantry Medal.

Australian, **Warrant Officer, Lawrence William Woods,**
    bomb aimer on 460 RAAF Squadron, raid on
    Wanne Eikel, on 9th November 1944.
    Distinguished Flying Cross. Immediate award